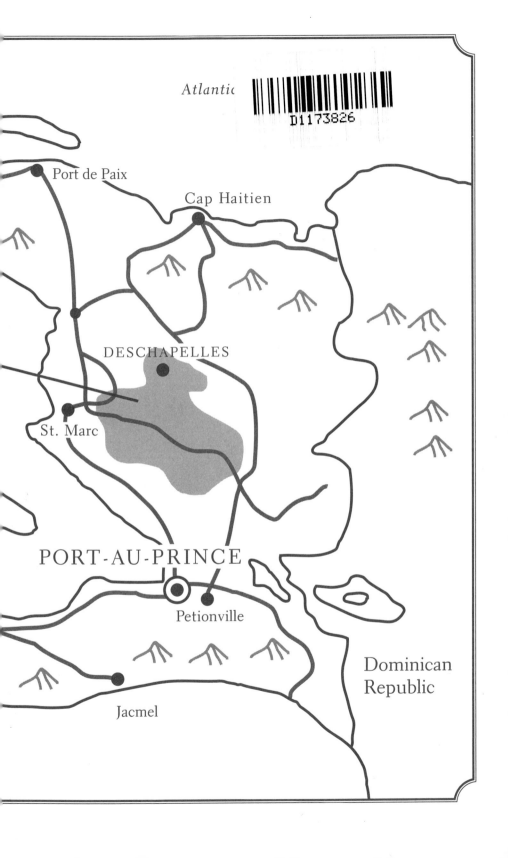

Atlantic

Port de Paix

Cap Haitien

DESCHAPELLES

St. Marc

PORT-AU-PRINCE

Petionville

Dominican
Republic

Jacmel

2 — 18   98

To Lois

My Road To
Deschapelles

With real wishes

Gwen Grant Mellon

My Road To Deschapelles

By

GWEN GRANT MELLON

HÔPITAL ALBERT SCHWEITZER
DESCHAPELLES, HAITI

CONTINUUM • NEW YORK

1998

The Continuum Publishing Company
370 Lexington Avenue
New York, NY 10017

Printed in the United States of America

ISBN 0-8264-1055-3

Library of Congress Card Number: 97-77024

For Larry
My lodestar for over half a century

This book has been produced at no cost to
Hôpital Albert Schweitzer
Deschapelles, Haiti

Gwen Grant Mellon is contributing her royalties to
Hôpital Albert Schweitzer
Deschapelles, Haiti

Table of Contents

Ian astride, with Jenny and Michael beside me.

me years later she thought I was dead when I arrived. Luckily the hospital was staffed by a young doctor who sent to Phoenix for a new medicine called sulfa. I was put in an oxygen tent, and Larry left.

Larry appeared later with the children. They were all clean and dressed, and Jenny's short, blond, pigtails were braided and tied with a blue ribbon to match her eyes. All four climbed the stairs to look in on me. I was so sick I had not worried about them, not even knowing that Larry had moved in with them. Each morning he dressed the three and sent them off to school.

The children left and I could hear the pickup door close, and then Larry ran back up the steps, looked into the tent, and said, "I want you to get bet-ter. It makes a difference to me." I had no friends and no plans for the future. You can imagine what those words meant to me. I got better fast and soon returned to Rimrock.

Larry invited the four of us for a supper of pancakes and cocoa at his ranch house. He sifted the weevils out of the flour, then used powdered milk and white lard instead of butter. The cakes were fat and beautiful. The syrup was Karo. The cocoa was made with condensed milk. The kids loved it. It was my first exposure to food on a working ranch.

7

Presents from Larry.

Larry took us all out to a sandy wash where we made traps for quail and panned for gold. Those days, Larry wore an Indian penny on a gold chain around his neck. He said that he would never be without money.

When Larry first knew me he never saw me wearing a dress. I was always ready to ride. He wondered if I was deliberately hiding my legs.

One day at Rimrock, Larry drove Ian and me to Apache Maid, his summer range in the mountains. While there, he used the forest ranger telephone to speak to Washington. He was to report to Washington for duty.

The two and a half weeks before Larry went back to Washington and the Office of Strategic Services were good days, and we learned a lot about each other. Larry would be gone for two years.

En route to Washington Larry stopped in New York and asked his sister Peggy to help him with some shopping. We received four big boxes. Jenny got a doll with magnetic hands, Mike, an airplane pilot's uniform, and Ian, a navy officer's suit. I received the most beautiful leather purse, almost like a saddle bag, from Phillips.

Before leaving to work with the OSS in Europe, Larry had a training session in Washington. He was told to meet a car at such and such a corner at such a time. Larry was to ask if it was so and so's car and get in and talk to no one. The chauffeur got out and Larry was about to ask the coded question when the chauffeur, wreathed in smiles, hugged Larry and said "Mr. Larimer!" He was the chauffeur who used to drive Larry, Porky Flynn, and other friends to dancing school. The incognito was blown at an early moment. He delivered Larry to a nearby farm outside Washington for further training. There they carefully avoided each other.

Larry was given lumber, tools, and a partner to build a one-room house. The helper was planted to cause confusion and annoyance and to test Larry's patience and good humor. Larry happily caught on immediately.

When Larry returned to Washington to await his assignment to the OSS, he rented a one-room apartment and included a good friend in his life, a dog chosen from the pound. He bought a hotplate for home cooking, and a bicycle which was used daily to go to and from the office, and on the weekends, to explore beautiful spots around Washington.

At a dinner party in Washington, his hostess, Helen Clark, told everyone of the time, ten years earlier, when Larry had joined his father on his boat for a trip to Peru. Because Larry had only blue jeans in his suitcase, Mr. Mellon cabled the Gulf Oil agent ashore, and asked him to buy and bring a suit for Larry on their arrival in Lima. As Helen told the story, Larry said, "Yep, that's right and I have it on!" He opened up his jacket to show everyone the label.

Aline Griffith was a Bergdorf Goodman model from Pearl River, New York. She and Larry traveled together on the flying boat to Europe for their jobs in the OSS. Aline enchanted all in Madrid in no time, particularly the matador, Manolete, who presented her with ears and capes at the bullfights. All Spain marveled at where she came from: Rio de las Perlas!

Aline was a beauty and a free spirit. One night at a big banquet at a hotel in New York, she wanted to speak to someone on the other side of the crowded room. She crawled under the long table to get there.

Years later she was giving a talk on Spain in New York City. She asked Larry to sit beside her. I was relegated to a lower level next to a dull luncheon partner. A cold seat! During lunch, Aline asked, "Do you think Gwennie is jealous?" Larry looked down and said, "I hope so."

I don't think that Larry would have chosen Aline over me but I might have lost him to Lola Flores, a lovely Spanish widow with two children. She had been forced to watch her husband's execution for being a member of the Resistance. This is one of the many instances of Larry being attracted to people he could help.

Our letters to each other were infrequent but we kept in touch. Larry sent me a picture of him feeding a tiger a bowl of milk. The tiger was a rug. I sent him a four-leaf clover and an arrowhead I had found, tiny and fine and sharp, obviously used for small birds. He sent me a picture of himself in Manolete's bullfighter uniform. Manolete was skinny, and Larry said he had to hold the bright pink cape in front to cover the gap. Larry's friendship with Manolete and Belmonte extended well beyond the bullfighting ring.

The care and concern Larry had shown me and my children before he left for Europe gave my life a focus and a strength that I needed. Larry had

Wrong side. No bucket.

told me what I was to do in his absence: make a forty-foot rawhide reata and learn how to be a good cowhand.

I gave myself a personal assignment to learn how to milk a cow. I needed to know how to approach on the left side, to push my right shoulder into the spot above the cow's flank, to place the stool in a position to be easily lifted out of range of any of the four flailing legs, and to always be on the lookout for the rattlesnake all too often coiled in the corner below the feed bin. The lesson was learned, and I asked someone to take my picture, which I proudly sent to Larry. He sent it back asking where the milk pail was. I returned it reminding him milking was done before dawn and after dusk, and the posed photo was taken long after the milk was placed in the cold room to set.

Larry left, for my use, his saddle, with blanket and saddle bags, his bridle, chest strap, cropper, boots, tapaderos, chaps, and the Stetson hat bought in Salt Lake City one Fourth of July. It had a tiny American flag tucked into the band. I used them all until his return.

He asked one of his old cowboys to keep his eye on me. Cuter Bach was a good mentor. He sat with me in the irrigation ditch and taught me how to

In Larry's chaps.

clean the fat and hair off the steer hide. Starting in the center of the hide, four sixty-foot leather strands were cut from a single skin with a sharp knife. After cleaning the strips, we had to bevel them, while working all the time underwater in the ditch. Then we coiled each one and started braiding the four strands. With the leather beveled, the braided strands turned into a round rope. It was indeed forty feet long, and we made a honda loop and a beautiful tassel. Cuter drew the rope down with his horse, Grey Goose. The reata was strong, and it was springy. It was a big, smelly, wet, and very long job, taking weeks. We then coiled it up and waited for Larry's return. When Larry did return, he was very pleased, and was soon to carry it over the pommel of his saddle on our next roundup. At the end of the drive, when the cowboys rode in to the ranch, Larry was not among them. They said he was delayed. When he came in two days later, I found he had been looking for the reata that had dropped off his saddle. Probably it was just as well, as it might have broken and someone gotten hurt. The fun for me was making it and giving it, and his pleasure in receiving it.

One day Cuter said, "Gwen, get out of the wet ditch and come have a cup of coffee." The cup was a can and the coffee was good. Then he took me inside his cabin to show me something. He hauled a wooden box out from under the bed and opened it; it was packed with socks filled tight with silver dollars. "It's all yours gal, but I reckon you're waiting on Larry." He said if Larry didn't return he would "pick me up." He was a good sixty years old but even so it was nice to be wanted.

Cuter taught me a lot. He had a telescope which he carried in a leather case on his saddle. I learned to read the brands and ear cuts on far off cattle. He showed me Indian ruins that I am sure others had not yet found. One was a huge flat rock on the top of a mesa. The rock had a couple of dozen shallow hollows with the metate stones still there. It had been a communal corn-grinding spot, and the Indians must have left in a hurry.

A Navajo, Pusher, lived on the creek near Cottonwood with his daughter, Mazie, and her family of black-eyed children. I rode down to buy a deer hide from him. Mazie said that Pusher was taking a bath, so I got off my horse to wait. After a couple of hours I got up and left. It turned out Pusher's bath was a steam one, from dawn to dusk, throwing water on hot rocks. Pusher was a graduate of Carlisle University, but it did not prevent him from enjoying a steambath and chewing deer hides to tan them.

The next trip to Pusher's I bought a deer hide, a beautiful one. I made myself moccasins which I beaded, and a leather riding skirt with a fringe. I made Larry a leather jacket. When Larry returned, we were at a powwow at Flagstaff. Someone who saw me with two pigtails, leather skirt, Stetson hat, and beaded moccasins asked Larry what tribe I was from. I think Larry was as proud of me that day as he ever was.

Cuter and Pusher were not my only friends while Larry was overseas. Fran Smith and her husband, who lived at the Rimrock ranger station, became close to me. They asked me and the children to stay with them in the spring for six weeks. We had a wonderful time, riding and fishing in Beaver Creek. We ate raspberries almost every night.

The beginning of the summer I rented a log cabin at Mormon Lake - pine country and cool. Mormon Lake was shallow and small, but it did have good catfish which we ate every day.

I got a job helping Yule Weems gathering wild horses. Yule was blind in one eye and had lost a forefinger while roping. He gave me a good mare to ride. Wild horses are swift runners but they are barefoot, and if you can keep up with them, they get sore-footed and tire fast. One day we came on a herd, and Yule went on one side of the low mountains and I the other side. We rounded the mountain and then held the herd between us. The trick was to keep the horses together and drive them back to the corral at Mormon Lake, a good twelve miles away. As we were moving them along, the stallion became aware of my mare and came at me with forefeet raised, nostrils red, and tail and mane flying. Yule yelled, "Hit him with your reata!" I tried and then rode away fast. I was able to get away because the horses we rode were shod. All the way down to Mormon Lake I kept an eye on that stallion. There is usually just one to a herd, and this one became busy with his own girls, and somewhat less interested in mine.

I was rounding Mormon Lake with Yule Weems another time when two men came by in a Ford coupe. The driver was Livy Burrill, ranch manager during Larry's absence. He stopped his car and I got off my horse. He said, "Here's someone you better meet." It was Addison Vestal, the Mellon family tax advisor, from Pittsburgh. He was my first and best Pittsburgh friend, and through the years, he supported Larry's and my life and work.

Livy Burrill had come to Arizona from Long Island, where he had a good wife, and a social life with all too much alcohol. He went West to start a new life. When Larry left for Europe and the war, he did not hesitate to leave Livy in charge of the whole operation. It was not the place to get a cure, but the responsibility and confidence Larry placed in him made him sober, busy, and happy.

Every Saturday night at Mormon Lake we had wonderful square dances with box supper raffles. Each girl packed a picnic for two, and her favorite cowboy would find out which was hers, and be sure to buy it. I remember getting dressed up to go to the square dance. It was tricky trying to put on lipstick in front of the mirror with an oil lamp in one hand.

It was a federal offense to shoot a wild turkey. The big heavy birds could make only two flights before they had to stop to roost. If your horse was swift, you could keep up with them, and with a small rock, easily kill one as it roosted. Sometimes you were lucky enough to find a feather on the ground, but it was still daring to wear the feather in your hat. I used the one I found to decorate my picnic basket, and I always seemed to have a taker.

At the end of the summer at Mormon Lake, I was saddling up horses for the children, when a man drove up in a station wagon. Leaning on the fence and watching me work in the corral, he asked if I would like a job. I grabbed at the chance to be in charge of the horses and riding at Squaw Peak, a dude ranch in Phoenix. School for the children was near.

My day at Squaw Peak was full. I was up early to feed the kids breakfast. Then I rode my horse about six miles to drive the horses back for the day. After that I took the kids to school, and returned to saddle up, and take the guests for a ride. I often took them to Taliesin West, Frank Lloyd Wright's school for young architects. One of the guests at the ranch was Jack Lord King, who had been a student of Frank Lloyd Wright's. He became a good friend, and later our hospital's architect.

In the evening, after the kids were fed, I acted as hostess to the guests. I had to see that everybody got drinks and was happy. At free moments I would run over to see that all was well in our cottage. The kids were always tucked quietly in bed. Michael told me later they could see me coming because I wore a skirt decorated with a thunderbird made of sequins and mirrors that glittered in the dark.

Rattlesnakes were a danger. They cause horses to buck and shy, and possibly throw you. If a snake strikes a horse, it is usually on the head as the horse grazes. The head may swell to the size of a hippopotamus', and, unable to eat or drink, the horse eventually dies. If one sees a snake when riding, it is not ethical to ride on without killing it with a rock. I used to worry about the kids. They all wore boots, and Larry told me not to worry, just to tell them not to put their hands down any holes.

One day in Phoenix when I was riding with the dudes, a rattlesnake was on the trail. One of the dudes, Edie Betts, was my good friend from Shipley School days. I got right off and killed the rattler with a rock. Edie was not surprised, but her friend from Tuxedo Park was horrified.

One night I entered our small bathroom at Squaw Peak and saw a rattler coiled in the corner. I slammed the door to keep it in the bathroom and jumped up on the toilet seat. The only available weapon was a squeegee mop with a soft sponge head. My battle was long and gruesome, but finally successful.

That summer, after Squaw Peak, I put Mike and Jenny and Ian in Captain Moss' camp near Prescott. There were a lot of nice kids, and it was a fun place for them. I went back to Rimrock to stay with Fran Smith. It was not long before the camp sent word to me that Ian had wandered off, and was lost in the pine woods. With the help of the sheriff and his posse, using horses and a jeep, Ian was finally found, thirty-six hours later, asleep on a dirt road. Ian was young, only six - a scary experience.

I had survived well the two years since my first look at Arizona on the ride down to Oak Creek Canyon in the Rimrock Ranch station wagon. I had no plans at that time. I was beginning a new chapter in my life.

On this second trip, I still had no plans, only that Larry had asked me to borrow Bill Jones' Ford coupe and come meet him in Flagstaff. The train, being twenty-four hours late, did not add to my glamour, but it did not seem to matter when Larry stepped off the train with his one small suitcase in hand. It was as if there had been no two-year interval. A quiet ride down the canyon gradually changed unknowns to the realities of the present.

Quickly, Larry and I were off to see Billy in California. As soon as we arrived, however, we received word from Fran Smith saying my husband would be in Prescott the following day. We immediately returned to Prescott. Having finished my years of residence in Arizona, my divorce was now completed.

The following summer, Billy came with a good friend to the Apache

Maid. That summer with the four children was a busy and happy time. It was cool pine country with green pastures for the cattle.

This was a hard time for Billy, as up to then he had been the center of Larry's life. Suddenly there was not only me but also three siblings. Billy's friend Bart proved to be a catalyst, and the summer ended well with the tensions of the early weeks forgotten. It was the beginning of a long and strong bond between the four, and Billy became a devoted child, as close to me as any of my own three children. When he moved to New Orleans to live with us, he became a solid member of the family.

Larry was glad to be shed of his OSS responsibilities. He considered his work in Europe confidential, and rarely talked about it. He did once say that he finally persuaded Mussolini's daughter to sell her father's diary at a big price. It contained nothing more important than dentist appointments. Later, when we went to Europe, we met friends with whom he had worked. They knew him as "Bill," the name he had used during the war. The bonds were strong, but they seldom spoke of their experiences.

When the war was over, before leaving Europe, Larry drove to Germany to take Truda Mellon's family sugar and coffee. He took pictures of them to bring back to his brother Matthew and his German wife.

He had left with one suitcase, and a heavy identification bracelet that Peggy gave him. Back in Arizona, he showed me his suitcase, a different one, with a false bottom. In it he carried black lace mantillas for Jenny and me, and Manolete's red satin cape for Billy to hang in his room. He also brought Patek Philippe wristwatches for his sisters Rachel and Peggy, and for me.

He returned with a spectacular collection of Basque books which he had gathered in Spain. He donated them to the library in Chicago when on his way to Arizona, but he kept his blue Basque beret which he would wear when not riding.

Larry also brought back from Spain two hand-blown glass *pellejos,* all too reminiscent of nursing home life, but also acceptable facsimiles of the traditional goatskin drinking bags found in every bar throughout Spain.

Undoubtedly, they had never before been seen in Arizona, and most certainly never before in Haiti. Later, the two *pellejos* first seen in the Caribbean were guaranteed to liven up any dull dinner party in Deschapelles.

The goatskin is held high by the forelegs, and a thin but strong stream of wine could be directed to one's mouth. The greater the space between the jug and the mouth, the greater the respect of the onlookers. A real aficionado could drink on one side of the mouth and speak from the other. Larry had learned the technique in Spain one evening, while drinking red wine and wearing a white linen suit.

On his return, Larry asked me to live with him, and we all did. Becoming Larry's favorite cowgirl was a strong step towards our future life.

We crowded into Breezy Bench, the winter headquarters of Larry's ranch. Several years earlier, Larry's mother, distressed at finding Larry living in a tent, had built the ranch house for him. With the ranch manager and his wife, the five of us, and sometimes six when Billy was with us, lived in the two bedroom, one bathroom house. We seldom used the big living room. Instead our lives centered around the kitchen and the screened-in porch that became sleeping quarters for the children. The demands on the bathroom were heavy.

Life within the walls of the house was brief and relatively unimportant compared to the time we spent in the corral and on horseback. We did make an effort to plant flowers around the house, and we discovered just in time that oleander leaves are lethal for horses and cattle.

We drove to Phoenix and Larry bought Mike, Jenny, Billy, and me new saddles, blankets and bridles. Ian inherited Billy's first saddle, and Larry got his own saddle back from me.

Larry shod his own horses and also the kids' and mine. It was heavy work but a beautiful job when done. We each had horses that suited us. Mike rode Arizona, a large golden horse with dark mane and tail. Jenny's horse, Snowball, was round, almost white and tractable. She used to ride with her dachshund, Goldie, behind the pommel of her saddle.

Ian had Combo, an old and wise Appaloosa. Combo was so thin that his hind legs and pelvic bones seemed almost separated from his long bony back.

His ears were small and his nose pink and sunburned. He carried himself in a stately and sure manner, and almost seemed to have been borrowed from Don Quixote. One spring when the cavy was brought in, Combo was not among the horses. No one talked about it much, but all seemed to understand his time had come to join his original master.

My horse, Bullet, was so named because of the bullet embedded under the cinch strap. Wild horses were often shot, because they were overgrazing the land granted for our beef. Bullet was lucky he survived, and he was roped and brought in to join our cavy. He was short-coupled, swift and wise. He carried me far and well.

Despite the fact that today Ian is the strongest and tallest of all three boys, I had often replaced his worn clothes with new ones of the same size. He loved riding but suddenly stopped going out with Jenny and Mike. He said it hurt his chin, which at that point of his life, was at the level of the pommel. He was small and slight until we got his tonsils removed, and all of a sudden he ate ravenously and grew.

Except for Bullet, our horses were quarter horses. They were strong and sure-footed, and easy to train. Each cowboy at our ranch had four apiece, which they kept shod. The horses were never broken. They were gentled.

When buying the stud horse, Larry chose among all the rest a Morgan with one eye. For years, Clipper threw wonderful colts. He made his mark on our remuda, one of the best in Arizona.

When I first met Larry I quickly joined the cowboy habit of carrying a package of Bull Durham tobacco with papers in my left hand shirt pocket. While riding we could roll and light a small limp cigarette, being careful not to let the match head fall in the hole behind the pommel.

When Larry came back from Europe, he said he would no longer smoke, but took vicarious pleasure in smelling my lighted cigarette.

Moving cattle across the drift fence was a semi-annual event. In the fall, all hands were needed to drive the cattle down to the winter pasture, Breezy Bench. I was delegated to drive the big truck carrying the cat, whom I hated, the saddles, the two milk cows, and all the things that could not be left behind. The three kids sat in front with me, and the cat sat on top of the load. Halfway down the Blue Grade the cat looked down at us from the top of the cab. I went fast so he would go into the back.

When we arrived, we unloaded the cow, the saddles, the bed rolls, and all the summer necessities, but no cat. He did not appear until two weeks later, sore-footed and thin, but he had survived.

The first job on arrival was to get the cow into the milk shed and milk her. As Michael threw a bale of hay down into the bin, we saw a rattlesnake hanging from a wire of the bale. It slithered off to the corner of the stall and coiled. I kept Mike up in the loft, the milk cow outside, and I went back and killed the snake. It was longer than Mike was tall.

I settled the cow down, brought in the pails, and tried to milk. The cow would have none of it. Jack Beau, our new ranch manager, was watching the whole routine and giving directions, carefully removed from the immediate scene, and sitting on top of the corral fence. The cow would not let me near her. Suddenly one of our cowboys rode in for fence pliers. He came near me and whispered, "Gwen, you are on the wrong side of the cow!"

Michael gathered the eggs and I milked the cow. I carried two full buckets to the house. On the trip back for the third bucket and the eggs, Jack offered to help and gallantly took my hat full of eggs. He might well ride a well-caparisoned horse, but he was no man for a ranch.

Jack Beau had been in the OSS with Larry. A French cavalryman, he wanted to be Larry's ranch manager after Livy Burrill moved to Prescott. He was no cowboy! He had a horse which he brushed and curried but rarely rode, and then with a flat saddle! He did not shoe his own horse. While we mended fence and gathered cattle, he counted sheets and made inventories; useless in a community where nothing got stolen or lost. Jack married a nurse, and she added to our crowded household. She saw that the bathroom was clean and the top on the toothpaste before Jack went in.

Jack was very excited when the telephone line started appearing from Cottonwood. He asked Larry what room he wanted the phone put in. Larry said the saddle shed (a good quarter mile from the house), where he could use it if he needed it, but would never hear it. Today in Deschapelles, fifty-some years later, we still live without a phone.

Larry would never say he wanted anything for his birthday. Once he admired a neighbor's brindle milk cow. I approached the owner, but he said it was his best and favorite and he didn't want to sell it. After many evening visits to help him milk, the neighbor finally sold it to me. Larry was pleased and called the cow Ingrid as she had such long eyelashes.

Larry taught Mike to shoot with a double-barreled shotgun. He under-estimated Mike's strength and enthusiasm and Michael pulled both barrels. The tin barn siding probably still bears the dent of eight-year old Michael.

Early one morning, Mousie, our best packhorse, was standing ready to be loaded with rolls of barbed wire for fencing. Larry said he would tie on the load with a diamond hitch. Much as he tried, he could not remember the knots. All morning he tried again and again, as Mousie and I waited patient-ly. Finally, when the sun was high, we were off. It was not only an example of Larry's patience, but also of mine and Mousie's.

Another day Larry said to pack a picnic, that we had a long ride to mend a place in the drift fence. With our sandwiches, we added a round flat bottle of Chilean Underagga wine. The two of us arrived at the fence and decided to eat and drink first. We woke up as the sun was setting, and never saw the hole in the drift fence. We got home late, when the cowboys had all eaten and retired to the bunkhouse.

Close to Breezy Bench was a wonderful prehistoric Indian ruin cut in a high cliff. With difficulty, we could climb up and explore the different rooms. The only things we found there were vestiges of bones, human or animal, we never knew.

One of our favorite picnic spots was Natural Bridge. It was a high stone arch that was cut thousands of years ago by a river that now ran far below it. Along the river was a beautiful ranch, with fruit trees and lots of water. We used to fish there, but never with success.

We all wore hats in Arizona, and they soon became a part of our per-sonalities. From a distance, you could distinguish whose hat was whose, and you could tell who was who by their hats. Ian was continually losing his. We got him a hat which we hoped would be the last one. He really treasured it. He came in from riding in the rain, and with special care placed it on the wood stove to dry. Later, what he grabbed up was a felt bowl, and left on the stove was a circular cinder.

One big ranch near Rimrock was owned by an Eastern businessman, Charlie Ward. His business was calendars, usually with bathing suit girls (some on horseback for the Arizona demand). The Ward group would appear with great prior preparations, equipped with clothes from Denver, saddles and buckles with lots of silver, and hats with chin straps. No real cowboy has any trouble keeping his hat on. On a sunny day you could spot these guests from miles away. You could follow their trail by the shine of the silver and by the Kleenex that was dropped along the way. Charlie Ward and his guests always had a big barbecue to which all from miles around were welcome. Everyone came to eat and to marvel. The ranch was again deserted once the long weekend was over.

Billy began boarding school in California. Larry and I drove over to see him. Tires were all retreads then, and we had four flat tires crossing the desert. We took the big truck, because we wished to bring our mare, Goldy, to be bred. That day we learned one should always unload a horse every five or six hours, as they cannot urinate in a moving truck.

We left the mare and drove on to Carpenteria to see Billy at Cate School. Poor Billy! All his friends' families would usually arrive in Mercedes and Jaguars. Up we drove in the big truck, with a bale of hay in the back and straw in our hair and dust on our clothes. Mr. Cate was great and hugged us both in a most unheadmasterly way! We took Billy and his friends to a good restaurant and started back to Los Angeles and Arizona.

Half way to Los Angeles, Larry suggested we go dancing that night. As he drove along the thruway, I crawled around the cab into the back of the truck and changed my clothes. Then I came in the driver's side and Larry went back and changed his clothes. Mocambo was the spot of the year, good food, good music. As we drove up to the *porte-cochère,* I jumped out to see if we could fit under it. Larry eased in as I beckoned. The doorman, a true gentleman, was glad to see us and parked the truck in the appropriate spot. No one had more fun that night than we did.

When winter ended, the cattle moved north to new pastures as the tiny blue flowers of the phillyrea began to appear. This dark green browse brought joy to the cattle growers. Even though each plant was separated by several feet, it was a strong enough feed that the herd survived the long drive, and arrived up on the summer range in good shape.

All ride slowly when moving cattle, allowing them time to graze so as not to lose weight. Only if one breaks away from the herd is it quickly brought back.

22

The herd was rested where water was available. On our range, water was held in man-made tanks. These were shallow ponds dug by a bulldozer, in spots that would be most likely to catch run-off rain water. When it rained, it was always exciting to ride out to see if the water held. Salt licks were put out near the water tanks. As the thirsty cattle reached the tank, the cowboys were plenty thirsty too. Tank water in the folded brim of a felt hat was eagerly swallowed.

At the end of the day's drive, the chuck wagon would await us. It was a bed truck, with sides that let down to make a shelf for a table. Sarah Killebrew would be inside with good food. We were hungry, hot, and tired. Coffee, beef, beans, and biscuits tasted just right.

Early morning before dawn is the coldest part of the twenty-four hours. We would be saddled and off by that time. Just before the sun rose, we could see puddles become ice, right in front of our eyes. Long, thin, white streaks raced across the water.

Cattle men had no respect for sheep owners. Browsing sheep tear up the roots of pasture grass. Sheep herders were given well-defined routes for their drives between their summer and winter pastures to isolate them from cattle country.

Our range was a checkerboard of mile square blocks of government and private holdings. The government lands were leased to us. One was always careful to drill a well, sometimes five hundred feet deep, on one's own property.

The tract of land holding our cattle was overseen by the government Forest Rangers, whose job was to control the size of the herd placed on the pasture. The Rangers' responsibility was to maintain a balance between the herd and the pasture available. Overgrazing results in permanent damage to pasture land. Rangers also protected certain animals. High on the list were the wild turkey and porcupine. Should a cattleman find himself isolated, or without his horse, the only food available was the porcupine. He was slow-moving and easy to overtake and kill.

The Apache Maid summer ranch house was a beautifully built log cabin with a porch on two sides. It housed all of us and the cowboys, and we ate our meals together around a large table.

One day Larry said we would have chicken for lunch. The only chicken

Apache Maid.

available was an old hen who had had wintered on the hill above the Maid. She was finally caught and put in the pot, cooked for twenty-five hours, and was still inedible.

There were no eggs at the Maid. I heard of some chickens up for sale, and went to Cottonwood to buy them. The three children sat in the front seat with me, and all thirty chickens were in the back of the station wagon with a tarp hung between us. Undaunted, the chickens came under the front seat and sat on our laps and shoulders all the way up the Blue Grade, some fifty miles. From then on we had eggs but also plenty of lice.

Hot water was an unknown luxury. At Apache Maid the water was espe-cially cold. One day Larry said we would all go and have a hot shower. The water pipe to the ranch went high above ground as it crossed a swale. Larry pulled a wooden plug in the under part of the pipe, and we all soaped and scrubbed in the hot water.

Among the ranch hands was Franklin Killebrew. One morning Billy reported that Franklin was in bed with his grandmother. We swallowed hard, because we realized it was Zona Mae, the cook's daughter, with her curlers on. She had been missing from the breakfast table!

Charlie Coon was an albino raccoon bought and brought from

California at Billy's request. When we arrived at the ranch, Larry put Charlie on a leash to walk him to the tank, where he could eat and swim. Larry was talking exquisite French to our potential tutor, Jacqueline Perynelle. We, all behind him, were laughing. With his hand high, his leash was empty and Charlie far gone.

One summer day, Larry handed us each a hatchet, and said he would pay us to clear the very young cedars in the big pasture. We started full of enthusiasm but stopped fast. The trunks were like hard rubber and could not be cut. Even Larry could not succeed.

We still kept going places on retreads. One day we had two flat tires but only one spare. All of a sudden we saw a car and we raced over to get help. It was a ranger car with train wheels, riding on the train track, and obviously of no help to us.

My life began to make sense when my three children and I joined Larry on his working ranch. It was over two years later that Larry asked me to marry him. I said he would be crazy to choose me with three kids. "Maybe that is why I ask you," he said. The respect and love the four children had for each other and for Larry made all their lives happy and full. Larry and I made plans to go East to get married and to meet each other's families.

One morning Larry put on a new pair of chaps made from a kangaroo hide someone had given him. Before starting off he sat in the water trough to thoroughly wet his new chaps, the intent being that at the end of an all-day ride the chaps fit the rider and no one else. They were heavy chaps and heavier when wet, and he had very heavy taps on his stirrups. He was riding Cowboy, a young quarter horse colt that he had been schooling. We were almost home from our long trip to Grandpa Wash, when Cowboy stepped on a tin can and bucked, and threw Larry in front of the pommel onto the horse's neck, his feet still in the heavy taps. I jumped off to grab the bridle, and that made the horse buck worse. Larry said, "I'll try to jump clear!" He got one foot out of the tap but the other hung up. Larry fell hard, but luckily, the cow pony stood, and Larry's other foot came free. I rode fast and got the pickup at the ranch house not too far away. I got Larry in the pickup and drove to Cottonwood Hospital. He had a broken shoulder, and was put into a full body cast, with his arm outstretched and elevated for seven weeks.

We kept our plans to go East. We had plane reservations and thought the trip would be quick and easy. We should have been in New York in ten hours, but we got grounded in Texarkana and ended up sharing an upper berth for two nights on the train. Larry, once up, was fairly comfortable, but I had to sleep curled up at his feet. The train was very crowded, because all the passengers from the plane needed space.

Mother, and my sister, Kathleen, loved Larry as everyone does. Mother was immediately charmed by Larry even in his full body cast. Kathleen asked me if I knew who I was marrying. "Sure," I said, "a cowboy from Arizona who had lived in Pittsburgh when young." Up to that moment I had no idea of the significance of the Mellon family. Of course I knew of Andrew Mellon and the National Gallery, but he was a distant relative.

Neither did the Mellon family have any idea who Larry was bringing from Arizona to marry. From the first moment I saw them they were wonderful to me, welcoming and warm. Larry's sisters, Peggy and Rachel, remain two of my most valued friends.

Peggy gave us a small party to meet close friends and family, and then we left for Miami to join Larry's father. Our plane didn't take off because of bad weather - rain and snow. We got in a taxi to go to the lodging the airline assigned us. On the throughway, the hind wheels of the taxi came off, and the driver told us to get out fast, as he had no lights. We stood by the roadside in the pouring rain, and Larry's cast began to melt!

We arrived in Miami. I was nervous about meeting Mr. Mellon, or "Big Pa", as he was known by the family. The plan was a fishing trip on his boat. I was somewhat surprised to find the fishing boat was not a fast Chris Craft with raised seats over a cabin and fishing poles placed high in the air. What I did see was *The Old River*, a shallow draft, flat bottom boat, equipped for all types of fishing, and large enough to accommodate a crew of eight, and up to ten guests. This type of craft gave access to many fishing areas inaccessible to most boats.

During the beginning years of the war, private seagoing boats were not allowed, so Mr. Mellon turned his over to the United States Navy for it to use. In exchange, the government allowed Mr. Mellon to have *The Old River*, suitable for use only in shallow waters. This houseboat was dependent

On *The Old River,* with Larry in a cast.

on good weather to make it across the Gulf Stream to Bimini, and to spend the winter in the calm fishing banks of the Bahamas.

Awaiting departure from the dock, I was standing on the deck of *The Old River* with Mr. Mellon and the captain from Brooklyn. The captain reported a delayed departure, saying the port "terlette" was underwater. This sounded to me like a nautical term, and somewhat in awe of both gentlemen, I asked what a "terlette" was. Nothing nautical about it! Larry never let me forget these introductory words I had with his father.

I fished each day and began a close relationship with "Big Pa." Landing a bonefish in the skiff by myself with the guide poling raised my prestige. Bonefishing is an art, demanding the right guide, the right skiff, the right tide, shrimp for bait, patience and silence. The tension is high when one sees the tails, as the fish feed on reeds, and the tide carries them close to you. A light bass rod, with a light, strong, and long line is used. You cast your bait in front of the advancing tail. You can feel if the bait is taken but you do not strike until the fish has had time to swallow the bait beyond its bony mouth. Then you strike hard, and the first of many runs begins. The fish is heavy and strong, and the battle is a big one. One earns a deserved crown if the fish ends up in the boat.

Each day we went to a different location, with different equipment for a different kind of fishing. In the mornings we started out, each in our own boat with our picnic basket and our fishing guide. Larry couldn't leave *The Old River.* In fact, no one even wanted him to lean on the rail lest he fall in with his heavy cast.

This was the last of a sequence of boats in the Mellon family. "Big Pa" had the first big *Vagabondia,* that was built in Kiel, Germany. It had Diesel motors, making it capable of crossing the Pacific or rounding the Horn. It was used by the W.L. Mellon family on trips to the South Seas. There were lifeboats and ample crew for fourteen passengers. Usually the trips included a scientist or an ornithologist, who always made an important contribution to a Pittsburgh museum. One time Larry left the ranch and joined this boat for a leg of the trip between Los Angeles and Peru. The boat then went on around windy and cold Tierra del Fuego. This same trip had been made five years earlier. There, at this windy spot at the tip of Patagonia, stood the same low stone houses with doors close to the ground. Remarkably, those who came out to welcome them were wearing the *Vagabondia* shirts that had been given to them five years prior.

On one of the trips to the South Seas, a tidal wave approached the *Vagabondia.* The Captain and Mr. Mellon immediately turned the boat to face the coming wave. It was a quick and wise decision as the yacht survived, but all lifeboats and many other things were ripped off the deck. They were able to make port and obtain repairs.

Later in Haiti, a doctor and his wife, who had seen pictures of the *Vagabondia,* were sailing a Sailfish in Saint Marc harbor. They saw a tramp steamer with a beautiful teak hull. To be sure the bowsprit had been sawed off, but the hull was intact. They sailed close to the stern and could see the screw holes of the ten brass letters long removed. A sad ending for a veritable princess of the seas.

When we returned to Miami, the seven weeks were up, and we went to get the cast off. Larry was going crazy, itching inside it, and trying to scratch with a wire coat hanger. We were so happy to get rid of it. As the cast fell, so did Larry, in a dead faint.

Right after our wedding.

We returned to New York, and to Wilton, where Kathleen lived and where the wedding was to be. Mr. Mellon gave me a beautiful fur coat, my first one. It was especially welcome, as it was winter, and it was cold. He also gave me Mrs. Mellon's ring as a wedding gift. We had it reset in Paris. I never take it off.

Larry woke up on his wedding day and said that this was the happiest day of his life. He had looked out the window and had seen the Gulf sign, the big orange disk. His one contribution to his father's company had been his and Buddy Evans' design of the sign, seen the world over.

The wedding was very small: Mother, my sisters Cornelia and Kathleen, my brother Glen, Peggy and Rachel, a few friends, and Larry's best man, Tony Lage, from Rio de Janeiro, with his wife Zette.

Our honeymoon included my first trip to Pittsburgh. The best man and his wife wanted to come too, so they were on the night train with us. Neither Zette nor Tony are more than four and a half feet tall. Zette was in a short leopard coat and a Scotch tam o' shanter. Tony was in a black Chesterfield and a Homburg hat and brown lizard shoes. When Larry went to the bank later that day, his cousin Dick said, "I saw you get off the train with two of your new children!"

We stayed a couple of days in Pittsburgh and met a lot of people at different parties given for us. I must say Larry took better care of Zette and Tony at these parties than he did of me.

Larry showed me parts of Pittsburgh. He showed me what is now known as the Carnegie Mellon Graduate School of Industrial Arts. "Big Pa" had founded it. It had recently opened, and was the first school of its kind. It is no longer the only one of its kind, but it is still one of the best. Down in the cellar of Carnegie Mellon we saw the first computer, run by a wild, red-haired Russian. The computer completely filled the Carnegie Mellon cellar, but a passable game of tic-tac-toe could be played with it.

When Larry and I left for Arizona, Tony and Zette wanted to come too. So once more we were together on the long train trip back to Arizona and Breezy Bench. After a few weeks Larry said we should go to Mexico, and started getting our pickup ready to camp out. Again Zette and Tony wanted to come. But this time Larry said we were going all the way to Tierra del Fuego, which caused them to pause just long enough for us to jump into the pickup and be off, with a bedroll, ten gallons of water, twelve gallons of gas, a cooking pot, and a coffeepot. They were good friends, but two or three weeks with good friends, especially on a honeymoon, is enough.

Our trip in Mexico was great: South from Tucson, down through central Mexico, and ending at Guaymas on the inland gulf of lower California. The roads were terrible. There was little traffic except to the important cities. We would stop at a hotel when it was convenient. Mostly it was camping out, always by the river where we could wash the dust out of our hair and clothes.

On the eighteen hour stretch from Chihuahua to Torreón, there was no road, so we followed the power line through billowing dust. We drove fast to keep ahead of it, but arriving in Torreón and registering at the hotel, everyone laughed at us. We were caked with dust, and in the room, when we opened our bags, the dust had entered everything. The shower looked great but it was only a look. Larry had a newspaper in his hand which told of an epidemic of meningitis. We repacked and left in minutes to head farther south.

At Tillet's, in Cuernavaca, we ordered painted siam for curtains for our new house in Fort Rock, and chose tile for the bathrooms. All eventually fit in the back of the pickup. One memorable night we camped under a full moon among the pre-Colombian ruins of Mitla.

Camping out in Mexico.

Larry shaving in the rear view mirror.

The Yucatan Peninsula. Ian, Larry, Michael and Jenny.

Mexico City. Jenny, Ian,
and Michael with me.

Heading home, there was no road north. We put our pickup on a freight car and took a plane to Guaymas, where we awaited the truck. Waiting, we had a happy few days in this beautiful spot. When the car finally came, we lost no time continuing on our way north. Halfway to the border, our car, full of tile and things for our new house, froze solid. We hired a flatbed truck to carry us, pickup and all, to the border. We slept in the pickup, on top of the truck, and finally got through the border, had our car repaired, and were on our way home. Some thirty-five years later Larry woke up in the middle of the night and said, "I know what happened to that car. When I put it on the freight car, I drained out all the gas and oil and when we received it, I put the gas and oil back in but I never screwed on the petcock."

One of my favorite memories of this camping trip is of Larry shaving at early morning sunrise, using the small round rear-view mirror on the driver's side.

In the winter months, our ranch could be left with fewer cowboys to ride the drift fence and to check on the cattle. This meant we could be away for two months. In 1946 we went to the Yucatan Peninsula in the days when the hotel in Chichén Itzá had hammocks. There were so few tourists that Sam, the tutor, gave the children lessons on the steps of the Mayan Castillo.

Driving from Mérida to Chichén Itzá, we stopped at a restaurant, and Jenny and I were entranced by a tame monkey that sat at the table with us. On our return several weeks later, Jenny and I produced a suit we had sewn for the monkey. It was very cute, but alas, no hole for the tail!

In Yucatan, the water supply was found in natural underground wells called *cenotes*. Sometimes they were still covered at ground level by the limestone strata, but often this had fallen in. The *cenote* not far from the hotel was a pool of black tropical water, surrounded by a circular wall rising twenty or even thirty feet from the water's edge.

The descent was perilous. We never attempted to take all three children, but brought them one at a time to swim, confiding in them not to tell the others. I often wondered if each child thought himself to be the only one chosen to make this descent.

The green tropical vegetation made a canopy overhead. At the water's edge we always hoped to get a glimpse of a prehistoric fish in this self-contained area.

The largest and most well-known *cenote* is called Thompson's Well. It is close to the Castillo, and has a Mayan altar at its edge. A man named Thompson began dredging the dark sludge by hand, but came up with nothing. A mechanical dredge from Boston was brought down, and it worked. The first find was a gold bell and a small sandal. This was the beginning of the valuable collection of artifacts of Mayan culture that can be seen at the Peabody Museum in Cambridge. The bell and sandal were the first evidence that the altar was used for the sacrifice of young maidens.

We would often ride in a *volanta,* a big heavy two-wheeled cart used for hauling sisal in season. It had space for five or six people, and was drawn by two feisty mules driven by a skinner who had a big moustache, and who wielded a long whip. Going into the jungle we would see ruins, as yet unexposed, but crying for investigation. They were always evident as mounds rising out of the flat Yucatan peninsula, but hard to discern because of the heavy jungle growth. It took only one carved rock to verify that the mound protected a prehistoric Mayan ruin. A pilot told me that throughout the whole Yucatan peninsula, and into Guatemala, there were hundreds of such small high hills.

Since our times there, many mounds have been uncovered, and the dirt road is now paved and full of tourist buses. The Castillo at Chichén Itzá, where the children sat with goats and had their school, is now alive with tourists waiting their turn to enter the temple of Chac Mool.

The evenings were full of beautiful guitar music and the singing of the songs of Palmyrin. Our hammocks, which we finally learned to sleep in on the diagonal, are now replaced by Simmons Innerspring mattresses, and the guitars by stereo music.

The following year we made a trip to Guatemala. This trip, planned with great enthusiasm, proved somewhat of a disappointment. Walls in Guatemala City were alive with precarious cracks. Sidewalks disappeared into deep holes, with the gaps filled by a board. All repairs within the city appeared temporary, which was probably wise. During our one meal in the capital, our table was quickly moved under the door frame. As the whole world seemed to rock and sway, our host unperturbedly put dishes back in their rightful place before us. We left quickly, considering the countryside safer than the city.

The edges of the city were crowded with buses filled with country people on their way from the market - a cacophony of goats, pigs, and chickens tethered to each roof. Even though clothing was so colorful, there was no other note of gaiety. No one smiled, no one sang. The only laughter we heard was from a group of small children, sliding down the steep steps into the market place on garbage pail lids.

The city of Antigua still had many old colonial buildings. They posed not the same threat, as they were lower, and the town was more open, with a large central park. The town was composed of continuous lines of houses on both sides of the street - the only break in the monotony being the number beside each door. We were afforded a lucky glimpse through an open door, which revealed real life behind those closed walls. Chickens, children, plants, and flowers were gathered around a central fountain.

We were entranced by the local looms and colorful weaving. Every small house had a family member who was spinning or weaving. It was there that our plans for establishing weaving in Deschapelles were born. I do have cloth and belts to remind me of the brighter aspects of our trip to Guatemala.

Returning by train to Mexico City, where we would pick up our car, was a thirty-six hour trip. We had a deluxe stateroom with private bath. It was a tight squeeze for the six of us, made even more so by a lacy bamboo double birdcage for our two parakeets in Arizona. The cage had been finished just in time to be handed in through the window. We were able to hang it up on a rope strung between the two shelves over the seats on either side of the compartment, but Larry and I had to be careful not to hit our heads on it.

The private bath, though small, was the only place for a large basket of tiny wild strawberries that was a last minute gift from a friend as we got on the train. As we climbed up to Mexico, the heat climbed too. Well knowing the time it took to gather that many wild strawberries, no one had the heart to throw them out. We just closed the bathroom door, bringing with us the birdcage and the beautiful smell of wild strawberries.

Larry was eager to take me to Beaumaris, the summer home that Mr. Mellon, in his wisdom, had chosen. It was a large tract of islands, and some mainland, on Lake Muskoka in Canada, ideal for fall hunting and fresh-water fishing. To this day the entire family gravitates there and spends vacation days, now each with his or her own home. The original houses were solidly built, often paneled with narrow strips of bass wood. As the family grew, so did the boathouse. Each generation has suitable transportation. One large boat could contain all three generations for a day's trip to the Upper Lake, with a picnic lunch on Blueberry Island - a happy day, all returning with blue teeth.

Larry prized highly a Parker pen that his mother had given him. It was filled by pressing the rubber bladder. It wrote smoothly and evenly, and he always carried it. Once, he realized he had dropped his pen en route around Rimrock Hill, wrangling the horses for the morning ride. It was a large hill, but he retraced his steps for two or three hours and returned happily with the pen clipped to his shirt pocket.

One Sunday during that summer in Beaumaris, Larry and I were on the way to church with Larry's father. We were getting into the boat, and as Larry leaned over to untie the painter, the Parker pen dropped into the small slip of water between the boat and the dock. Larry explained that the pen would float upright because of the pocket of air at the top. If, even in the dark black water of Lake Muskoka, he could catch a glimpse of the metal clip, he would know it was the top of the pen. Larry did see it. He took off his clothes and jumped into the water. His father sat in the boat watching him. Larry dove down and returned with the pen. He then put on his pants, put on his shirt, and tied his tie. We started up the motor and were off to church, Larry with the pen, once again safely clipped in his shirt pocket.

Back at Fort Rock we had approved plans for a new house, and the foundations had gone in while we were away, but the house was a long way from finished. We moved into a bunkhouse, with Larry and me in one room, Sam Brown, the tutor, in another, Angie, the cook, in another, the three children with Elvarado, Angie's son, on the screened porch. The icebox was a screened outdoor shelf. Living was close and tight, but we were all busy outside, and there were not many rainy days. During this time I refinished all my furniture I had brought from the East.

Larry wanted a big house: a room for us, a room for each of the four children, a room with a piano for Sam, and each with its own bathroom.

The house was stone with a slate roof. The living room was large, with a huge fireplace. The dining table was at one end. Windows were on both sides. Our view out the front was an always green sub-irrigated meadow. The other side looked out on a walled garden courtyard.

The floors were slate. The furniture was covered in off-white white. The rugs were the same color, with Navajo rugs in between. The white rugs and furniture covers were a wise choice, as they were washable, and rarely showed dirt in Arizona. Larry studied Arabic in the library, where, over the fireplace, a niche held our Aztec stone figure. A farmer in Mexico had found it in his garden, and sold it to us. The kitchen was large and roomy. A wood-working shop was in the back part of the garage. Up the hill was the water tower and beyond the courtyard a pool.

The schoolhouse was in an old blacksmith's shop, a stone building with a wide and high fireplace that burned big logs for warmth during the winter months. School was the Calvert correspondence system. Sam, the tutor, had a life full of arthritic pain. He used either two canes or two crutches. Michael frustrated him probably the most, because he was always an inch or two beyond the end of Sam's outstretched crutch.

At Fort Rock, the cowboys lived in an old stage coach inn with narrow tall windows on the second floor. The windows had been designed to serve as protection against Indian attacks. One could follow the route of the stage coach, as the iron wheels had cut deep ruts into the white tufa rock. We found two stage coach lanterns that I made into lamps for the living room of the new house.

Larry interviewed and chose Habeeb Massabni to come from Brooklyn to teach him Arabic. His wife and two sons unexpectedly came with him. Each morning, Habeeb, in his Homburg hat and black Chesterfield, would walk the half mile from the bunkhouse, where he stayed with his wife and two sons, to our new house, to give Larry his daily lesson. His wife feared the antelope would kill him on the way. His two boys, however, fearlessly approached a "big pussycat", which was in reality a bobcat.

Roundup meant gathering, sorting, cutting, branding, and vaccinating all of the cattle, and there were a lot with the new calf crop. The bulls were always kept in a separate pasture, one that had good feed. Early in the spring they were turned in with the cows and heifers. This assured all the calves being dropped on the summer range within weeks of each other, thereby simplifying branding and cutting of the new crop.

Everyone had his job as the cattle went through the chute. My job was to give an injection against Black Leg to each calf. Amidst all the roping, cutting, tying down, and bawling of the cattle, I gave Larry a complete dose of Black Leg through his blue jeans, instead of to the struggling calf. I worried, but he was unconcerned, saying that a dose did not kill a calf.

At roundup I sometimes cooked for a dozen or more cowboys. I would go into the storeroom, remove the tarp, and cut meat from the hanging quarter of beef. I'd fry the meat, bake the biscuits, fry the eggs, make coffee, oatmeal and pancakes. The men would be fed and saddled and off by dawn. While they ate, Larry would gather all the horses. It went pretty well at first, and they felt Larry was lucky he married a good cook. But then the stove began to put out less and less heat. I asked Lyman, one of the cowboys, to see if it was broken. He asked me if I had ever dumped the ashes. I had just stuffed in more and more wood and never thought about ashes.

There was only one thing I did not like about life in Arizona. It was Sunday morning breakfast. From the moment I lit the wood stove I began to hear about last night's movie. Frame by frame it was recounted - each door was opened, each shot was fired, and each cattle rustler overtaken. Lots of alternate suggestions for better solutions of the main problem were freely offered and discussed. It continued well after the dishes were washed and dried.

For our meat a young steer would be chosen and butchered in the cool of nightfall to avoid the flies. It was done quite far from the house in a place where the carcass could be left for the coyotes. The hide and the quartered meat were placed on a tarp in the back of the pickup. Once, when the job was finished, Larry told us all to get in the back of the truck. As Ian ran to catch up with his brother and sister, he stepped onto the cow's stomach. Even with green grassy liquid covering his face and clothes, he was assured of our love.

Beef was a steady and necessary source of protein for a cowboy. We began losing young steers and found a hide, marked with our T-bar Lazy S, hidden in a draw. Not too much later, someone came upon a boy skinning a steer. It was Franklin, the son of one of our cowboys, old enough to be a good cowhand. There was a ready market for beef, but stealing cattle carried a heavy jail sentence plus a fine. Larry said he would handle it. All but Franklin ate the beef, and a few days later Larry called in Franklin and told the boy he was to ride with him each day for a year. A simple and successful solution to a potentially tragic incident.

Winds were cold and strong at Fort Rock. Sometimes a cowboy would ride in with a big white sheet, frozen stiff, blown miles from the ranch, and now folded and tied tight on the back of his saddle. It was a wild and dangerous item to pick up when riding a skittish colt.

Two of the things that kept Larry and me close were music and the transit. We could work on both together, and hopefully produce good results. I first encountered the transit and the stadia rod in Arizona. It was here I became Larry's rod man. One day he pointed to a tree on a hill about a mile away. He told me to stand by the tree and watch for his signal. When I saw him wave his handkerchief, I was to stand up, face the stadia rod towards him, hold it steady and straight, and when he waved his handkerchief again, I could sit down. I never saw the handkerchief, but what I did see was Larry approaching me. He had looked down the transit and had found me lying sound asleep. He walked back up, waved his handkerchief and I held the rod steady and straight.

Larry took my sister Kathleen and me on a pack trip to the Indian Place on the lowest part of our ranch, with three horses for us, and Mousie as the packhorse. We had to cross a smooth, steeply sloping rock ledge that abruptly fell off to a deep canyon below. Larry was ahead leading Mousie. Halfway across, I jumped off my horse, and looking back, I saw Kathleen was off even before me. We crawled the rest of the way. Larry returned twice on his horse to lead ours across, saying four feet were better than two.

On the return, Larry decided to go home a shorter but steeper and more difficult way. We were most grateful to our good friend Mousie who refused categorically to climb the steep and dangerous cinder mountain for the trip home. We had to turn around and return by an alternate route.

Once Larry asked me to haul water to Coyote Basin. Our water truck had no baffles. The road was dirt, and it turned to the left and right as it steeply descended. The water in the half-filled truck rushed from one side to the other at every turn, and at each turn the road dropped further. Larry thought I could do anything, but I was pretty scared that day.

The road up from Fort Rock to Highway #1 is twenty-five miles. When it rained it became almost impassable with heavy, black mud that rolled up in balls around the tires. Because of the children I said we must have something reliable to drive in and out. I think we had the first double transmission, four-wheel drive Dodge, with a cable winch in the front. It later was the truck we brought to Haiti.

Larry loved the *Grapes of Wrath*. Every time we left the ranch and were on Highway #1 to Seligman, he relived the Joad family's long trip. His heart always ached for Rose of Sharon.

Each spring we looked forward to the trip south to Prescott, though it meant a visit to the dentist. The first stop was the Green Frog for pancakes and watermelon. We used to shoot the seeds across the restaurant. There was jukebox music and lots of noise. Then we saw the dentist before we went on to buy blue jeans in a store where money went into a box on a string to the office upstairs. Haircuts, and last and best, were the ice cream cones to start the long trip home to Fort Rock.

Years ago, when only cowboys wore blue jeans, the general store in Seligman had them piled high to the ceiling, each pile separated by waist and leg measurements. Every pair had a leather Levi ticket; no other was acceptable. Cowboys were lean and wiry. Every cowboy knew his size and length, and no matter how much some ate, the jean size never changed. The jeans had copper rivets identically placed, no extra pockets, no full legs. They were rolled out the same year after year, and shame on any man who could not fit into his. Sometimes the winter months, when there was not so much riding, caused the waistband to fall below the belly.

Frontier pants were light wool with slash pockets, and a pressed line down each leg. They were acceptable for the Cattle Growers Association meetings or a trip to Phoenix or Tucson.

Special shirts, that were custom-made in Denver, were worn on special occasions. They had snaps for buttons, with eight or ten down the front and four on each cuff. As I remember, they had two breast pockets with flaps and snap buttons again. The material could be flannel or fine cotton, depending on where you would be wearing them. They were always dry-cleaned in Phoenix or Tucson!

No working cowboy would be caught in frontier pants, dress shirts, and fancy boots. On the range, boots were unshined, with the heels worn down from digging in the ground while roping.

In Arizona the backbone of the country was broken-boned cowboys who were used to heavy daily work. Two I know had lost their thumbs roping cattle. Many had pains and aches from past riding injuries, but none stopped working. Larry was one of them.

In those days, every cowboy had a pickup truck with a single horse trailer, or double if he had a wife beside him. The bed of the truck had a bale of hay, saddles and bridles, a bed roll, cooking pot, and coffeepot. They were mobile, and would accept work almost anywhere. I don't remember seeing any of them being paid, but I know they were well fed.

Years later, we made a trip back to Arizona to see how our head cowboy, Bill Jones, was faring. Bill used to be the one who picked out the morning horses from the cavy of forty. On horseback, in the middle of the corral, he could rope, one by one, the needed horse, as the cavy quickly rotated around him. We found him alone in a trailer, with a radio and an oil stove. When we asked him where the cattle were, he said they were all in feed lots, and all the ranch lands had been given over to development. There were houses everywhere.

On that trip we saw pickups but no saddles, no bridles and no horse trailers. All too often it was a closed car, the driver wearing shiny boots, with no mud and no worn-down heels. They had ironed blue jeans, twelve-button shirts, big Stetson hats, silver belt buckles and leather neckties. Bill Jones was right. The era of the cowboy was over. Except for a chance news article, Larry might well have become one of the best cowboys, but also one of the last.

CHAPTER 2

Our Mentor Is Chosen

I had begun to feel that Arizona, the ranch, and the limited life it involved, was not big enough for Larry. If it had been, I would have happily stayed with him in Arizona.

Providentially, the October 6, 1947 copy of *Life* magazine arrived. In it was an article about Albert Schweitzer, calling him the greatest man in the world, and describing his medical mission in Africa. Larry read it carefully and said, "I think I will go to medical school." I said, "Great. I will go too."

Since we had already made plans to take Michael, Jenny, Ian, and Sam, the tutor, on a trip to Peru in early 1948, Larry chose Jack Beau to go to Lambaréné. He would carry a letter to Dr. Schweitzer, explaining Larry's plans and asking for wisdom.

The six of us went on to Peru via a Gulf Oil freight boat, the *Santa Flavia*. But our trip was now purposeful. We were looking for a place to build our hospital.

The freight boat left from the port of Los Angeles. It was cold when we left the ranch, and we all had on winter clothes. Also we had the school books and big rollermaps that Sam, the tutor, insisted on bringing. The children had formal classes each day at sea but time off in port because of the noisy donkey engines. Larry and I had biology books, as we were to stop in New Orleans on our return to apply to Tulane Medical School.

Recently I received a letter from a passenger on that freight boat. He remembered Larry and me studying biology and hoping to get into medical school, and then build a hospital. Forty-five years later he saw an article about the hospital and wrote to congratulate us.

Sam and his crutches could descend the gangplank easily when the tide was in, but by nightfall it was a steep climb with each step of the gangway at an acute slope.

At sea, if it were rough, the captain would not allow the kids on deck. There were no railings, only ropes that swung out over the sea.

When we hit the Japanese current, we started shedding our winter clothes. I took one look at the children's long underwear, and decided I would not carry them down and back across the equator. I asked Mike to throw them overboard. With very little meteorological background he threw them from the windward side. All three pairs flew high in the air, and with bent knees and dropped seats, caught and hung, firmly intact, high up in the rigging. The captain later learned to love all three children.

Arriving in Lima we rented a car and driver to take us to Arequipa. The trip was a wonderful experience. A series of arroyos, each presenting a special problem, swept from high in the mountains to the sea. The car was large and the driver, excellent. He took care of us and prayed at every roadside shrine, leaving coins at the bottom of wooden crosses that were mute evidence of those who had not passed well. At the top of each gorge there seemed to be a treeless, sandswept desert. One had crescent-shaped dunes, all facing the same way. Another had straight paths in the sand, going in different angles as far as the eye could see. Later, air surveys interpreted them to be prehistoric astronomical reckonings. Unfortunately, due to these explanations, and paved roads, tourists have almost obliterated the beginnings of these trails.

After two days on the road we arrived in Arequipa, a beautiful colonial city with Spanish architecture and colonnades. The cathedral was large, and so was the market that was close by. The center square was filled with trees and plants and was bordered by a wide, mosaic walkway. True of all South American countries, Sunday was the big day. The park benches were filled with entire families, and there was a festive air with the frescoes, balloons, and baby carriages. On the walkway, eligible girls, dressed in Sunday finery, walked two by two, clockwise. All the young males, equally well dressed, walked counter clockwise. None got but a passing glance. The *duenna* seating regally on the park bench never took her eyes off her responsibility.

We stayed at Casa Bates, a charming and rickety old wooden hotel with eight or ten cottages and a garden.

It was cold in the mornings, and a man would wake us by putting a piece of moss as big as a pumpkin in the fireplace and throwing rum and a lighted match on top. He would then leave, slamming the door behind him. The room was warm in no time.

Breakfast was served on the roof of the old hotel. We ate in wicker chairs that fell apart when you pulled them up to the table. Boiled eggs were a gamble. Three times, Mike had one with a chicken inside. He still, to this day, does not eat boiled eggs. The view made up for all this, however, for three snow-capped mountains surrounded us. Mount Misti was the most beautiful.

I must say that whenever we travelled, especially with the kids, Larry had a Stillson wrench in his baggage. In Arequipa it stood us in good stead. Owner Tia Bates put us into three nice cottages, and one by one Larry fixed up the plumbing. And one by one she moved us all to more "comfortable" cottages, and one by one Larry's Stillson wrench was called into service. Despite the high quality copper tubing, the plumbing was obsolete. "Gwen," he said, "come up on the roof and I'll show you something you will never see again." It was indeed complicated, a plumbing system that even Rube Goldberg would have envied.

Tia Bates had gone as a young bride to join her husband who was administrator of an isolated tin mine high in the mountains of Peru. It was a cold, windy and barren part of the world, and social life was almost non-existent. Tia would sit with the local girls and help them roll cigars. At the same time, she learned a variation of the Spanish language that, years later, compelled her servants at Casa Bates to cover their ears when she spoke. She always asked us to her bedroom which reminded us of everything but the beautiful outdoors.

Larry wished all the children to learn Spanish. He quickly found a woman with several children, and my three spent each afternoon with the family. Mornings they devoted to Sam and school. Larry took daily Russian lessons from a Russian lady, while I went to the market with Tia. Tia also used to take Larry and me down to the prison to visit. She would give cigarettes to me and tell me to break them in two to hand around. One of the prisoners said the aerial was broken. Tia said, "Oh, that's all right, Mr. Mellon can fix it." Larry had to climb up on the high, tiled roof and fix the aerial. No prisoner would have been allowed to do it.

Tia would confirm reservations, and then sit and wait and watch the newcomers as they came up the steps. If she didn't like their looks, she just said there was no room. It was hard, as alternatives were not pleasant. As unexpected as life was at Casa Bates, it was a unique place that many loved, and it attracted people like Noel Coward and Ernest Hemingway.

One day a missionary arrived at the Casa Bates, with his wife and small seven year old boy. They could speak no Spanish, and were on their way to a mission station in the Andes. That night the child got a high fever, and Larry was delegated to bring the three of them down to the town and to find a doctor. The doctor said the child had to be operated on immediately for appendicitis. Larry translated all of this and helped the family to the operating room. Larry kept being sent into the town to get more gauze, cotton, anesthetic, and needles, each time having to explain to the parents what he needed. I sat with the parents, watching Larry dart in and out at high speed.

A half a day later, the child, pale as a ghost, was rolled out of the OR. Larry whispered, "I don't think he'll make it." Larry and I took turns for the next two or three days with the family and helped translate. The child did survive. It gave us an idea what one could go through if a child needed surgery in a foreign country. We were lucky.

We had given Sam a trip to Cuzco, and when he returned, Larry and I, leaving the children with him, were off on a trip to the headwaters of the Amazon, to a place called Tingo Maria.

We first flew to Lima. Lima was a beautiful, colonial city built on a sloping hill, with parks and city squares surrounded by covered colonnades. Lima is noted for its *chifa,* or Chinese restaurants. They are proud to have you enter through the kitchen so that you may order and eat with a free mind.

The United States Embassy residence was in the center of the largest park. In the middle of dinner there one evening, all conversation stopped as dogs began barking, cocks began crowing, and then there was a huge deep-throated rumble. The chandelier shook, the glasses rattled, and the guests jumped up and stood in the door frames. An earthquake is an expect-ed and periodic occurrence in Peru, and even though it is often repeated, it still strikes terror in the hearts of those who have seen what it can do. The shaking and noise stopped, but the dinner did not continue and everyone drove soberly home.

We wanted to visit Tingo Maria because we were thinking it might be a possible site for our hospital. This meant crossing the *altiplano*, the highest point in the world where people manage to live. We were told we couldn't get into the Amazon basin at this rainy season time. Dauntless as always, Larry found a taxi willing to make the climb up to Cerro de Pasco, across the *altiplano* and down into the Amazon valley below.

When the taxi came, we were shocked to see that it had a huge oxygen tank in the back seat. It made us a bit nervous, but we managed to ignore it until we reached the high plateau, when we both grabbed the masks and gulped oxygen. The people who walk on foot to these high altitudes have no trouble with *soroche*, or altitude sickness, if they follow the trails of llamas or alpacas.

Cerro de Pasco is a cold and heartless city. It is set in the middle of a treeless plateau where the wind blows continuously. Houses have low roofs and few windows or doors in order to conserve warmth. People huddle under heavy blankets and black hats, and they do not seem to move much.

Life seemed slow and uninspired, the people dour, no music and no laughter. The city of Cerro de Pasco was built on top of the richest tin lode in the world, but this did all too little to affect the well being of the people.

Everyone seemed to be drinking a hot drink called café. We soon dis-covered it was coco, or cocaine. Without it these people could not survive. Our driver would stop for a drink, drive wildly, and then after gradually slow-ing down, he would stop and drink again. We did not understand this sequence until the trip was over.

Once, on the edge of the plateau, we were told it was the day for the traffic to descend. We were lucky, we thought, until we periodically encoun-tered some *hombre valiente*, a macho man who risked lives and vehicles by going against the traffic, hugging the inside wall. The sides of the canyon were wet and quivering. We hesitated to blow the horn for fear of a landslide.

Billy and LeGrand on the Amazon River near Pucallpa, Peru.

When we arrived in Tingo Maria, we found a beautiful spot, lush and tropical, where the Amazon was swift and narrow. It had a small but good agricultural center. The people were friendly and healthy, and there were not many of them. Hardly the place to build our hospital.

We saw quite quickly all we needed to see, then found we were unable to reach Pucallpa, a town down the river, another spot we had considered for our hospital. Years later, Dr. Theo Binder came to visit us in Haiti. He had also been looking for a location to build a hospital, and had been in Pucallpa the same year, the same month, and same day that we were in Tingo Maria. He did build El Hospital Albert Schweitzer, in Pucallpa. Imagine if there had been two hospitals of the same name, only one hundred miles apart.

Later, Billy and his wife, LeGrand, made an excellent movie of Theo Binder's medical mission in Pucallpa. It depicted the life and work done in this corner of Peru, but also confirmed our original impression of this area of the upper Amazon, with its few and comparatively healthy people. It would not have been a good place to build our hospital.

Not too many years ago, a Catholic priest came to Deschapelles. He was compelled to leave his mission station in Tingo Maria because it had become the transhipment center for drugs from Bolivia and Colombia. What a calamity if we had chosen to build there!

Arequipa. Swinging
in the basket from
cliff to boat.

When we were ready to return to Lima, the chauffeur could not be found. He did appear two days later, a shadow of his former self which had not been very good to begin with. We returned, going with the traffic.

We rejoined Sam and the kids at Arequipa, and we left Peru via Mollendo. Euphemistically called a port, it is one in name only. It sits on top of a high, rocky cliff that is continuously beaten by angry waves, pacific in name only. It is termed an open roadstead with no dock and no tenders. Goods and passengers are transferred between boat and shore by a shoulder high, woven basket. On top of the cliff, a crane operated by a donkey engine swung the basket high over the waves to the boat, where it was caught by two sailors on the boat's upsurge. Two by two, the Mellon group tumbled out onto the deck, feeling much safer there than in the basket.

The trip continued to be one of ups and downs. Meals were served in the galley, on a table with raised edges to keep plates out of one's lap. The water in the glasses, continually seeking its level, did not whet our appetites. Once we reached the edge of the Japanese current, however, all was calm, and our spirits rose as we reached Panama City and entered the Panama Canal en route to New Orleans. Undaunted by not yet finding a place for our hospital, we were full of resolve to get into medical school and to pursue our chosen goal.

When Jack Beau had arrived in Lambaréné, he learned that, as always, visitors were asked to wait for Dr. Schweitzer to be available. But the whole day Dr. Schweitzer had reserved for Jack Beau was spent by Dr. Schweitzer in trying to find Jack and his wife river transportation to Port Gentil. Jack and Annie had few words with Dr. Schweitzer. Larry's letter, however, was well received, and Dr. Schweitzer spent the whole night before the Beaus' early morning departure writing his reply.

When we returned to the ranch, we found that Jack Beau had brought gifts from Dr. Schweitzer. The stone mask has been the first thing we hang in a new home. It is hung by a fine copper wire at the hair line, and mounted on a background of woven African straw cloth attached to a New Orleans cupboard door. Jack also brought a hippo tooth, the size of a small garbage pail. We placed this on the fireplace mantel. In a matter of weeks, due to the climate change from damp tropical Africa, to dry Arizona, this massive molar exploded in the middle of the night with a shattering noise, throwing shards of bone to every corner of the living room.

The real treasure that Jack brought was the hand-carried reply from Dr. Schweitzer. The care with which Dr. Schweitzer's letter was opened and the care with which it was read was touching to see. The letter was tightly written on one side of legal-sized, airmail weight paper. The five pages of this first letter were neatly sewn together in the upper left-hand corner. As we later learned, paper clips and staples are quick to rust in the tropics.

When asked what he thought of our following his path, and establishing a medical mission in a needy spot, Dr. Schweitzer pointed out the pitfalls and the disappointments we would face, but in no way did he discourage us.

49

A letter from Dr. Schweitzer.

From that day forward, our lives changed. We now had a goal and a mentor. It was the beginning of eighteen years of correspondence between Larry and Dr. Schweitzer, and it continued to strengthen our resolve to find our own expression of Dr. Schweitzer's ethic: *Reverence for Life.* He understood our hospital would not be a copy of his. It was the footprint of his philosophy that we were to follow.

The letters between Larry and Dr. Schweitzer over the years show that the wisdom Dr. Schweitzer gave was so basic and wise. They reveal an understanding of the difference between his beginning problems and those we had ahead of us.

CHAPTER 3

Anopheles And Stethoscope

Our initial choice of New Orleans and Tulane Medical School was based on the fact that the city's outlook might well be towards South America and the Caribbean, places we thought could contain a possible site for our hospital. Therefore our stop in New Orleans held great importance. A lot had to be covered fast: An interview with Dean Lapham of Tulane Medical School, a school for the two youngest children, and a house for seven years.

We had an appointment with Dean Lapham. He hesitated over Larry, with three years of pre-med still ahead of him, and we left his office. I ran back upstairs and said, "If you don't see your way clear to admit Larry Mellon and myself to medical school, you will make a big mistake." He did see his way clear, and Larry began making up three university years in just a year and a half.

Even though things were still uncertain about our admission to Tulane, we went ahead like it was a fait accompli. We saw three houses. I chose one and went back the next day to measure and plan. We got Jenny and Ian into a good school. Billy and Mike were to be at St. Paul's in Concord, New Hampshire. The whole sequence took two days, and we were on our way back to Arizona. Larry got ready for summer school, but we made a fast one-day trip to Los Angeles to see Billy, and then to choose the wallpaper and curtain material for the New Orleans house.

I was elected to close the ranch, as it was to be put up for sale - furniture, cats, cows, horses, saddles, you name it - and to move our possessions to New Orleans to meet Larry at the end of the summer. We had just settled into the new Arizona house. It was lovely, but I had little nostalgia in leaving it. I was looking forward to the New Orleans house with the lovely garden, and to adding the necessary pre-med credits to my Smith degree. Still, Mike shed tears with me, as we saw the Mayflower moving van enter the road to the Fort Rock house.

At the end of the summer, Larry met us at the train in New Orleans. His first words, after a big hug for us all, were, "Don't do it Gwennie. It is too hard." Secretly I was relieved. Four children and two parents in med school didn't bode a happy home life.

One of my first wishes, I told Larry, was to go to hear jazz in the French Quarter. He said there was nothing to it, and calling the district sad and dingy, said he would not take me. It seems while I was packing up the ranch, he had a surfeit of the noise and clamor of Bourbon Street. The only time I really heard much jazz in New Orleans was the night of Larry's graduation party, when Papa Celestin played from seven p.m. to seven a.m. in our garden.

Having chosen to not go to medical school, I began to seek other ways to prepare to be helpful in our new life, wherever it would take us. I went to lab school briefly, but was easily lured away by a malariologist at Tulane School of Tropical Medicine. Johnny Walker had a pointed nose and quite strongly resembled a mosquito. He wished someone to help him with the induced malaria therapy that was being used, along with electric shock and also insulin shock, on paretic patients at Charity Hospital. I had to raise anopheles mosquitoes, feed them a blood meal on the shaved back of a rabbit, infect them, put them in a plastic cage, and then take them to the psychiatric ward at Charity Hospital. To be sure they were infected, I had to use a dissecting microscope. Working in a drop of water, I examined the salivary glands for spirochetes, and the stomachs for oöcytes. To keep your hands from shaking when working in a drop of water, you handled your needlelike tools as if they were crowbars.

My first lesson with Johnny Walker was to take down and clean his personal old microscope. It was a Zeiss and looked like a Bofors World War I gun.

I worked hard and learned a lot, and I enjoyed Dr. Walker's office. One day I told him I had to stop working for him, because Larry and I had forgotten our wedding anniversary. I said that I thought I'd better stay home and take care of my family. Larry, however, said there should be no problem, since we had both forgotten it.

Medical students had some classes in the School of Tropical Medicine. Since I set up the slides for the tropical blood diseases, I was Larry's instructor for a brief time.

Dean Lapham of Tulane Medical School became a good friend. Because I worked in the lab, I could call him Max at the coffee hour. Larry had to call him Dr. Lapham, and never made it to the coffee hour.

The induced malaria therapy project at Tulane ended, and I chose to go to the Veterans' Hospital to work with Dr. Pizzalato. This hospital was a tumor center. My first job was filing lab slips. In my indoctrination into this new medical world, I was terrified that I would get cancer from the pieces of paper. I carried my sandwich to work, carefully wrapped in paper. I would eat my lunch outside, firmly isolating the sandwich from my hands with the wrapping paper. I learned a lot there, but what comforted me most was that cancer was not contagious.

Dr. Pizzalato knew Larry had to repeat the head and neck part of his anatomy course. He offered to help Larry, said that he had a good brain, and offered to bring it to the house on Sunday. He came on Sunday with the brain, and small, unruly twin sons, who were put in my charge to entertain and keep from drowning in the pool. Larry and Dr. Pizzalato sat at the dining room table using my new carving knife, which sharpened itself as it fit tightly into its wooden case. After that day, I never used the knife again, but Larry knew his brain pathology. Today Jenny, Ian, and I can still recite most of head and neck structure and muscles.

I also had a course as a nurse's aide. The Catholic sister who was the OR head nurse of Charity Hospital let me learn and work as a rotating aide in the enormous operating theaters of that great hospital. Sister Patricia was so good to me. The hospital had great appeal to Larry and me, because

Governor Huey Long had built it with the understanding that blacks and whites would have equal treatment. The building was divided into two mirror halves. The treatment that patients received was identical. The only spot where segregation was not observed was in the elevator down to, and within the morgue, where blacks and whites lay side by side and were treated with equal respect.

Larry had a mole on his groin. Jenny had one on her scalp. Working in the Veterans' Hospital tumor center lab, I persuaded Larry and Jenny to let me make an appointment with an oncologist. They went together. Larry said his problem was here, as he pointed to his groin. Jenny said her problem was here, as she pointed to her head. This was a strange moment, and the doctor was bewildered. It seemed that there were two Dr. Owens. One was an oncologist and one was a psychiatrist. Larry and Jenny eventually saw the oncologist who removed both moles.

At medical school, Larry carried his books in a big leather postman's bag that Peggy had given him. I don't know what became of it. We are great at not keeping things we don't use.

During Larry's first days of medical school, Thomas Jimenez was asked how many Puerto Ricans were in the class. He replied, "Four. Paco, Stephan, me, and Mellon." Larry had chosen a spot at the table with them, and all of his anatomy was learned in Spanish. It was more for the three Puerto Ricans than himself, as Larry's Spanish was impeccable.

After Larry's first year of medical school, during two months off for the summer, we went to Marcus Lawrence Hospital to get our feet wet with medical and surgical friends.

Marcus Lawrence had been a young man who came to Arizona from the East to make a new life and fortune. He had died tragically, because there were no medical facilities available. Larry initiated and supported the building of a small general hospital in his name. It was here that Larry's shoulder had been set. During that summer at Marcus Lawrence Hospital, we were exposed to many aspects of what would be our future life.

By the pool in New Orleans. Michael and Billy with Larry on the top step.
Jenny and Ian with me one step below.

Angie Caballero was a Mexican nurses' aide at the hospital in Cottonwood. When our motel stove failed, she would invite us to her house for a good meal. Her garden was full of flowers, and she served wonderful Mexican dinners with tortillas, refritos, and rum. She later came to Haiti to work in the hospital. She bought a house there, and gave it to Haitian friends when she left.

In their last year, medical students are asked to choose something in their diet that they can completely do without for one week. Some chose salt, some sugar, some meat, etc., but our housemate chose to do without everything except water. We would try to slip away for meals but no such luck. Larry insisted on sitting with us to watch us enjoy, or try to enjoy, our meal.

Max, among many others, was proud of Larry. Larry was the oldest in the class by far, but served as president in his junior year.

The New Orleans house was lovely, and the garden and the swimming pool were great. I cut out the wallpaper magnolia blossoms, big white ones with green leaves, and pasted them on the lower part of the wall on the winding stairway.

Ian was big into photography, and I gave him and his friend Deanie the third floor bathroom to use as a dark room. If the water did not run in the faucet, it meant we were filling the swimming pool. With the faucet open, Ian left for another project. That night we awoke to water pouring down the front stairs, damaging all the cut-out magnolias and my clothes closet. Larry came home, and unperturbed, told us to get the damage fixed. Before the swimming pool season ended, it happened a second time, and equally unperturbed Larry had it repaired once again.

Our garden was large, and it was beautiful due to the efforts of our gardener, Mr. Kepke, and his wife. They both worked long and hard hours, and wore work gloves with gauntlets. They asked to be paid in cash and not by check. They never told us where they had come from, and we never asked.

They once asked us for dinner. The table was small, but the cloth was of fine, white linen. There was one silver candlestick. The two sets of knives, forks, and spoons by our places were heavy silver. This evening, without their gloves, we saw tattooed numbers on their wrists. Mr. Kepke died during one of our absences from New Orleans, but his wife continued to work alone until we left. I am sure this friendship was equally valued by all four of us.

From the Kepkes we learned that old Christmas trees had a special value in New Orleans. They were gathered up willingly in the streets and thrown in certain spots along the river and bayous. They made ideal breeding and nesting areas for the famous Mississippi shrimp of the local restaurants.

Larry used to worry about the nursemaids walking round and round our block with their little charges, so we put a fountain and a circular seat around a big tree in front of our house. It was close to the sidewalk so the nursemaids and children could drink and sit and rest in the shade.

We had an old cleaning man, Henri, who came once a week and polished floors. Ian used to meet him at the door and carry his suitcase up to the third floor, where Henri would change his clothes. One day I drove him home. His home was a big cardboard crate, with an oil stove to keep him warm. We were able to move him into a great house for old and indigent gentlemen of color. My friend, Izzie Ewing, had founded it, and it had just opened.

One night our cook, Lily Belle, answered the phone and told Larry that Peter Rabbit wanted to speak to him. It was Palmer Abbott, who wanted to sell us a new Buick. I told Palmer the story, and he has used it ever since, and no one ever forgets his name.

Jenny had two fat, short, blond pigtails. When she mentioned bangs I was adamantly against then. Suddenly she appeared with a blond fringe across her forehead. I was heartbroken. It was a feather from her cocker spaniel's tail and could be placed and removed at will.

Billy came to live with us to work at the Whitney Bank. We fixed a lovely apartment for him in the brick garage. Usually, when awakened, he would jump up fighting mad. I said I would no longer call him and handed him an alarm clock. After that he was never late for breakfast or for work.

Bahislav Hruby was in the OSS with Larry during the war. As a priest, he had a good cover. He joined us in New Orleans and moved into the garage apartment when Billy returned to school. After looking for a job, he found his CV was not particularly applicable in Louisiana, so he returned to Czechoslovakia for a few days. He contacted a school teacher friend and asked him to name three students who would make good marriage prospects. He called the first, who was not home. The second one, Olga, was, and he asked her to go swimming. The following day, Hub and Olga were married and they returned together to New Orleans. Finally, Hub got a job in New York. Olga stayed on, pregnant, and knowing just enough English to be able to complain about it, until she was able to join Hub. In New York they did a remarkable job managing a program which rescued Christians from behind the Iron Curtain. Their child was named Susie Gwen. The baptism and reception were in our hotel rooms at the Savoy Plaza. Czech President Jan Masaryk's sister was present along with other Czech friends, as was Gregory Thomas, a colorful friend from the war years.

The famous St. Charles Streetcar passed Tulane University. At one end of the run was the Camellia Grill, where, on rare occasions when our whole family was together, we would have hot fudge sundaes. At the other end were the famous restaurants of the French Quarter.

Larry was a wonderful parent, beloved by all four children. He would always consider and wait before punishment, which was rare and therefore very impressive. He had great patience with the two older boys, both of whom presented challenges. When they were searching for their identities, Larry took Mike on a trip along the coast of Florida, fishing and camping. After Larry graduated from medical school, he was diagnosed as having an ulcer. "A very small one," Larry said. I think the doctors wanted him to get away from all pressures. A trip with Billy to South America proved to be a cure!

Our good friend Emory Ross came to see us one day. He said he had a wonderful opportunity to offer us. There were no doctors in the Gabon, but three Gabonese students were qualified to go to medical school. If we could send them, they would be the first Gabonese doctors in their country. We did, thinking subconsciously that they would serve at the hospital in Lambaréné, but the lure of a lucrative medical practice in Brazzaville was too hard to resist.

Both Mike and Billy were each given the chance to travel the length of Africa with Doctor Emory Ross. Being a missionary, and a close friend of Dr. Schweitzer's, Emory was able to show them the hospital at Lambaréné. This wonderful association with Dr. Ross made the fact that they were couriers for a group of missionaries acceptable.

Dr. Schweitzer asked Emma Haussknecht to visit us in New Orleans. She was one of the original staff at Lambaréné. One day I took her to the Marine Leprosy Hospital in Carville. She was used to seeing Africans of no education in Dr. Schweitzer's leprosy village, but seeing doctors and nurses and mission personnel living with the disease at Carville, in an almost closed community, really upset her. Until then, she thought leprosy was a disease of forest people. With this traumatic revelation, she missed her footing and fell. She was in bed in our house for two to three weeks with a sprained knee. This time was for us a joy, as we saw and spoke with her daily and learned, not only about her, but also learned of life in Lambaréné and the important part Albert Schweitzer played in the lives of his staff.

During her visit she gave me a copper bracelet that had been given to her at the time of her stay with a tribe in Africa. I was proud to wear it, and gave it to my granddaughter Susannah when she graduated from college.

Tom Hitchcock, Larry's brother-in-law, gave the ushers at his wedding gold cufflinks with their initials as well as with his own. Larry prized his set. His shirts always were sent to the laundry. The driver returned the cufflinks three times, but the fourth time they never surfaced and disappeared for good.

In New Orleans, Larry gave me a black Jaguar with red leather seats. I loved it, until the medical students I was teaching in Dr. Walker's lab started to tease me. Larry was great. He turned his Ford coupe over to me and tried to hide behind the wheel of my car.

During those years in New Orleans, Larry and I seldom went out together, but people were good to me. In the evenings my friends would take me out and bring me home. But it was not the same without Larry.

1951 GGM Valentine to WLM

My Valentine
He has no time.
His stethoscope
It blasts my hope
Of a day in the sun
And, "you are the one."
My student prince
He never stints
His lab or books
With half-way looks.
But I have no peeve
I await the eve
When the evening is mine
From 6:30 to 6:39
When in between bites
He often recites
The PH for something very alkaline.

My Valentine
He is devine
But his percussion hammer
It chills my manner.
And when on his lap
My knee he'll tap
He'll hold my hand
But not as planned.
He drops it fast
Lest the blood go past
The 0.5 (point five) line
For a white count fine.
He'll look into my eyes at night
But with a little machine and a little light.
My ears are small and devastate
But it's the drums alone that really rate.
I hope you may, this 14th day
Have time to read this as I say
"I'm glad you're mine
My Valentine."
That you are suitable
To me is indisputable.
I'd find it hard, I must admit
To find another who would fit.

The area where we lived was termed "restricted," which we did not understand at first. We soon learned that some of our international friends were not welcome. We resigned from a particular country club when we were criticized for taking our friends, Al and Nena Lavender, for dinner and dancing. It was the first and only time we were ever in that club.

We had a rare treat. The Beverly Country Club was run by a Mafia boss, Phil Kastel, who lived next door to us. He was a good neighbor and always sent my mother flowers and things to eat when she was so sick. The Beverly Country Club was really a big attractive casino, with a huge gambling area. They had the best bands and wonderful food. We would arrive early, eat well, dance once, and leave. Mr. Kastel would almost cry to see us leave without entering the Casino.

Once he had the Brazilian, Carmen Miranda, come to the club, and he had an outdoor Easter party for her at his house next door to ours. Among the decorations were chocolate rabbits six feet tall. Carmen Miranda was adorable but could speak only Portuguese. So could we, which well may be why we were invited. We went into the garden to meet a person everyone called BoBo, who had just been sprung from the pen. He had a diamond zipper, diamond cuff links, a diamond ring, and he was highly respected by everyone present.

Our neighbor eventually was found guilty on some count, and he died in a federal prison. He was, however, as I said, a good neighbor.

When Larry graduated from Tulane, we gave our only party in New Orleans. It was an all night blast, with Papa Celestin and his band playing, and we danced in our garden with family and friends from Europe, Arizona, Pittsburgh, and all over. Even the state troopers, who were there to control the parking, had such a good time that they too stayed until early morning.

At the party, dancing with Max Lapham, I said, "I was so scared years ago, when I told you that you would make a big mistake if you didn't accept Larry." He said, "You were scared? I was scared to death!"

Up The Ogowe River

Duncing medical school years, we did have certain free times together as a family. One Christmas vacation we all went to Nassau. The children had a room near the end of the wing of the hotel. Next door, intermittently, a male voice said, "Oh Boy!" clearly and loudly at all hours. It was a mystery and somewhat disturbing, until we saw a man hanging a cage with a Mynah bird on the balcony.

We also all went to Hawaii. Larry considered we were halfway there when we arrived in San Francisco to discuss the hospital plans with architect Jack King. We were really in Hawaii the minute we stepped on the boat, for the passengers were mostly tourists or returning residents. The evenings were spent learning to dance the Hukilau. Hawaii was filled with days of sun and leisure on the beach of the Hotel Halikulani, with the kids surfing and swimming all day, and dancing all night.

Jack had given us a letter to Mr. Fairchild in Kauai. He had turned his whole end of the island into an area full of every variety of tropical plant. The property had a narrow-gauge railroad that brought you through two altitudes of vegetation. One evening before dinner he told us to go into a room to choose our costumes. There were closets full of traditional dress from all countries in the Far East. We each made our choice and had an identity far removed from reality for the entire evening.

All six of us went to Europe on the *Île de France*. We had two state-rooms, so one of the boys had to double up with a stranger. We chose Ian to move in with an Iranian diplomat. I was allowed in twice, the first time to unpack, and the second time to repack Ian's things. Ian, more than any of us, had a good time. On arriving in Le Havre, I discovered that he had not opened his toothbrush or changed his underclothes during the entire trip.

Jenny had new dresses, and all three boys had new dress suits for the evenings at sea. One rainy day before our departure from New Orleans, I said that we should all go to Arthur Murray's for samba lessons. During our first dinner on the boat, with the first strains of samba music, the band discovered that we were a good floor show. Thereafter, as soon as we entered the room, that rhythm started. We all danced and loved it, and I guess a few others enjoyed it too!

In Paris we stayed in a lovely old fashioned hotel, Hôtel de France et Choiseulle. We all went to Notre Dame, and climbed the highest tower with an intrepid friend of Larry's from the OSS.

While in Paris Larry took me to Patou, and chose for me a black and brown suit with a black velvet collar, and a sapphire blue satin evening dress. Both the dress and the suit ended their useful lives in the deluge from Ian's attic darkroom spigot in New Orleans.

We also went to Cartier and chose the setting for my ring. We had it reset in gold wires which made it acceptable to wear day and night. Someone asked me if it was real. I said I did not know, because it had been given to me.

On arrival in Paris, Jenny and I went for a walk. I explained that sometimes men pinched and talked to young girls. While we going down the street, a man followed us, plucked at my arm and spoke. I told Jenny to watch me, and I would show her just how to handle it. The persistent follower turned out to be Romeo, the driver Larry had hired for our stay in France. At the time we had engaged two cars. Larry and Billy and I often rode together in the smaller car, with the three others in the larger car with Romeo.

All together in Paris, we went to the Marché aux Puces. There we saw, and Larry bought, two small gilded bird cages with keys to wind the birds, and levers to release them. One cage held a bird that sang a beautiful song and lifted its wings. The second and slightly larger cage had two birds that sang back and forth to each other. My bird still sings but no longer flies. Larry also bought Jenny and me ball watches that we wore on fine gold chains.

We saw so many things, from the Bateaux Mouches, to Montmartre with Scott Lockwood, another OSS friend, to Le Chien Qui Rit, and Le Lapin Agile where a chanteuse sang bawdy songs; all were Paris highlights.

We went to visit Combourg where Larry's family had stayed when Larry was very young. Larry took us to the beach where, on his fifth birthday, the family had buried his presents in the sand for him to find. As we walked past the front of the hotel, he pointed out the room on the top floor where he and his nurse had stayed. He told us how each morning he kept hearing someone calling, "Larimer," and he would jump out of bed, run to the window and say, "Here I am!" The man would pay no attention. He was selling the morning newspaper which was called *La Rumeur*. As Larry told this story to us, along came a newspaper man, selling the same paper, a later edition by some years to be sure.

That day there was a marching band and a parade, with the beauty queen in an open car full of flowers. Lots of enthusiasm came from the watching crowds. Later in the evening at the hotel, there was music and people danced. Billy saw the beauty queen dance by and, with the assurance of a Princeton junior, proceeded to cut in. He was refused, there was a lot of noise, and Larry jumped up. The beauty queen was dancing with her father, who was not about to give his daughter to a stranger. Apologies were forthcoming with accompanying embarrassment, especially so for Larry, as the father turned out to be someone he had worked with in the OSS.

We left early the next day. After an omelet we were off on the climb up Mont-Saint-Michel. Then we motored down the Loire Valley through the chateau country. We crossed into Spain by way of the Basque country. It seemed like each day Larry remembered a spot or a friend.

Just before we crossed the border into Spain, we stopped at a farm house to get water for the car. In the barn we saw a Dusenberg convertible, piled high with expensive luggage but covered with dust. The farmer said a woman had come by and asked to leave the car there. Then she had quickly left on foot. It had been seven years, and she had not returned.

In the north of Spain we overtook a wonderful scene, a story in itself. An old man holding the reins was driving a two-wheeled, horse-drawn gypsy cart, with a cloth overhead for protection from the sun. Lying on the bed of the cart, with legs crossed, and playing a guitar, was a young girl with lots of black hair. A little dog, attached by a leash, was following, trotting along underneath the cart. Behind, and bringing up the rear, was a handsome young man on a beautiful black horse. He was wearing a large black hat, tight riding pants, and evil-looking spurs on his bare feet in the leather stirrups.

In Southern Spain one hears the *fado,* a wailing, gutteral, atonal, long drawn-out song of tragic love. It is usually sung by a woman of large proportions. That assures a bellow power strong enough to reach Portugal, the land of the *fado's* birth. The song requires intricate finger work on the guitar, as well as a large tumbling of black hair, and the ultimate loosening of a blouse.

Villa Rosa is an outdoor restaurant high above the city of Barcelona. We arrived late in the evening, and the tables were full. Everyone was drinking Fundador, patiently waiting to hear the tale of the evening song. We secured a table but someone advised us not to sit there. It was a bad spot, since the morning sun would get in our eyes!

Our time in Madrid was unexpectedly extended due to Mike's earache. We stayed at the Hotel Ritz, the best in Europe. Every day for two weeks I crossed the stone courtyard of the hotel garden and entered the wonderful Prado Museum. It took many trips to begin to understand Hieronymus Bosch, and to realize what those high-ceilinged walls contained, with their three-tier hangings. The children of the Spanish royalty became our good friends.

The bullfights were an education to us all, with music, color, excitement, skill, and danger all in one package.

Aline, from Pearl River, New York, now the Condesa de Quintanilla, had a summer cottage on the Basque coast. We had a picnic on the sand, served by a waiter wearing white gloves. He poured water from a silver pitcher onto green grapes and then tossed them to us. Very Bacchanalian! That night we went to the village square and danced the *paso doble*, with the dancers rotating faster and faster in one direction. As Larry passed me he shouted, "Don't fall Gwennie, or you will be killed!"

The trip ended in Cadiz where we saw Lola Flores and her two girls, who now had their own families. Three generations of Flores were living in an old and beautiful house that was four stories high. The entire ground floor, originally stables for horses and carriages, was now a garage for cars. The second, third, and fourth floors were around a large open courtyard full of flowers and trees and shade. Each generation had a floor, and each floor had a balcony that overlooked the courtyard. They could communicate from the balconies above and below and across, making for close family ties. Few details of daily life passed unnoticed.

We met many of Larry's associates from the war. There were friends in Paris, Barcelona, and Cadiz, as well as members of the Maquis in the Basque country.

On another trip Larry and I visited Sir Hugh Foote, former Governor General of Jamaica, and his wife, Lady Foote. They were long-time friends of ours. Our stay in Jamaica with them had been filled with British discipline and fanfare. They had fulfilled their post well, and had lent great dignity at the time of British exodus from that colony in the Caribbean.

It was easy for Larry and me to be persuaded to stop and visit them in Cyprus when we were en route to Israel. The tone on arrival was decidedly subdued. Cyprus with Archbishop Makarios was divided into two camps, with the British playing a holding game between the two. We were met by an equerry who whisked us off to Government House. We stayed at the Residence, with its beautiful gardens, but now the staff were all enlisted men.

It was the Footes' second assignment in Cyprus. Early in their marriage,

Sir Hugh had been a member of the Embassy staff, but as a minor official. They had endeared themselves to those with whom they had come in contact, and they were well known, as they were often seen riding together each morning.

This second tour was very different due to the precarious political situation. Now Sir Hugh's early morning ride required two extra riders; an equerry in front of him and another following behind. But the Footes were still loved and remembered. Fruit and jars of honey were left at the gate of Government House, anonymous gifts from those who cared.

Guests at dinner were only members of the small legation, and Lady Foote and I were the only women. One evening, Sir Hugh asked me to watch as he pushed a button beside his plate. One whole side of the room slowly raised, and the dining area became the size of a banquet hall.

Lady Foote took us off for a day, just the three of us in one car with a chauffeur. Our first stop was by the seaside, and atop a rocky, craggy, wild cliff was perched a Crusader castle. It was like a fairy tale illustration, with five spires and crenelated battlements on top of a rough pinnacle that pierced the sky.

We continued to a small seaside town to visit an ancient Byzantine church. In the town square sat four men playing chess. They were dressed in black, and wearing miter hats. As we drove in, they did not look up. As we entered the church, the bells in the tower rang out, echoing with shattering cacophony. The equerry rushed us out to the car, and we sped away. To be "rung out" of an ancient Byzantine church in a sleepy peaceful village square was a frightening experience. Only then did we realize that our trip had been made with three cars, one in front and another behind.

We bid the Footes good-bye. As we departed, Makarios was arriving to confer with Sir Hugh.

The flight to Israel was short but eventful. All passengers crowded to the left side of the plane to get a first glimpse of their promised land. Emotions were high, and as we entered the terminal, we were "Welcomed Home."

We were allowed to rent a car, but obliged to have a driver. Each morning he listened to the radio for a possible alert. He was ready to put on his uniform, pick up his gun, leave his car at an appointed place, and report for duty. The whole country was prepared to be mobilized at a moment's notice.

From our arrival until our departure, we saw that this new country was full of marvel. The new Tel Aviv was built on top of an ancient civilization. On our visit to the hospital there, we found that the the doctors represented many different nationalities, and were therefore prepared to translate for patients who gravitated from all corners of the world. We saw original kibbutzim, and others in process of change. Golan Heights was filled with heartbreaking memories, but with irrigation, reforestation, and agricultural production, it could be seen at its best, with fruit trees, vegetables, chickens, and eggs, that were being produced in quantity for world markets. We swam in the Jordan, a muddy uninspiring entry to the Dead Sea. From the top of the first skyscraper in Israel, we were allowed a faraway glimpse of Jerusalem and The Wall.

We left the country, full of respect and admiration for this courageous and productive nation.

Our plans to go to Lambaréné during two months that summer fell through, when we received a cable from Dr. Schweitzer asking us to postpone our trip until the following year. My boss, Dr. Johnny Walker, came to the rescue and said he would plan a trip to Liberia, where he had worked for many years on the Firestone plantation. We were to do a malaria survey.

Dr. Walker was organized, and we were at his beck and call. Not only had Dr. Walker shown me how to disassemble our microscopes and put them in cardboard boxes twelve inches square, but how to clean (really clean) the slides, and number and package them in groups of ten for survey purposes. Then I had to measure and weigh stains for the slides. These would be mixed at each station where we would be gathering blood.

On our way to Liberia, we stopped on Long Island for Larry's niece Louise's coming-out party. Her aunt and uncle, Avey and Helen Clark, welcomed us for our night's stay, and the bags were taken to our room while we had a drink on the porch. Suddenly, I jumped up, ran to our room, and found that my worst fears had been realized. A maid was unpacking all of our carefully prepared survey equipment. Packaged slides were put next to shaving brushes in the medicine cabinet. We repacked everything before going to the party.

Dr. Walker was well-loved at the Firestone plantation, so we were off to a good start. Larry and I shared a two-room cottage with a bachelor. A bath-

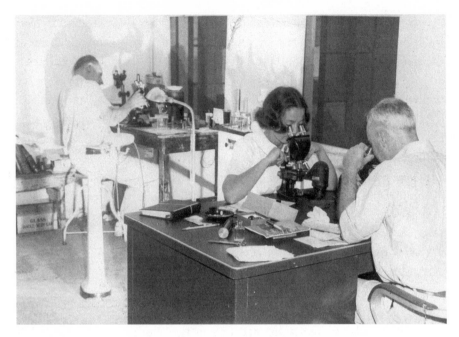

On the Firestone Plantation. Liberia.

room was between the two bedrooms. Invariably, we were wakened in the night, as we seemed always to fail to unlock the bathroom door on his side.

For our lab we were given a dentist's office, with a spitoon in the middle. The administrator was about to take it out, but Dr. Walker said that we could use it when staining our slides. It was great, with lots of room around the basin, and a tiny fountain in the middle to wash and dry our stained slides.

Labor on the plantation was recruited from all over Africa. The workers arrived in fairly large groups, and then built their own styles of houses. And they came with their own diseases. Our malaria survey suddenly began to include leprosy, sleeping sickness, schistosomiasis, and guinea worms.

The reason for all these workers was the tapping of the rubber trees each morning. The whole plantation was filled for miles with orderly planted trees, and each group of workers had its own allotted plot of the plantation to work. Every morning a tapper would first empty the can at the end of the sloping gash in a tree trunk. Then, with a special V-shaped tool, he would clean the hardened latex, so the raw rubber could run freely again on the next day. The raw rubber was collected and brought to a central processing place, where it was made into large sheets of crepe rubber that were easy to ship.

The doctor at Harbel asked us to go with him to Monrovia to see his hospital. Monrovia was a sleepy port city whose raison d'être seemed to be the Firestone Company. The docks, the shipping, and the bank all existed for the rubber industry. The medium of exchange was American money and the Kissi penny, a stick of iron eight or ten inches long.

President Tubman and his wife, he in a black morning coat and top hat, and she in an evening dress, walked to the presidential office each morning. They were very loved and very dignified, walking in the unpaved streets.

On the road from Monrovia to Harbel, we passed a huge three-story brick house surrounded by galleries. Each gallery was filled with women and children. Each floor was for a paramount chief with his wives and family while he travelled to the city.

When we left the Firestone plantation, they gave us a farewell party of native food. One of the managers came up to Larry and asked if he was all packed and ready to leave for the airport early the following morning. "All ready," said Larry. "And your tickets and passports?" Larry felt his hip pocket. It seemed that the tickets and passports had been found in the bushes off the road that morning, and brought to the main office by one of the workers who had no idea of their importance.

We finished the survey, and left the plantation to take a trip to Northern Liberia. En route we planned to stay at Dr. Harley's hospital for lepers. On our arrival, our host was nowhere to be seen. He was in the kitchen trying to get the kerosene icebox to run, and was on his knees, hot and mad. Larry offered his help and being a good Arizona ranch hand, he fixed it in no time. Those iceboxes have diabolic little motors. One has to have a personal approach, and move in on the right side of them.

We were given a room in a cottage nearby. Early the next morning we went outside and discovered lines of skulls under our porch. It was a bit unnerving, until someone explained that they were orangutan skulls that were being cleaned by ants before being sent to Dr. Hooten of Harvard.

At the leprosy hospital, I had a birthday. Dr. Harley asked us to come up to the attic. In a huge trunk were masks, some new, some old. He asked me to choose one, and I ended up with four beautiful old masks. It seems that people would come at night and offer packages for Dr. Harley to buy. He never opened the packages but paid five dollars for each one. He had a wonderful collection, most of which is now in the Peabody Museum in Cambridge.

We moved on to Baöe on the northernmost edge of Liberia. On the way, we picked up a passenger who came from that town. He was anxious for us to meet his family. It turned out he was the son of a paramount chief. We went to the palaver house where five old bearded gentlemen were seated, waiting to welcome the son and his guests. A huge drum easily five feet high was behind them, and several other drums, somewhat shorter, were on either side. Larry asked the gentlemen if they had good health, or if they harbored some illness. They cackled together, laughed, and said, "Only old age." That night we stayed with missionaries, and all through the night we could hear the Assota drums celebrating the homecoming of the son.

Leaving Liberia, we continued to the Gabon and to Lambaréné. Though Dr. Schweitzer would not be there, he told us we would be welcomed. A plane took us to Port Gentil, where our passports and visas were declared incorrect. At a table sat a secretary wearing big heavy boots. He was working on an ancient one-foot high typewriter. Both were very noisy. We were left in the hands of a Corsican police chief, who had a small monkey sitting on his desk.

Port Gentil, in spite of its name, was no place to be stranded, and we were literally trapped there until the police chief gave us permission to leave. There was a cafe called Café de Wharf. Larry was hopeful. He thought it was called Café du Roi. It was a long bar full of tough loggers. There was nothing much to eat, but we could have drunk to our hearts' content. There was no hotel, but we finally got a room in an empty shell of a hospital. We had a bathroom, but no water and no sheets. We went back and forth to the police station, competing with the small monkey for the attention of the police chief. We were hoping to be released for the trip up the Ogowe River to Lambaréné. The chief would poke the monkey with his pencil, and ask him if this was the day they would let the Mellons go up the river.

Late one afternoon, as we were sitting on the dock, a big passenger boat appeared in the ways. Larry grabbed me and we jumped on a bumboat. That night we drank wine and ate well in the dining room of the passenger boat. There was music and dancing, but we kept bumping into the police chief.

He was now separated from his monkey, who had been replaced by a denizen from Marseilles.

We returned via bumboat to shore and to our bed in the hospital. The next morning, we found ourselves in the open boat on our way to Lambaréné.

The river was wide, black, and quite swift, with the jungle right at the edge. These trees along the river were full of many birds. Our Diesel motor disturbed them, and as we passed, they took to the air.

There was one stop, where one missionary family replaced another, without a spoken word between them - spooky.

As we were nearing the Lambaréné dock, Mlle. Kottman, wearing a white cork hat, white dress, white stockings and white shoes, came to meet us. She was standing in a dugout canoe paddled by three lepers. We arrived at the hospital landing, and were greeted by Dr. Naegle and Dr. Percy.

Dr. Schweitzer was not there, but very much present. Nothing was done in the following days that was not according to his wishes and routines. Even our offer to send fly screens for the OR required Dr. Schweitzer's approval.

The hospital had five European nurses, two European doctors, and loyal long-time local employees, who had learned their jobs on the spot. Two of the nurses, Mlle. Kottman and Emma Haussknecht, had come to Africa almost at the same time the hospital opened.

The hospital was very basic, with wooden buildings, each with two tiers of beds. Patients came with family members, who cooked and cared for them.

The hospital lab was a dark corner. As he was working by my side, Joseph Bizongoi said he wished to show me something. From a shelf overhead he produced a basin that had a one-foot long embryo of an elephant floating inside it. As I marveled at the tiny trunk and the toenails, he said he had something else to show me, and he produced the same size embryo of a hippopotamus. I worked on the counter beneath these two treasures.

When I needed light for my microscope, I would take it outside and sit under the tropical sun.

Dr. Schweitzer's storeroom was partially underground. The shelving held pharmaceutical supplies meticulously labeled on six sides, so there was always one side that the ants could not reach.

There was a leper village with small wooden houses, where patients could live with their families. And there were lots of fruit trees planted by Dr. Schweitzer. The huge vegetable garden was on a piece of land brought down by the river at the end of each rainy season. Its care was completely overseen by Mlle. Kottman, and for all too short a season it provided vegetables for the hospital staff. There was also a small, touching cemetery for staff members.

All the foreign staff ate together at one long table. Dr. Schweitzer's place at the head was kept empty. At one meal we were offered hippo meat. Another time they served crocodile tail.

At one end of the room stood the small portable organ. With bellows eaten by ants, the organ could no longer sing, but Dr. Schweitzer used it daily to keep his fingers limber for his European concerts.

Each evening we were given a pitcher of water and a wash basin in which to bathe. After my minimal bath, I used the water to scrub my moccasins inside and out. Before I jumped into my narrow iron cot, I realized I had been brushing my teeth with the same toothbrush I had used on my moccasins.

Our return to Brazzaville was not by boat down the Ogowe, but instead by a small single-motor plane. It was piloted by two dashing Frenchmen who wore blue tam o' shanters with red pompons. We whizzed close to the jungle treetops on our first stop for gas. We all got out, and Larry asked the pilots if we could take them to lunch. They replied that they had expected us to do so. We were driven to a small colonial hotel with wide porches, and spent a good four hours waiting, eating, and drinking before we returned to the plane. We rolled on down to Brazzaville, arriving just before nightfall.

We were lucky enough to be able to stay with the Carpenters, a missionary couple who were great people. They were printing school books and bibles in the African language.

In Brazzaville, after months without a shampoo, I needed my hair washed. We took a taxi and directed the driver to a recommended spot. This hairdresser was unable to take me and suggested another place. This second place said a third place would be better. Larry left me there and went off in the taxi, after saying he would return for me. His taxi broke down, and the driver found him another. Brazzaville was full of wide dirt roads with no signs. In his new taxi, with great difficulty, Larry finally found the first place and was again directed to the second place and again to the third. Just as I had finished, Larry dashed in. Surprised, I wondered why he was so glad to see me.

Dr. Schweitzer with Larry.

The wild Congo, an untamed river even in the dry season,ran between Brazzaville and Leopoldville. No boat ventured to cross alone, always two at a time. Just below the crossing, rapids began, and spume and spray reached the town fifty feet above. We went one day to cross a tributary via a bridge hanging from one rock to another. Larry walked across, but I crawled, saying I wanted to watch the water through the slats!

Sitting on the woodpile.

We left in a small plane from Leopoldville, to go on to Günsbach to stay with Dr. Schweitzer. His was a strong and lovely Alsatian village house, ivy-covered stone with a slate roof. We walked to the Münster where Dr. Schweitzer played the organ. He asked me to sit on the bench beside him. Dr. Schweitzer was built like a peasant, with large hands, large feet, and a huge head with lots of hair. As he played the organ, he was transformed. I was fascinated by his huge feet, which in their heavy shoes became those of a ballet dancer as he pushed the pedals. His hands pushed and pulled the stops and played the keys with the delicacy of the artist that he was.

We ate with both Dr. and Mrs. Schweitzer. Twice during our visit, Mrs. Schweitzer asked me what my place would be at our hospital. She seemed to want assurance of my role in Haiti, remembering all too well the times she spent in Europe while Dr. Schweitzer was in Africa.

One day we went for a walk and sat on Dr. Schweitzer's brother's wood-pile. Dr. Schweitzer advised me to always marry a man with a big woodpile! He admired my blue wool dress because it had big pockets.

At Dr. Schweitzer's request, his nurse, Emmy Martin, took us to his friend's nearby vineyard. The friend proudly opened the underground cave and showed us the huge wooden *tonneaux,* or barrels bound in bands of iron. When we returned for lunch, Dr. Schweitzer remarked that he hoped we had not *frappé sur les tonneaux,* or knocked on the barrels. Larry was speechless with shame at even being asked. He knew that to do so was comparable to asking a cattleman how many cattle he ran in his herd, or how much money one had in the bank.

During our stay, Larry opened a blister on my big toe. Inside was a coiled guinea worm. Uncoiled, it was a foot long, and snapping and twisting in the air. We flushed it down the toilet, and up to fifty years later I still have had no sequela. This is probably why all the staff at Lambaréné was requested to wear white stockings.

Dr. Schweitzer put us on the little narrow gauge railroad train in Günsbach. It had arrived steaming and screaming from behind a mountain. We went to the next town, Colmar, where we had left our car. We were on our way to Paris, and home to New Orleans, full of good memories and assurances that Larry had chosen his mentor well.

CHAPTER 5

Gene Pool

It was while we were living in New Orleans that Mother became very ill. Since Father died, she had been living alone in Englewood, New Jersey, where she had hoped to find old friends. She had bad arthritis, but even in snowy weather she walked to market on her crutches. Larry said to me, "New Orleans is the place for her to be," and we sent for her. She lived in Ian's room with three nurses, happy and uncomplaining for over a year. It contributed much to the latter part of her life to have Ian, Jenny, Larry, and me around her.

Larry and someone else would often carry her on a stretcher down a winding staircase to the garden. She adored both the garden and hearing the children and their friends in the swimming pool. She was in a loving and comfortable atmosphere. I am so grateful we were able to bring her joy, comfort, and affection at this time of her life.

Mike had cried when we left Arizona. I promised I would return with him and a friend during the summer. Mother knew about this and implored me to go. She was in a coma when we left for Arizona.

Mother always said she wished to be cremated at her death as she did not want to be a bother to anyone. None of us knew there were legal restrictions on cremation in Louisiana. It was Dr. Mayo Emory who accompanied her in the hearse to Mississippi for cremation, since I was in Arizona and Larry was on OR service.

Dr. Mayo Emory, mother's devoted physician, wrote recently to tell me that he has a brass duck's head with a long beak that holds his important papers on his desk. Mother gave it to him, and it reminds him of her and of all our family in New Orleans.

Mother died and left my life, but I have clear and vivid memories of her warmth and devotion to me. She always understood big decisions in my life, even when unexpected: a divorce when divorces were unheard of, a move to a cattle ranch in Arizona, a plan to build a hospital. She and my father had heritages that were different, but both had tremendous strength. The mix produced a devoted and stable family.

My sisters Cornelia and Kathleen and I have shared memories of our grandparents' lives in New York City and Tarrytown, and what we heard of past generations.

In my great-grandfather's generation the new world was young, and opportunities were varied and many. There were no conglomerates or corporations. Business was healthy with individual opportunities and without any social onus. While Mr. Astor was buying furs from Russia, my grandfather was buying various findings from Paris. It was a time when one's choice could be unique, and popular demand could soon make it prosper.

My great-grandfather, Henry Augustus Ward, was reputed to be the most handsome man in New York and the first millionaire to make his fortune by importing the braid buttons and laces of the day's fashions. His wife, Gertrude Cornelia Ward, was born in 1838, was well educated, and evidenced the good upbringing typical of that generation.

Dear Gran, my grandmother, lived with her widowed father at 559 Fifth Avenue, and did not marry until after his death. At the advanced age, for those years, of thirty-three, she married John Hudson Hall and they continued to live in the family house.

The house covered a whole block including quarters for carriages and horses in the back. Almost all of our treasured possessions came from this household via my mother: Irish linen sheets and tablecloths, dinnerware, silver, Baccarat glasses, china boxes, beautiful large oriental rugs, and jewelry.

Each spring the horse-drawn carriages moved my mother's family to their summer home in Tarrytown on the Hudson. I remember visiting Dear Gran there one time. Dear Gran was a tiny, fragile, little old lady and she and her bedroom smelled of lavender. I remember trying to hear her "leaking" heart that Mother had told me about.

The house had wide lawns and big tall pines with tiny cones. It was full of many lovely treasures: painted glass boxes, a silver saltcellar that was a coach and horses, lace curtains, and well-polished silver. The furniture was covered with loose-fitting unbleached muslin slipcovers for the summer. The house had many porches with wicker furniture. On each visit, we were invited next door to Mr. Rockefeller's estate for a ride on his small railroad.

The coachman had a daughter, but I was not allowed to go to her house over the stables because her father drank. But I was allowed to sit with him behind the beautifully matched pair of horses.

There was a nice kitchen with a porch that was level with the lawn. I liked it down there, but the cook was always hugging me and she smelled of garlic.

My grandfather died at an early age, but Dear Gran continued a life that was full of interest. Besides the usual trips to Europe, my mother often spoke of the four children being taken to Russia at the time of Czar Nicholas, and of their trip up the Nile to the second cataract. These were adventurous trips for those days, even with a courier to keep track of the trunks and hat boxes, and a maid to unpack them. They had a box at the opera during the season, and spent summers in Tarrytown.

Even though Dear Gran was a widow with four children, she had many friends and was not limited in her choice of plans. The family's life was spent around a box at the opera and "at homes" where the children were introduced to good music, family friends, and eligible suitors.

Today, a large beautiful portrait of Dear Gran and the four children hangs in the Museum of the City of New York. Mother is the youngest, in a white dress with a blue sash.

Mother's brothers were well-educated and bright. Uncle Hudson from Harvard was a lawyer. He and Aunt Mabel lived on 57th Street in a big apartment full of portraits and furniture from Dear Gran. Aunt Mabel had a "condition"; no one was sure what. She would rise late and be waited on by two servants: a Chinese chef and Julie, the French maid. The two servants never learned to communicate verbally, so peace always reigned below stairs. Each year, Aunt Mabel and Uncle Hud went to Aix-les-Bains for the "cure." Their trunks were always packed and their traveling clothes ready, but they never had a pre-determined departure date. Instead, they had an arrangement with Cunard that they could pick up a late cancellation and leave on a moment's notice. In this way they could travel at half fare.

Uncle Charlie had an engineering degree from Cornell. He was interested in aeronautics, and built the first airplane made of aluminum. He used it to become the first to fly from Buffalo to Geneva, New York.

Mother had lots of attractive suitors, among them a penniless Canadian who became my father. He would arrive early for an "at home" and would ring the doorbell, and then put a pin in it so it would no longer announce those who came later. Mother's mother was not entranced by Father, probably because she knew no Canadians. Father was not to be discouraged. One day he saw smoke on the roof of the house next door. He climbed up on the roof and used his jacket to beat off the sparks that fell on our house. Father did not talk about it, but while drinking tea later in the day, he had to explain why his jacket smelled of smoke.

Mother definitely refused him, but he slipped a note into a big rosewood cabinet which ended up in our home in Geneva. That note read, "On to victory." Happily he succeeded.

Billy Grant was one of thirteen children. Born in 1866, the infant was placed in the trundle bed in the Ottawa, Canada home. Father graduated from the Royal Military College. Instead of taking a commission in the army, he went to Pittsburgh with his engineering degree to seek his fortune with Westinghouse Electric. There he became an American citizen. After ten years in Pittsburgh, Father worked on the Panama Canal and in Costa Rica. He then moved to New York where he met my mother.

My father was a product of hardy Highland Scots from the rocky hills of Inverness. Over the years the clan survived debt and famine. This heritage gave me a father of tremendous energy and will to fill well the span of life granted to him.

A symbol of this hardy group is the Corimony cup, a fragile, two-handled, silver goblet passed down to the oldest living male of the Grant clan. Today the cup is held high and the tartan worn with pride at all weddings and funerals.

Father's father was Sir James Alexander Grant KCMG, a leading physi-

My grandmother, Cornelia Katherine Hall, with her children, Charles Augustus, John Hudson, Martha, and Katherine, my mother.

My mother, Katherine Hall Grant, with her children, Cornelia, me, Kathleen, and Glen.

82

cian in Ottawa and a member of Parliament. Sir James was the doctor for the Governor Generals who were appointed by Queen Victoria.

As a member of Parliament, he was one of four cavaliers knighted by Queen Victoria in her Jubilee Year. It did him no harm professionally when Princess Alice broke her arm when she was thrown from her carriage in front of his office. He was given the keys to the city of Edinburgh for his medical work. A portrait of him in his court clothes was painted when he went to London to receive his knighthood. He had come a long way from his simple home in Ottawa.

The Prince of Wales spent a weekend with Father's brother, Harry Grant, in his house overlooking Niagara Falls. Uncle Harry was never again the same person. He wore spats and carried a cane ever after. The visit remained the pinnacle of his life.

Mother and Father were married and lived in New York with her mother, Dear Gran. Soon they moved to Englewood, to a lovely home that was a joy to Mother's heart. It was a happy household with Kathleen 8, Glen 7, and Cornelia 5. One day, Father took all three children to hunt eagle eggs on the high Palisades overlooking the Hudson River. The three children were tied together with a rope. Many years later my brother told me that Father had hung him over the edge of the cliff to reach a nest. All four, happy with the egg for the Museum of Natural History, returned home to find Mother had a surprise for them. It was July 22, 1911, and Gwendolyn Frances Grant lay in Mother's arms. The adored youngest sibling must have been a bitter pill for Kathleen and Cornelia.

I never had to succumb to the indignity of orange, high-laced shoes and serge bloomers. All three elders wore heavy mackinaws and knitted caps from the Hudson Bay Store in Ottawa, while Gwennie had a white rabbit fur coat and bonnet. Perhaps it was lucky that no one discovered until much later in my life that Gwendolyn means "Little Princess."

Father was always full of plans. He took us all to England to see what life offered the family there. I was in a baby carriage when we were in Malvern. Mother was not happy at the idea of being a gentleman farmer's wife in England, so they moved back to the States to Geneva, New York. Father studied Shorthorn cattle raising at Cornell, but by the end of the course, had reduced his dream of a farm of two hundred acres to one of sixty acres. He finally settled on six.

He bought a rambling brick Victorian house on Castle Street. His six acre decision turned out to be practical, since he needed all available family hands to help him. My job was the least demanding because I was the youngest.

I remember that first small wooden house on Castle Street in Geneva. One day, when we were all prepared to go on a picnic, it rained. Our gloomy spirits were brightened, however, when Father began placing planks on trestles for us to use as picnic tables in the garage. There were thousands of flies to be shooed away.

I remember better our house at 600 Castle Street. It was a large, three-story, red brick house with a cellar, an attic, and a cupola. A winding staircase led from the front door to the second floor.

To the right of the entrance was the living room, which had a bay window and a large table that bore a big Webster's dictionary. There were bookcases along one wall filled with books of the century. Among them were *The Book of Knowledge, The Swiss Family Robinson,* Christopher Morley's *Parnassus on Wheels,* and works by Rudyard Kipling.

On the mantle was a round-faced clock that was supported by four columns. It had a swinging brass pendulum. Father was the only one who would wind this clock, and the same went for the Seth Thomas clock in the kitchen. There was a player piano and a hand-winding Victrola. Inside the lid was a print of a small white dog listening to a speaker. Among the well-used records were "Oh Frenchy, Frenchy," "Good Morning Mr. Zip Zip Zip," and "How're You Gonna Keep Them Down on the Farm After They've Seen Paree."

I never did know the drawing room very well. No one ever seemed to sit there, but we used to pass through it on our way to the dining room. It had gold-painted furniture with pastel needlepoint upholstery done by Dear Gran. A lovely gold-framed mirror hung over the mantel. The half shades of pleated silk for the small side lights were made by Mother.

In the dining room, there was a round table with Adam chairs. For me, there was a mahogany high chair with a black leather seat. With the leaves of the table removed, there were many complicated, smoothly articulated wooden runners that made perfect shelves for hiding unwanted fat, gristle, spinach, Indian corn pudding, and raisins. Whenever the leaves of the table had to be used, it would have to be pulled apart, and lo! all the hidden evidence fell on the rug!

The sideboard held a five-gallon tin of maple syrup, a five-gallon tin of clover honey, and a high round tin of hard candies. Mother always ate the black ones as no one else liked licorice. Also kept in the sideboard was a bottle of Maltine of cod liver oil: one tablespoon once a day!

We had round white Philippine-embroidered doilies with napkins to match, and we used blue, onion-pattern china. I had a silver bowl, plate, cup, fork, knife, and spoon. One day, I came down to breakfast and the plate was on top of the bowl. I lifted the plate and found five pink baby field mice. They were all too quickly replaced by my daily bowl of prunes. At breakfast one morning, I informed my family I had just swallowed a prune pit. Quick as a wink, Father pulled me up and shook me by the heels. Everyone was so surprised, I don't think they ever looked for the pit.

Dinner parties meant opening up the safe to bring out the finery. The tablecloth and napkins with the large embroidered "H" would be washed, as well as the best dishes and the gold Baccarat glasses and finger bowls. The candlesticks with beaded shades would be set out. Dinner always ended with blancmange, which required a late trip to the bakery to get the specially ordered ladyfingers. There were flat round pink and white peppermints, and wintergreen candies.

There were no alcoholic beverages in our house. Once, Father served his buddies what he thought was wine, a gift from his Italian gardener friend. He did not drink any himself, so he did not realize that what he had served his bridge guests was olive oil! Father did not smoke except for an occasional "stogie".

There were two doors off the kitchen. One led to the back porch, and one to the back hall, where there was a shoe-shine box with brushes and polish. We had to shine our shoes each morning before school. We kept our overcoats, galoshes, rubbers, and mittens in boxes with our names on them.

The kitchen was huge with a big black coal stove. In the middle of the room was a large tin-covered table. On the side facing the porch, the brown wooden icebox had an opening for putting in the ice. A copper tray beneath caught the melted ice. This was emptied each day by Father, who also emptied the ashes from the stove.

Coal and ice were delivered by the same driver in a horse-drawn cart. In the winter, the cart was on runners, and the horses wore rubber shocks on their hooves to steady them on the icy road. When the snow melted, the runners were replaced by wheels. In the summer, we were always eager for ice chips that flew off when the driver would cut a large piece with his pick. He would weigh it on a hanging scale and heave it onto his shoulders with heavy tongs. His shoulders were covered by a gunny sack for protection. He would brake the cart with a curved piece of metal applied against the wheels.

Twelve empty bottles were replaced by full ones each morning by the milkman from White Springs Farm. When he stepped out of his wagon to deliver the milk in the wire baskets, he carefully placed on the ground a big iron ball on a rope attached to the cart to keep the horses from leaving. In winter, the frozen milk pushed the bottle caps and a couple of inches of frozen cream up out of the bottles.

Another vehicle that came to the kitchen was a horse-drawn coupe with two people who sold brown eggs and crocks piled high with fresh butter. They must have been Dunkards as they dressed in black.

Anna, our cook, had a room off the kitchen. She was fresh from Ireland and had never seen a carrot or a lemon. Mother never learned to cook anything other than creamed mushrooms. Needless to say, our diet was limited and dull. Anna always kept her door locked, but on her day off, Father would crawl through the transom to see if she kept food in her room. She usually did. I figured she came at the time of the potato famine and knew what hunger was. She never wanted to be left without food, especially sugar.

I was occasionally invited to Anna's room, and I can vividly remember the crucifix, the rosary, the large color lithograph of the Pope, and the covered glass for her teeth. These items were her life. I shudder to think how devoid of warmth and affection Anna's life was, and how little we as a family contributed to it. Once a week, she would go to church.

She was very good to me, and her white, starched apron had big pockets that were often stuffed with gingersnaps for all four of us. She did not wish to "make chalk of one and cheese of another."

I remember a trip to Ottawa to visit Sir James and Lady Grant. Father rode on a motorcycle, and I rode with Mother in the sidecar. Both grandparents were dressed completely in black. Granny wore a small cap. Granny and Sir James lived in a house much too small for the thirteen children. Father showed me where he slept on the top floor. He told us how he would pinch the little ones when he got scared in the night so they would cry and cause an adult to come upstairs. The living room was small and full of ugly furniture, lace curtains with heavy drapes added to keep out the winter cold, and a small coal-burning fireplace that did not succeed. We had high tea with crumpets and honey. Father, who, as always, departed early in the morning, brought me upstairs to say good-bye to Granny. She was in her bedroom in the process of dressing. Her corset strings were tied to the bedpost and she was pulling against it. A beautiful piece of articulated mechanism, the strings slipped evenly through the sprockets like honey from a spoon.

Mother was fastidious. She always kept the silver articles on her dressing table well polished, and her bureau drawers neat and in order. In the bottom drawer of the mahogany bureau were carefully-wrapped vestiges of her youthful life that included evenings at the opera. Wrapped in tissue paper were long white kid gloves with three pearl buttons at the wrist, the carved ivory blades of a fan from which the ostrich feathers had long since disappeared, and a small pair of mother-of-pearl opera glasses.

Mother sewed a great deal. She did the mending of Father's socks and shirts. I was in charge of the button box. She loved to make sachet bags with cotton stuffing, satin ribbon, and lavender sachet powder.

Father always took very good care of Mother. He was always ready to drive her anywhere. He was ready with her breakfast each morning. Once a week he turned the mattress of the big bed. Mother and Father always dressed for dinner. One evening, watching them change, I saw a fairy that seemed to be dancing on the outside of the window sill. Mother saw it too.

For years, May Cowdrey, my nurse, ate dinner with me. We were served on a tray in the nursery. There was too much junket, Indian pudding, and more junket.

There were four other bedrooms and a sleeping porch on the second floor. Glen's room had a small closet that was under the attic stairs. The closet door had no knob on the inside. I was once closed in there all too long with Barbara Graves, and to this day I carry the scar of the panicked scratch she gave me before we were finally found.

Glen's room was tiny but full of treasures. Among them were a cocoon, some snake skins, an oriole's nest, and a tiny vireo's nest lined with smooth and silky milkweed. His window opened onto the kitchen porch roof where we had built bird feeders. Glen and I worked hard to get the peanuts out of the suet for them. He also used to make and sell bird houses.

Glen had Dan Beard's book for Boy Scouts and a book on tying knots. It was in his tiny room at the end of the hall that I first learned to tie knots, and also how to write on birch bark and on a fungus, like a flat shelf. Once, he returned from Camp Dudley with a string of lucky stones that he had made into a necklace. I loved it and wore it often. The weight made my head look like a turtle's coming out of its shell. We also struggled to hammer garnets out of the big rock in the garden.

I have another vivid recollection of his room. I was isolated in it with scarlet fever, for what seemed to be weeks. The doors were hung with wet sheets reeking with carbolic acid solution. I can remember overhearing Mother say, "She has had another," referring to a convulsion. She was with me constantly, and I remember Father carrying, boiling, and washing sheets. I don't think there were any maids to be had in those days during the war, and I guess Mother and Father had to do everything. At first, there was only Mother, Father, and Dr. Stebbins, who took good care of me. Then a lovely redhead, Nurse Theodocia, arrived from Painted Post to help.

Cornelia, Kathleen, and Glen were sent away during my quarantine. I was later told about the big red sign on the front door.

Our neighbor, Warren Smith, sent me a lovely bunch of blooming purple violets during my ordeal. When I was in Geneva some fifty years later, I got the chance to tell him how much those flowers had pleased me.

All four of us slept on the sleeping porch under large heavy blankets from the Hudson Bay Company. Mine had big red and black squares. The blankets were sewn into our sleeping bags. We all wore toboggans, knitted hats with tassels on top. Father always opened and closed the windows for us, and sometimes we would wake up with our sleeping bags covered with snow.

Beyond the wood shed at 600 Castle Street was the icehouse. Behind the big thick door was lots of wet sawdust.

The large wooden barn was full of hay. And it had a cupola, a tiny square structure perched on the high ridge pole. The cupola could be accessed only by a ladder that hung six feet above the garage floor, but the bottom rung could be reached by a step ladder. The precipitous climb took courage, but the view out of the four windows was well worth it. There were two shelves that could be used as seats. Glen and I would face each other and brace our feet on the opposite shelf. We avoided looking down the hole we had climbed up. The whole trip was a challenge we met, but we had no desire to repeat it.

Beyond was a smaller barn that held wood. This was the barn that we re-shingled. I did the ground work of picking up the old shingles and piling them neatly to use for kindling.

Father had a big roll of sisal string which was not wound very tightly and therefore always giving off whiskers. He used to store things in paper bags and hang them from the rafters with the sisal. He did not label the bags and would quickly forget what he had put in each. He usually ended up opening them all before finding what he was looking for.

The floor of the garage was stained with grease from changing the oil in the Pierce-Arrow. In the Pierce-Arrow there was room for five, but not six, so I sat on a wooden stool made from orange crates. If you turned the stool over you saw a sticker of a laughing clown who was tossing and catching oranges in the air. When we went out in the car, Mother wore a hat and a veil, and so did I. Father wore his goggles and a long white coat.

There was an observatory on our place. Instead of a telescope there was a sink and a small coal stove. Glen used to cook fried eggs and pancakes in his scout equipment folding pan. We ate with the one-piece combination fork, knife, and spoon.

There were in fact three observatories in the neighborhood; ours, and one in each of the yards of our neighbors, the Smiths and Professor Brooks.

Professor Brooks was head of astronomy at Hobart College, and was evidently well known as he had many people coming and going. The Professor always wore a black gown and black skull cap. He looked like Merlin.

I have often wondered why there were three observatories so close together. Was it because of Professor Brooks, or was it because of a special constellation, or an expected meteor? Unfortunately, I shall never know, but then I was more interested in Glen's fried eggs than in those telescopes. Today I realize what I missed, but those eggs were good!

We had an abundance of fruit trees around the back of our place. There were black cherries behind the icehouse and sour cherries in front, and we also had sickle pears and yellow pears. The peaches were not very good, but the yellow and purple plums were. We had gooseberries, currants, raspberries, and strawberries. There was an asparagus bed and also a big rhubarb bed.

During the war years, we had potatoes, corn, and wheat, as well as other vegetables. We all worked hard in the garden and kept the place neat. Our yard had nice trees and flowers. In early spring came the tulips and iris. Then there were the forsythia and bridal wreath in the front of the house. A thick bed of lily of the valley was just outside the kitchen door. Nearby were purple violets. Later, there were bleeding hearts, and sweet Williams. The rose bushes had many spines, furry leaves and tight pale pink buds. The peony bed was full of red, pink, and white, heavy-headed blossoms that were alive with ants. On the dining room side of the house were two enormous horse chestnut trees. All too often, it was my job to pick up the nuts and the burrs so they would not stick in the blades of the lawn mower. Once up in the tree, it was like a covered nest. I would often sit there, until one day I fell and Glen found me with a broken arm!

The chestnuts could become weapons in the autumn. With a hole bored through the center and threaded with a string, we would wind them in a fast circle over our head, and they would travel high and far when released at top speed. An encounter en route could be as lethal as an Australian boomerang.

There was a large copper beech and a cluster of white birches. In the early spring, the magnolias had no leaves but were covered with large waxy sweet-smelling white flowers. The ginkgo tree had leaves like fans and foul-smelling yellow plums which made good fighting ammunition. Happily, I was an onlooker to these fights.

Spring was beautiful and summer was too, but there was lots of work to be done. We cut the grass and weeded the driveway, which was made of gravel. We had to pour old motor oil on the driveway weeds to kill them before hoeing them. We picked and canned the fruit and berries. During the war years, we planted wheat on the front lawn. We cut it and then flailed it with a leather strap that held two pieces of wood. We did this on the garage floor, and there was always a taste of motor oil in the cereal. Worse yet were the pieces of hard chaff after Father ground the grain in the coffee mill. There were other bad eating experiences like applesauce that was made by straining our apples through Father's wool socks. And sparrow pie. Father hated the English sparrows and trapped them.

I used to get tired of working, whether it was putting soft and hard potato bugs in a can of kerosene, or picking up chestnuts. With a cane in my hand, I would duck-walk up to Father and say, "Charlie Chaplin is tired." This usually had the desired effect and I was allowed to go back to the house.

The pride of the place were the three huge Norway pines that stood tall in front of the house. These trees had lots of pine cones that were sticky with pitch. We gathered these cones in the fall for use in the fireplaces.

Kathleen had long, black, wavy hair, that was beautiful to look at until she got involved with the pitch from the pine trees. One tree had a witches' broom, and horticulturists came from miles around to get a look at it. The broom was in the highest part of the tree. Once I reached it and sat in it. It was a thick thatch of a different kind of pine that had tiny fat needles. Beneath the pine's dark brown needles, a deep, dry, springy carpet was formed.

The whole area behind our property was called Smith Park. There was a wealth of trees and bushes of all varieties growing in this area. Neat gravel roads curved through the whole property, and the lawns were always trim and neat. All around the park was a fence of metal with hollow posts that were beginning to rust out at the ground level. On some Saturdays, the Smiths would ask us to go for a drive through the grounds in their buggy drawn by two horses.

Smith Nursery shipped trees and bushes all over the world. The empty shipping crates were stacked next to our fence line where we would crawl through the bushes to reach them. They were made of light pine wood and we could break the boards and pass from box to box to find ourselves in a world of endless catacombs. They were very springy if you ran along the top.

My father, like all good Scotsmen, wore knickerbockers, wool socks, and heavy leather shoes. He usually wore pepper-and-salt tweed jackets. The jackets were belted all around, with two straps in front and two in back. He wore a bow tie. He wore a tweed cap with a beak, and in the winter, a mackinaw and his astrakhan fur hat from his Royal Military College days. When it got really cold, under rubber boots, Father would wear heavy felt shoes that reached half-way to his knees. He was seldom without his Zeiss field glasses for bird watching, and he almost always carried a walking stick. He tried to dress Glen the same way, in pepper-and-salt tweed knickers.

Father and Glen once had a picture taken for Mother. For Glen, Father took a pair of long pants out on approval. The picture was taken and the pants returned.

He was an avid walker and wanted us all to be. He paid me to walk ten miles a day. When you see the intensity with which present day people walk and run, my father was well ahead of his day.

Father loved golf and hoped I would too. Glen Eagles was notable for its three challenging golf courses. The terrain was unusual in that it was practically flat, but the courses were rumored to be among the most cleverly trapped in the world. Unfortunately, Father's enthusiasm for eighteen holes in the morning and eighteen in the afternoon was never shared by me.

Father really knew how to whistle. He had three kinds. One was made by putting the ends of his forefinger and thumb together in the front of his mouth. Another was made by using his two smallest fingers in each corner of his mouth to pull it into a wide, straight slit. The third was a no-hands kind. He used it when he lost track of Mother in a crowd, or when the family count was not six. Glen tried hard to learn all three, but without success. They remained Father's alone, and no one ever came close to matching him!

Father had a kidney-shaped desk, and he kept a book of postage stamps in the left-hand drawer. He used a stenographic pen which he would refill with a medicine dropper. There was a metal bear with a bristly-back that was used to clean the nib of his pen. No one could sharpen pencils better than my father. His fine sharpener with a handle was screwed onto the inside of the closet door. Father kept a diary which was dull but factual. In the back, he had a list of jokes he liked to tell.

In Father's library window was a glass transparency that was just the size of one of the small window panes. It had a picture of a road runner on it. Father had a heavy bunch of key rings with at least fifty keys on it. I wonder where they all came from.

Father's effort to persuade mother to like camping gave birth to what residents of Geneva called the Vander-Billy-Built. It was something like a house that was built on the flat bed of an Reo Speed Wagon truck. It was painted olive green with black trim. Inside, the ceiling was high enough for one to stand upright. It contained a narrow sofa, an icebox, a folding card table, and four folding chairs with arms and chintz cushions. The legs of Father's wicker chair were shortened to enable him to sit behind the steering wheel. Mother sat beside him in her own wicker chair. It was Father's greatest joy to invite friends for a drive to some shady countryside spot for bridge and a picnic.

Frankly, we children were embarrassed by it. In our eyes, its uniqueness held no value. Our dreams were of roadsters with raised, removable tops. Once, he took Glen to Pittsburgh in it and parked on the golf course. Poor Glen was a wreck, since his best girl lived in Pittsburgh. Father may well

The Vander-Billy-Built. Father, Mother, and Amy Hedrick.

have heralded the campers and mobile homes of today, but only Father heard the bugle.

Father was ahead of his time. Long before other people were aware of the need to separate and re-use waste products, Father experimented making ensilage. Corn stalks were cut into short lengths and thrown into an unused and empty underground water cistern. Fermentation occurs fast in such a small contained space, and the fumes become lethal. When the time came to turn the stalks, Glen was lowered, fortunately with a rope around his waist, and was quickly pulled out to fresh air.

My father also offered a prize to the person in Geneva who could collect the most tin cans, and the response was spectacular. People arrived pulling long lines of cans tied together, and put them into a huge wire cage at the foot of Seneca Street.

Father's choice of hard physical work resulted in "lumbago," known simply as acute lower back pain today. The cures he chose were self-inflicted. One "cure" was to bare his back in front of the bee hive and stir the entrance

The Tin Can Parade

with a stick. Another was to lie on his stomach with a box containing electric light bulbs placed over his back. The heat quickly became intense, especially if heavy blankets were placed on top of the box. Whether these were
cures, or whether the lumbago became preferable to the cures, we never
knew.

His lumbago, however, never stopped him or dampened his enthusiasm.
No task ever seemed too big for him to tackle: moving piles of matted pine
brush, gathering thousands of tin cans, taking six people on a year's trip
around the world, or learning to play bridge. The latter was one of the few
things he never did well.

Glen finally got his first pair of long pants and his Indian bicycle at the
same time. The bike was a real beauty. It was red and had coaster brakes. It
had a sliding toolbox on the bar and a kit to fix punctures. Glen shined and
oiled it daily.

Later, Glen had a Harley Davidson motorcycle that was also red, but big and heavy. It became the joy of his life. When we returned from the Far East, he brought a leopard skin that he used it to cover the seat of the motorcycle. That seat turned into a thing of beauty, appropriate for the maharajah that he was. Luckily, it was always outdoors, but even so, the smell of the Far East stayed close to it and to him.

My bike was an Ivor Johnson with hand brakes and a tiny leather toolbox strapped behind the seat. Glen gave me a basket that hung on the handlebars. He taught me to ride by letting me go from the top of the hill in Smith Park. I kept riding and never had any trouble from that day on.

Glen taught me to sail a boat. I was the crew and worked hard. The first boat he had was a Barnegat. Later, he got a Star with a thousand-pound keel. The only race he ever won was a Jack and Jill race, and he was my crew. He screamed at me but I did not cut the buoy chain. It was close but we came in first.

Glen also taught me to ride, and to curry and saddle a horse. Bea Hoskins used to ride with us. I was aware that my presence served as chaperon, but it did not dim my pleasure at being with them.

Kathleen was very kind and patient with me. She helped and encouraged me with my stamp collection. Father gave me great impetus by leading me to the front door of Mr. Gulbinkiam's rug store in Rochester. There, he pushed me in to ask someone, unknown to us both, to help with my collection. I stood in his office and asked him if he received mail from Egypt, Syria, Persia, and Turkey, the places from which his rugs came. He was a kind man, and he took an interest in the little girl standing in front of him with a large, blue Scott Stamp Book in her hand. His friendship produced a veritable lode of Near Eastern stamps.

One summer, Father decided that Kathleen had to teach me to tell time. He made a cardboard clock with moveable hands. I was to tell the hour correctly twelve times in a row. If there was an error, then five more times were added.

With swimming, it was different. Father threw me into the creek at Chipmunk Lodge with a rope around my waist. To this day, I panic if I do not feel the bottom under my feet when I am in the water. I still see that creek with white foam bubbling around.

With my snake.

I used to go with Father to visit the prison in Auburn when he showed lantern slides of Costa Rica. It was while he was working in Costa Rica that he discovered his great interest in ornithology. He was given a complete set of Elephant Folio Audubon prints with engravings by Havel. Each of us, as we left for school and college, could choose one from the pile to hang in our room, much the same as students today hang travel posters. Today, some eighty years later, in my living room in Deschapelles, hang the Great Blue Heron and the Fish Osprey. Both are residents of Haiti, but both are now almost extinct.

I used to look for owl pellets with Father, and then we would separate the bones from the fur and feathers, and mount the bones on boards. One pellet might contain a complete set of mice bones or a garter snake. Early in life Father told me not to be afraid of snakes, and he taught me how to hold them.

While we were traveling on the train one day, Father pulled out his black-faced Ingersoll watch that he had bought for a dollar. He asked me to count the number of clicks made by the train in one minute as it passed over the rail sections. At the next station, we paced off the length of an iron rail. It was thirty feet long. Back in the train, we multiplied the number of clicks per minute by sixty minutes, and then multiplied that number by the length of the iron rail. Dividing by 5,280 feet, we were able to figure the train's speed in miles per hour.

The winters in Geneva were very long and very cold. The snowdrifts were high and there were long icicles on the roof gutters. The front steps and those by the kitchen were slippery with ice, and Father used to sprinkle the wood ashes on them to keep us from falling. The tin and wood shovels were in constant use. We seemed to wear long underwear for months.

I had double-runner ice skates and a Flexible Flyer sled, which had a back to it so Father could pull me. There was a sequence of three terraces behind a neighbor's house. These were just fine for my sled and skis. We all had skis but no binders, just a single strap across the toe. One challenge was to go down turned around backwards with the skis going forward. The ground dropped off steeply, and one had the feeling of flying. The trick was to avoid going through the thin ice on Castle Creek that ran at the bottom of these terraces. You could see the water flowing in and out from under the slabs of ice.

The early spring brought patches of bright green grass still edged with snow. The skunk cabbages were among the first plants to appear, then jack-in-the-pulpits, and violets that were yellow, purple, and white. There were red and white trillium. We could cut pussy willows by the creek and watch the leaves and lovely furry blossoms appear. Indian paint brush grew in profusion, as did beautiful white daisies with yellow centers. I remember Queen Anne's lace. I brought a big white beautiful bouquet to Mother who tried to act pleased. I later learned they gave her hay fever.

I am sure Father started raising bees because he was so fond of honey. The hives were behind the house. In the spring, Father would put on his bee suit and change the supers. When the bees swarmed, we were kept out of school to follow and not lose track of them. The new queens would arrive by mail in a tiny wooden box with a fine, metal grill. Sometimes we went to Ithaca to buy a queen from Cornell University. We loved honey, and paid a big price. We all got stung, but Glen seemed to get stung the most.

My first taste of the Orient was at Willard Straight cafeteria, where we would eat lunch and see dozens of Chinese and Japanese students who were studying at Cornell in those days. They always looked interesting and attractive to me.

We had another good friend in Ithaca, Mr. Louis Fuertes. He traveled all over Mexico and Central America, collecting tropical birds of beautiful iridescent colors. They filled his trays, as they lay on their sides with their dried feet and claws drawn up into balls.

In the summer, with the help of friends, we would cut and rake our big front lawn. Father would then walk us all down to the movies. He was crazy about Harold Lloyd. Sometimes, we would go to Duffy's restaurant where we had small round salty crackers called Oysterettes, I think, with half and half served in thick white bowls.

Summertime was also a time for picnics. We went often on these all-day affairs, with the food and plates in a big wicker basket that had leather straps. Father drove the Pierce Arrow with Mother beside him in a hat and veil. The rest of us sat in the back. Glen was always at the ready to help change and pump up the inevitable two or three flat tires of a day-long trip.

Early one spring, Glen and I found a mossy mound about three feet high. It was full of tiny, tiny frogs. We tried to bring them home, but they died on the way.

One of our favorite places was Slate Rock. It had a high waterfall that splashed down over big, flat slabs of blue slate. At the foot of the falls was a deep pool where we swam. Along the walls of this gorge, one could separate the flakes of slate and find many tiny fossils. We had a fine collection of them. These were placed in Glen's bookcase with the bird's nest, cocoons, snake skins, and other treasures.

When I was very young, Nurse would take me to school, and I really suffered. First, because my nurse was with me, and second, because I was the only one who had leggings with some thirty-odd buttons on each leg. Nurse had a button hook to do my leggings up, and she often caught my fat legs in the buttonholes. Later, Herman Unger was my hero, and he always helped me. We would cross Castle Creek over the Brook Street Bridge on the way to school. Some days, the creek would run bright red from the chemicals they used at the Shuron Optical Company.

While walking with Father along the sidewalk near our house, we would often see a neighbor sitting alone on his porch. As we walked by, my father would urge me to wave to him, saying he had been in prison and was lonely. After many passings, Father persuaded me to go up the steps and speak with him. For me it was a good lesson: his punishment had been carried out and should be a punishment completed.

I used to dream I was in the bathroom, and on especially cold nights, I would wet my bed. My mother would get me up to try to avoid this, and once, Father sent me to school with a sign on my back. I was distressed. But Glen put me on his bicycle and said not to worry. He told me that the sign said I was a good girl.

Often, cosmetics and drug houses offered samples in magazines. Sometimes the samples were free, sometimes they cost ten cents. I had a doll with real hair, and the needs of my beautiful doll were well taken care of. It was a sad moment when I realized I had combed and brushed her so much that she was bald. Miraculously, Mother heard of a doll's hospital. It was the first stop on our next trip to Rochester.

I had curls, round fat tubes of hair. They fell from straight hair on top, and were about ten in number. It was only with considerable effort on May Cowdrey's part, and a fair amount of suffering on my part, that these curls existed. Each night, my hair would be wound on cotton-stuffed ribbons, that were then tied in knots on my head.

Curls.

I always remember feeling inadequately dressed, both in quality and in style. The biennial seamstress did what she could for us in the spare room. Mother had a shopper from Best and Company who would send things like coats. There was no choice involved.

On lower Castle Street, there was a more sophisticated dressmaker who had imported materials, but the results seemed equally uninspired.

Later in our lives, we would make a twice-yearly trip to Rochester to shop for clothes. It would be a long day, up before dawn and back after nightfall, though Rochester was only fifty miles away. Our first stop was always the Genesee Valley Club, where we would sometimes return for lunch. It was at Sibley's that I first had a decision-making part in the clothes I was to wear. This really made me happy, except for the shoes. In fact, I was sent away to school wearing a pair of high-laced shoes, the only one at Shipley so shod.

Nora, an "at-home" hair dresser, washed and curled the hair of Geneva's elite. When she arrived in her Ford coupe to do Mother's hair, she came complete with her bag containing an alcohol lamp, curling iron, shampoo, and hair tonic. In Nora's hands, gossip traveled faster than the speed of light. There was little that she didn't distribute on her visits.

I had lessons in sewing, carpentry, cooking, and typing. I have many times in my life been extremely grateful for this. I learned to type with a cloth tied over my hands and a Sousa march on the Victrola.

Mother began my sewing lessons. Aprons seemed to be the most daring challenge. It was not until I arrived at boarding school that I ventured into making dresses. I remember a red sleeveless silk dress I made to go with a Roman sash that Mother and Father had brought me from Italy.

My sex education was scanty: the book in Father's third bureau drawer, with fetus, complete in color, at all stages to actual childbirth; Mother getting out the gauze and cotton and working at the card table; and the mare and the stallion that Father stopped the car for me to watch. About the only other exposure was a brief glimpse of the *Police Gazette* on days when I was with Glen at Art Kenny's while he was getting his shoes shined. There was the *National Geographic* collection with their wonderful photos, and a statue of Narcissus in the stair niche. Going fast up the stairs one could flick off his fig leaf!

Religion in my life was also scarce. I remember Father taking me once to the Presbyterian Church on Park Place. We left before the sermon. When I stayed with our neighbors the Hedricks, Amy taught Sunday School, and I was always in her class. Once, Bishop Brent came to the Episcopal Church in Geneva. He was a tall impressive man in his purple sash, and his index finger bore a large amethyst ring that a lot of people kissed. The Bishop was on his way to start a school in Bagio in the Philippines. It was almost fifty years later that my son, Ian, taught there and met and married Lucy Theissen. At Shipley, I went to church regularly and owned a Bible. I became head of the Christian Society, and I had to contact Sunday speakers and introduce them in Chapel.

Geneva had beautiful old block houses on Park Place, and many lovely old Greek revival houses on Main Street. Most of the houses on the lake side of Main Street had wide porches across the back, and big lawns that dropped abruptly down towards the lake. The houses on the other side of the street were architecturally just as interesting, but had no view of the lake.

Father refused to let us swim in Seneca Lake because all sewage was dropped directly from Main Street houses into the beautiful lake below.

I would often go shopping with Mother. We went to Mr. Catchpole for fish and Mr. Baumgartener for meat. Mr. Catchpole had eyes that looked like a cod's. He sold fish, and oysters that were shucked and in a big barrel. Mother and I never went into the Greek ice cream parlor with its tiny round tables and wire chairs, but Glen took me there once for a banana split served in a long, glass dish. Mother would stop with me at Appleton's, where they had pink peppermint, white evergreen candies, and ice cream cones.

Periodically, Mother would go to the Geneva First National Bank to open her safe deposit box. As a treat, she would ask me to go with her. The president opened the heavy metal door, and used both his and Mother's keys to remove the deposit box. We followed the president to a small room where he left us alone with the box.

Mother's first job was to cut her coupons. In the box was a pair of long sharp scissors kept there solely for that purpose. The real treat came when she brought out her jewels, and they were just that. There were leather or velvet boxes that had forms to fit each piece of jewelry. The boxes themselves were things of beauty, but what lay inside was even more enchanting. The treasures came from her grandmother and mother, and they were from the days when one's jewelry was designed and set in Paris. Among the finest pieces were Mother's pink topaz collar and belt which had been set in Russia. Today, many of these are remade into rings with the same settings for the twelve grandchildren and great-grandchildren. There is other jewelry that adorns the necks and wrists of beautiful young girls at family weddings and engagement parties. They serve as periodic reminders of a past age and past relatives that many of us never knew.

In the spring, the Barnum and Bailey Circus was a big occasion. Father would take us down to see the train come in, and we would watch the elephants pull up the big top. The parade would take place at about noon. It would turn the corner at the head of Seneca Street with the calliope blasting. The tigers paced in their cages, and the lions were hot and panting in theirs. The clowns, with white gloves and white faces, walked alongside. The horses were sleek and well kept, and their riders were in excellent form. You could buy lizards wearing little collars attached to chains that could be pinned to your shirt. Of course there were balloons and spun sugar for sale.

The circus people ate in a tent together, and it was always fascinating to see that the freaks and the clowns had home lives, and did their laundry just like other people. Father never took us to a circus performance, but he would take us to comb the grounds the next day to look for money that might have been dropped after the circus train had pulled out.

Once Sousa's band played at the lake front. He was a short fat man with a stiff mustache. He was leading a large band of mostly brass instruments.

I was often left behind in the winter, when Mother and Father were off to Europe, and sometimes I lived with the Hedricks when my parents were traveling. The Hedricks were our dearest friends and neighbors. He was Director of the Experiment Station. Their house was always full of flowers and fresh fruit, and on one occasion, we had strawberries frozen by a man named Charlie Birdseye, who was starting his experiments.

The Hedricks were establishing a new breed of Jersey cows. Everyone who worked at the Station carried two covered hand pails on the way to work, and returned in the evening with one full of milk and the other of cream. I stayed three times with the Hedricks, and it was real bliss compared to other places.

Once, Cornelia and I stayed at Mrs. Hemiup's, with its dark wood, steep narrow stairs, and gaslights. It was a bleak boarding house. We had a room on the top floor and were miserable, not only together, but also to each other. We had our meals with the other boarders in the dining room, which was in the basement, with its little narrow windows near the ceiling. We could see the feet of people passing by. The only joy I can remember in these months was the candy I bought at Appleton's with my spending money. I did have roller skates, and I can conjure up that deep-throated noise made by the skates on the slate walks and cement slabs.

Another winter, Cornelia and I stayed at the Browns'. And one time, I stayed alone at the Stukeys'. Mrs. Stukey was a school teacher who had a lovely baby boy called Loren, who put a bit of joy into those winter months. Every day I had to hang for a specified length of time from a trapeze that Father had hung in one of the doorways. Someone had told him that I had a curved spine.

There was one winter when Father, Mother, and Cornelia were in Majorca. Those winter months were long and lonely, and for the most part, pretty miserable. Father had left stamped addressed penny postcards for me to send off regularly. The mail service was most undependable. It took my cards seven or eight days to go to Europe via the Canadian Pacific. Then there would be another eight days for their letters to cross the ocean, and then they had to make the trip on the Lehigh Valley to get to me in Geneva. I remember the time when no mail seemed to come. I think I must have been a very brave child. I never remember crying or complaining.

Mother often said that she hated to leave me, and I am sure it was desperately hard on her. She called me "Sunshine," "Lambie," and "Lamb-pie."

Father had enough of a British background to feel that children should go away to school at an early age. He had a hard job convincing Mother, but I was sent to Shipley School at the age of eleven. It seemed like a good idea, considering how I had spent many unhappy winters with other people.

On the day I was to leave for school, I developed a felon on my index finger. Father put several bread poultices on it and the throbbing seemed to subside, but by the time I was put on the train that evening it had begun again. In the middle of the night, I summoned up my nerve and called the porter, who in turn called the conductor. Both of them gave me sympathy, but were able to do little else.

When the chaperon met me at North Philadelphia Station, the finger was twice its normal size, and I had angry red marks up my forearm. Without stopping to eat breakfast, we got on the Paoli local to Shipley School, where I was rushed up to the infirmary. My finger was lanced, resulting in immediate bliss.

I went to school with a bank account of my own. It was my bête noire, as I never had enough money for my wants, and I had plenty of needs. The first question Father would put to me when I arrived at the train station at Lyons was, "How's your bank account?" I always knew, and Father always suspected, that it was overdrawn, but he was good about bailing me out. Still, his question, and the smell of the sauerkraut that was made in Lyons, dimmed my enthusiasm about returning home.

I was always a bit of a misfit at Shipley. When I began, I was too young for the school. All the other boarders were in higher grades. However, after returning from a year's trip to the Orient, I was much more exposed to life than the others.

Boarding school opened up a new world of literature, music, ancient studies, and foreign languages. I had a wealth of books and so many new things to learn. Miss Rott taught me Ancient History, and she made it come alive. We made models of Egyptian tombs, and drawings from the *Book of the Dead* in the correct colors. The civilization of the Tigris and the Euphrates Valley became alive and full of meaning through my religion teacher's efforts. We made chronological time sheets of the ancient worlds, and could compare what was happening where and when. English Literature began with *Beowulf* and ended with Thomas Hardy. It was a speedy but broad exposure.

The world of music opened to me in these years. We went to hear the Philadelphia Orchestra along with the Main Line residents, with all of us in evening dress and white gloves. We took the Paoli Special almost to the door of The Academy of Music.

During one concert, Stokowski stopped when someone in the audience coughed. He began again. The same person coughed again, and Stokowski asked the man to leave the auditorium. Then Stokowski began once again.

We also went to museums and to the theatre, where we saw Shakespeare with scenery designed by Gordon Craig.

I did have two good New York friends in boarding school, Edie Betts and Doris Havemeyer. I often visited them. Edie lived in Tuxedo Park, a secluded, protected enclave of close friends who lived in big houses with beautiful gardens. The entire community was surrounded by a high wall with a security gate and a guard. It was a lovely place, where the privacy of each family was guaranteed. There were trails for horseback riding, and squash and tennis courts. It seemed a lonely place, and Edie was glad to have my company. We caught up with each other years later when she rode with me in Phoenix.

Doris Havemeyer lived opposite the Metropolitan Museum. Her house was connected by an art gallery to her grandmother's house. We used to roller skate up and down the wide sidewalks of Fifth Avenue. When we returned home, the door would be opened by a butler in a striped vest. We entered the marble entrance hall and, still on roller skates, took a door to the right to go see Grandmother. As I passed through this door, my right hand could have touched the tutu of a Degas ballet dancer. A world of art passed by our eyes on our way to the adjoining house.

The wonders did not cease there. Upstairs in Doris' bedroom were two grand pianos. Doris and her father played duets, both classical and jazz. Every weekend Mr. Havemeyer would take us to the opera, or to the newest musicals. After the theater we would hurry home, and with her father at one piano and Doris at the other, they would play the new pieces we had just heard. Up to that time, my musical education had been the player piano, the Victrola, and Sousa's band.

For three years in a row my roommate, Mary Dick, invited me to Norfolk, Virginia, for Easter vacation. It was there that I had my first dates and went to my first dances. On Easter we wore bunches of purple violets to church. We used to have daily morning prayers in the drawing room. These were long kneeling sessions!

On October 16, 1925, Mother and Father's twenty-fifth wedding anniversary, the whole family was off on a year's trip around the world. Kathleen had graduated from Smith, Glen had left Williams, Cornelia had graduated from Miss Hall's Finishing School, and I was taken out of Shipley for the year. I was fourteen and had already spent two years at boarding school.

We left Montreal on a Canadian Pacific boat. Each of us had a steamer trunk and a suitcase. Then the group shared a square suitcase for hats and still another for shoes. We were to be gone for a year, and would be facing very hot and extremely cold weather. When we arrived in Liverpool, Father quickly decided fourteen pieces of luggage were too many. At Selfridges he asked for the strongest suitcase. The salesman showed him one and claimed that a man could stand on it. Father jumped up and down on it, then said he would take half a dozen, one for each of us. And except for one square hat-box, this was the total number of suitcases for the rest of the trip. They were indeed big and strong, made of bright orange fiberglass. We never saw the other fourteen pieces until they were returned to Geneva a year later. My orange suitcase came to Haiti with me in 1954, and was given suitable thanks and burial.

Father had the tickets, passports, money, and baggage tags on a belt around his waist. In those days most people traveled with a courier. Father did without. It was Father who had to make plans and reservations, and change money at each stop.

One day, with alarm, Father said he could not find his letter of credit. After a few panicked moments it was found. It had been so hot in the Far East tropics, that the letter of credit that he carried in his pocket had lost all of its original color. It was almost unrecognizable but still viable.

People made the trip from England to the Far East on Pacific and Oriental steamships. A veteran traveler would quickly ask for a port cabin going out and a starboard on the way home to avoid the sun. But port and starboard made no difference where ants were concerned. They were equally busy and equally in evidence on either side of the boat.

Our first taste of the Far East was the sight of shivering cold Lascar seamen in their turbans, who were loading the boat in Liverpool. Our P&O steamship left England and stopped in Algiers, Port Said, and arrived in Colombo, Ceylon, on Christmas Day. It was a five week trip. Most of the passengers were British civil service employees returning after a year in England. There was lots of rice and curry, and with luck, at each stop, a can of Huntley and Palmer digestive biscuits which we rushed to buy.

In those days, there were no planes. One traveled by sea or by train, and in towns and cities by rickshaw.

Our first day on land in the Far East was at the Galle Face Hotel in Colombo. All of the rooms faced the sea, and along the inland side was a continuous gallery, where an untouchable was always on duty to carry the waste water away. It was our first contact with small bright green lizards, mosquitoes, mosquito nets, baskets with cobras that would rise and sway to the sound of a flute, and big black ravens that would steal bright things off your bureau. The women wore veils and saris. The men wore white trousers with long white shirts, and their hair was long and coiled in big knots on top of their heads. If they wore shoes, they were embroidered, and flat with pointed toes that ended in curved tails.

It was a wonderful trip which included India, Java, the Philippines, China, and Japan. In India we went to Bombay, Calcutta, Agra, and Benares. On the train to Peshawar, on the Northwest Frontier, all six of us spent three days in one compartment with food, water, and bedding.

In China, we went to Hong Kong, Canton, and Nanking, staying quite a

The Taj Mahal. I'm on the step, with Kathleen, Mother, and Cornelia.

while in each place. But the most popular place of all for world travelers was Shanghai, the Paris of the Orient. Mother took Kathleen and Cornelia to a couturier, fresh from France, and chose two beautiful dresses for them to wear that evening to the British Embassy. Glen and I were left behind in the hotel.

In Nanking, we stayed with the Loudermilks. Mr. Loudermilk was studying the effects of the loss of loess, a productive soil that was so fine and light that is was easily blown far away by daily winds at great loss to the farmlands in that part of China. This was my first exposure to the real importance of ecology.

The Imperial Hotel in Tokyo was more of a marvel than Mount Fuji or the gardens of Nikko. It was built by Frank Lloyd Wright, who had accepted the challenge of designing an earthquake-proof hotel. It was made of lava rock with no reinforcing steel. It had thick walls, closed corridors, and low doors and windows. Strangely enough, it was a thing of beauty and in many respects reminiscent of a Mayan temple.

Both the hotel and the walled moat around the Imperial Palace had been untouched by the big tremor that completely flattened the rest of the city in 1923. The moat wall was built of tightly-fitted stone using no mortar.

One saw so much more by slow land travel. Although the presence of Great Britain was still pretty much in evidence throughout the Far East, we always stayed at a local hotel and ate what local people ate. We did drink only bottled water, however. We were never sick and we had fun.

At no time on our trip did we have a threatening or unpleasant experience. However, in a hotel in Yokohama, Mother said to Father, "Come and see what I found in the bureau drawer." Father went and looked, and immediately moved us all out of the hotel. At the time we were too shy to ask what it was, and never did ask in the intervening years. It remained a secret that Mother and Father took to their graves.

In many ways this trip prepared me well for my future life. I was exposed to the size of the world and its many varieties. It was a wonderful gift to be received at an early age, and I observed and appreciated cultures, religions, and people radically different from those I had previously seen. What courage my parents must have had to travel all the way to the Far East with four teenagers!

I learned early in my life that all people are equal. This was not taught to me by words alone, but by active living. My father's kindness to those with whom he worked was an example to us all. In our travels I was even more conscious of this, especially in 1925 when we all were together on the world trip.

After our trip around the world, I returned to Shipley School, one year behind my old classmates. Glen came to call on me one Saturday. He wanted to take me, in his roadster with the top down, to a nearby town for lunch. Miss Brownell, the headmistress, said no. The students were not allowed to ride in cars. Glen appeared an hour or so later with a horse and bug. Miss Brownell relented, and off we went together.

One year when I returned from boarding school, Father thought I looked "peaked," and daily placed a block of Fleischmann's yeast by my cereal bowl. Once taste was enough. The yeast continued to appear, but was thrown into the snow outside the dining room window. When spring came, there were many large spots on the lawn, all equal in size and all equally yellow.

Wanamaker's in Philadelphia was a beautiful department store comparable to Macy's in New York City. It was the first store to go all out for Christmas. It had a Norway pine that reached up four floors. Many came to see the tree, with its lights and decorations, and to enjoy the Christmas music. At that time, it was a unique expression of yuletide spirit.

On Saturdays, small groups of seniors were allowed to go unchaperoned to Philadelphia. Invariably, our first stop was at a shoe store, where we immediately bought and wore shoes with three-inch heels. We would hobble onto the train at five p.m., footsore but happy. Our new shoes were put away until our next trip to town.

The day before graduation, at a picnic luncheon on the lawn, the headmistress read aloud an article from the newspaper. It described the first trans-atlantic solo flight made by Charles Lindbergh the day before. We were all in awe of the feat.

When I graduated from Shipley, Mother and Father gave me a Ford roadster. What a joy! I came into lunch one day and said that I had a flat tire. Father asked how I had changed it. I said I hadn't. Without a word he took me to the garage, handed me the jack and lug wrench, told me to change all four tires, and left me.

Edmund Keedy, a dashing Annapolis graduate in full uniform, cast his eyes on me, much to my pleasure and my father's distress. We spent weekends in New York, where went to the theater, and stayed at his sister-in-law's apartment. She was married to Eddie's brother, who was one of the Four Horsemen of the Notre Dame football team. It was a pretty heady group for a Shipley girl. Back in Geneva, Father tore the Navy overcoat off my bed and told me he wanted to take me for a ride. We drove to Lodi and passed a clapboard house. Sitting on the front porch was a grey-haired woman in bedroom slippers and a chenille wrapper. "That," said Father, "would be your mother-in-law."

In retrospect, I feel that I was given the gift of independence and self sufficiency at an early age. I was shoved from the nest as a fledgling with few feathers, but regardless of where a situation put me, I was always busy and happy with something I enjoyed doing, and it was usually something worth-while.

Life in Geneva could have been insular, but Mother, and especially Father, did not let it be. Our lives could have been tight and circumscribed, but Billy Grant had the vision to open other vistas to us.

Evidence of this was my refusal to join my friends and "come out" in New York as I was urged to do. Mother, having been brought up in New York, would have been happy to see me do what she had done. New York was fresh and new and exciting in those days, and it easily could have become an important part of my life. Instead, I chose to go to college, and I may have been the only one in my Shipley class to do so.

It was Kathleen who urged me to go to Smith College. She had gone there, and her claim to fame was having been a member of the college's first polo team, although the team never got any closer to Long Island or Saratoga than Northampton, Massachusetts.

A semester of sports was compulsory for Smith students. I chose lacrosse and was rated absent. I tried crew, figuring the pond was small and could not involve the Connecticut River. I just passed. I had no trouble with my own choice of exercising on the roller skating rink, where you could get waltzing lessons.

Picnics were often and good. Sometimes we went to a river with fast racing rapids called "The Tubs." Other times we went to a marble quarry in Vermont, where we would dive into the black water of unknown depth and unknown shelving. Both were fairly dangerous, but not nearly as dangerous as the race back to Smith to meet the ten p.m. curfew on Saturday nights.

Easter vacation was a part of my college life, and I usually spent it with my good friend Marty Wheeler. Her father, Dr. Wheeler, was a distinguished ophthalmologist. We were terribly excited when the King of Siam came to the States for eye surgery, and we were included in the festivities at which the King thanked Dr. Wheeler for the fine work he had done.

Dr. Wheeler was fun. After operating all day, he needed exercise, and would take Marty and me to Arthur Murray's for dancing lessons. He was not above taking us on to Roseland, where we danced the evening away with unknown partners. We bought rolls of tickets which were quickly used up because the dances were so short!

The Grant Family. Front row: Jane Grant, Michael, and Jenny.
Second row: Kathleen Van Wyck, Grankitty holding Ian, and Gael Grant.
Third row: Tim Mahan, John Rawson, and Cornelia Mahan.
Back row: Gwen, Glen, and Billy Grant.

One Easter, Marty and I drove to Tabby Manse in Beaufort, South
Carolina, which had been casually recommended to us as a sleepy but fun
town. It was all of that, and we kept putting off our departure. This left us
twenty-four hours for a twenty-four hour drive. It seemed all right. Both of
us would drive, and our car was Marty's mother's Cadillac. We made an early
morning start on Easter, but as we got into the car, Marty dropped and broke
her glasses. That meant twenty-four hours with me at the wheel. As dawn
rose we met a car at a dirt crossroads, and I called out, "Happy Easter!" A
man got out and asked us to stop at his church and look at his flowers and
garden. Pressed as we were, we did stop. I wrote later to thank him, and
began a correspondence that kept on all through and beyond my college
days.

From the second term of my freshman year at Smith, to the last term of

1934, I was on the registrar's list. The last semester I squeaked through with an A, B, C, D, and E. Most of my Northampton days were spent either in or on the way up to, or back from, Williamstown. I never could have dreamed that they would give me an honorary degree some years later.

Still, my memories of Smith College are few. The one course I enjoyed was Sociology, and I idolized Margaret Mead and envied her years spent in Samoa. Little did I know that I would precede her by several years in receiving the Elizabeth Blackwell Award from Hobart College.

New York in the 1930's was beautiful and full of activity. There were flowering trees and colorful flower beds that ran the length of Park Avenue in the spring. Central Park was a haven of peace, with trails for horseback riding and bicycling. Art and music attracted the rest of the world. It was considered daring but not dangerous to go to Harlem to enjoy music and to dance. The best place was the Crystal Ballroom. Cab Calloway and his band were our choice. In white tails, tall and lithe and elegant, he set the tempo and style of the whole evening. We never felt unwelcome, even though the only other white things in evidence were the teeth, and the beautifully tailored tails of the band master.

In the spring of 1934, I was happily and safely having dinner with college friends, Jim and Sally Linen, at their house in Greenwich, Connecticut. The talk turned to the parachute jump at Steeplechase Park. I said I would love to go on it. Jim grabbed me from the table, put me in the car, and we drove off to Coney Island. There was no turning back. I would get what I asked for! It was Jim's third or fourth trip, but my first, and when it was over, I would have definitely told you it was my last.

When at Smith College, I had attended a lecture by Walter White, who was the Secretary of the N.A.A.C.P., a progressive but conservative and thoughtful organization that stressed equality of opportunity. I was smart enough to realize that a door was opening to me. In the Virgin Islands there were children who needed help. I applied for a job there, and a lunch meeting was set up with Paul Pearson, Governor of the Virgin Islands, and Walter White. We met at the Hotel Algonquin in New York City, at that time, one of the rare spots where blacks and whites could eat at the same table. Our meeting lasted nearly three hours, while my fiancé waited impatiently. When I told John that I had been offered a two-year contract, he said he would not wait for me. So instead of going to the Virgin Islands, I married him, and we had three children.

It is strange how close I came in 1934 to doing what I finally did twenty years later. Here I sit, very close to the Virgin Islands. In Haiti, I worked for almost forty years with a man who had the same ideals that I had in 1934. The web of life is intricate, but it does seem to have a design.

CHAPTER 6

The Cornerstone Is Laid —
Reverence For Life To Be Carved
Over The Entrance

Once again, travel was in my future. We had a mentor, and a goal, but we had not yet decided where to build our hospital. We had considered several spots in Africa, Central America, Mexico, Guatemala, and at the headwaters of the Amazon in Peru.

One summer, Larry's thesis on tropical ulcers for Tulane Medical School brought us all to Haiti. We packed the Dodge Powerwagon with our needs for a summer of camping. Three could sit in the front, and three would be delegated to the cage in the back, which had to be locked on the outside to keep the door from swinging open.

In Port-au-Prince, we had a bottom apartment in the Hôtel Citadelle. We had a small lawn and one of the rooms could serve as a lab. The first thing we needed was material for Larry's thesis. SCISP, the international health organization, directed us to the old folks' home in Signeau, and assigned a doctor and his assistant to drive us there. The doctor was François Duvalier, and his assistant was Orelle Joseph. These contacts served us well in the future. We took scrapings and blood from the residents, and also did a malaria survey at a big school nearby. When Larry saw Dr. Duvalier in later years, the President always asked what happened to the little boy who gave out the jellybeans with each prick of the finger. It had been Ian.

We became very attached to the old folks at Signeau, and invited them to our place for lunch. Michael picked them up, and they arrived all dressed up in hats, ties, and shoes from somewhere. It was a lovely affair, and a few lonely old ladies and gentlemen had a good meal and a good time.

Most social life took place within an extended family, especially Sunday dinner after church. This is how we met our good friends Dr. Elie Villard, Mr. Georges Léger, and Dr. Maurice Armand and their families. There were also restaurants, and they were good, but mostly we preferred the family groups.

Night life, with good food and good *mereng* music, did exist. The popular choice was Cabane Choucoune, a large round structure with a high thatched roof off the square in Petionville. The President could often be seen there on Saturday nights. People would wait in their homes, dressed and ready to go, their cars ready to roll. When they heard the sound of the President's siren, they would race to follow it to secure a space at his nightclub of choice for the evening. Getting a good table had disadvantages, however. Even though the music and food were good, one could not leave before the President, who could dance every dance until three or four in the morning.

One day that summer, on the lower side of Port-au-Prince, an Austrian asked me to visit the factory he had established. It was in a big warehouse that had a floor made of slate that had been ballast in boats from Europe. The boats would then return to Europe carrying Haitian exports. On this hot sweltering day, I saw a pile of discarded old fur coats on one side of the room. They had been washed in a big machine, and looked like large wet cats. Girls sat at tables and plucked hairs one by one, until they had enough to be made into an artist's paintbrush.

The Austrian said that he had been short of water for his factory, but had been lucky when he drilled only one foot and found all of the water he needed. He must have hit a water main.

Nothing went to waste in Haiti. Pieces of paper were saved and tin cans were made into drinking cups. The era of plastics has changed all that. Now, plastic wrapping and empty Gina bottles are littered everywhere.

With the survey finished, we packed up for camping trips, and went on every road marked on the 1950 Esso map. Within an hour's drive of leaving Port-au-Prince, we discovered our French was useless, so we were all quick to learn *kreyòl* (creole).

We always laid our bedrolls by the side of the road, and when there was no breeze we would hang mosquito nets in a single line above them. Once, in the middle of the night, a man rode by singing happily. His horse's head broke the mosquito cord and all of the nets came tumbling down. This frightened him, and he cut off his song to shout, "*Zonbi* (the living dead)!"

Periodically, we would return to our place in Port-au-Prince for baths, laundry, some good meals, and food supplies for our next foray. We didn't want to get sick, so we carried our own water. The only bottled kind was Vichy. That summer we drank and brushed our teeth with bubbles!

In Port-au-Prince, we had met Timothy Kane, a coffee exporter. Haitian coffee was known to be of exceptional quality, and was used to upgrade coffees of less quality. In Tim's office was a round marble table that rotated. Tiny coffee cups rested in depressions around the edge of the table. These were used for buyers to evaluate the quality of various coffees. We carried letters from Tim to coffee growers in each of the towns that we visited, making our trips useful as well as interesting.

In those days, one had to report to the police when passing through a town. This was a good way for them to keep track of travelers, but also an unspoken comfort for us to know that we would be missed if we dropped down a canyon.

Wherever we stopped, people offered to help us. They would bring us fruit and sugar cane, or wood shavings to help start our fires.

In the south, people were especially hospitable. In Aux Cayes, the Blanchets and the Sansariques invited us to Sunday dinner. The Sansariques had five boys and one girl and weren't a bit upset to include our four. We took a trip with them to three neighboring islands in their *chaloup* (motorboat). One of the islands was nothing more than a small sandy spit that held back the sea with empty conch shells. We saw islanders dig in the sand for drinking water. That day, I saw a big long log *boumba* (dugout canoe), the only one of that size I had ever seen. It required six paddlers.

Years later, tragedy struck the beautiful Sansarique family. Four of the five boys were involved in a plot for political change. A priest betrayed them. All four were shot and killed. The youngest boy and the girl were too young to take part in the plans. Today that boy is a senator. Not long ago he came to see me. Now in his fifties, he said he still remembered our visit to Aux Cayes.

Our visit with the Blanchets was equally pleasant. Recently, the youngest Blanchet boy came to Deschapelles. He was now an engineer, working with a European construction company that had the plans and the money, but no contract to rebuild the road from Pont Sondé to Mirebalais. At lunch that day I reminded him of our Sunday in Aux Cayes. He said, "I was too young to remember, but my father often spoke of the American family that had come to Haiti to build a hospital in a place of greatest need."

Jacmel is a beautiful town perched on a bluff high above the sea. It has old gingerbread houses, an impressive Catholic cathedral, a large town square, and an iron marketplace. In those days few foreigners ventured very far from Port-au-Prince, so we were a conspicuous group. A man named Max Bolté introduced himself and asked if we needed help. Larry said yes. He needed to borrow a jeep to go up the mountain to La Voute. Our own truck was too heavy and large to make the steep climb. Max called his yardboy, "Hydrogene! *Vin' ou* (Come you)!" After no response, he called the yardboy's brother. It was Oxygene who appeared with the jeep, and we were off to La Voute.

Max, delighted with us as visitors, said he wished to give all six of us a party the following evening. Larry said it was not possible because we were leaving early the next morning. In those days, the road was a riverbed which was passable only if there had been no rain. But nothing daunted Max, and we were invited to his house before we departed. It was breakfast time, and as we arrived a band started playing. All the ladies and gentlemen of the town greeted us in dinner clothes. Later, after a big meal and several good meringue dances, we piled into the Powerwagon and made it back to Port-au-Prince before the rains.

While in Jacmel, Ian busied himself making a do-it-yourself voodoo kit. In the tobacco tin was a dried lizard, nutmeg, toenail clippings, a dog's tooth, and a piece of a mirror.

The roads were bad and at one point, Larry waved to someone. The front wheel went into a hole, and all three other wheels were lifted off the ground. It was the only situation from which our Dodge Powerwagon could not extricate itself. It was unable to use even one hind wheel. Without a tree

The Artibonite River.

close enough to winch us out, we couldn't move! A man nearby saw our predicament, took down a post from his porch, and with the help of his sons pried us out of the hole. Then off we went leaving tracks and a friend behind.

Each day we became more entranced by the country and the charm of its people. And each day we became more aware of their desperate needs.

It was at this point that Larry decided Haiti was the place for our hospital. Now we had chosen a country, but not the spot where we would build. We were told of a piece of property that had recently been abandoned by Standard Fruit. After twenty-five years in Haiti, the company had left because of rising taxes. This property, about fifty acres, had been returned to the Haitian government. We drove out to the Artibonite Valley, saw the spot, and found it ideal. It was halfway between Port-au-Prince and Cap-Haïtien, and halfway between the Caribbean Sea and the Dominican Republic border. It was on the edge of the fertile Artibonite Valley where, because of the newly-finished Péligre Dam on the Dominican border, good irrigation projects were under way. This was Deschapelles.

Dr. Elie Villard made it possible for us to see President Magloire. He had us invited to a huge dinner-dance at La Boule for President Anastasio Somoza of Nicaragua. In the receiving line, Larry had time to speak of his hopes to President Magloire. President Magloire said to come to his office the next day. With those words of encouragement, we were ready to go home to bed but that was in no way possible. No one left before the President. It was a gala evening. President Somoza brought his wife, his elite guard, and his own band. President Magloire was equally well-equipped and everyone danced away the evening, which lasted until 4:00 a.m. We survived, but just.

Larry saw the President, not the next day but one day later. The President agreed to let us use the fruit company's property for the hospital.

Our lawyer was Georges Léger, a true aristocrat and eminent *avoka* (attorney), trained in the Code de Napoléon.

The Haitian government drew up the contract and sent it to us in New Orleans. One stipulation was that we were guaranteed use of the land for only twenty-five years. Larry found this unacceptable and he stopped plans for the hospital. I was sent back to Haiti to have the time limit removed. It took a couple of weeks but the contract was re-drawn, signed, and printed in the official government newspaper, *Le Moniteur*. This made our contract a law of the land. Under the terms we were granted the rights to the fruit company farm and an additional piece of land on which there were the ruins of a colonial aqueduct.

The contract gave us a franchise that allowed us to bring in all hospital supplies, excluding food, duty-free. This is a rare privilege, and we value it highly and are careful never to abuse it. We were also given the right to bring in foreign staff. This contract, through all the changes of the government and their accompanying vicissitudes, has never been questioned or threatened.

While I was awaiting the redrawing of the contract in Port-au-Prince, the Episcopal nun, Sister Joan, became my good friend. She found me a job at the Baptist Mission in Fermathe, above the city. Due to Hurricane Hazel help was needed. All crops and trees in the South had been destroyed, and malnourished children were being carried up to Fermathe to be fed, clothed, and given shelter. Each day I brought three or four of the sickest to

Port-au-Prince where the General Hospital could provide better medical care than the mission.

The heart of the whole mission was Granny, with whom I shared sleeping quarters during my time there. She was a person of tremendous faith, and not only the religious type. When we were living in Deschapelles she sent us a lemon pie. It travelled some one hundred miles over dusty and hot roads, on the top of a public bus! It arrived safely, but we had the wisdom not to eat such a culture medium.

When we told the children of our plans to go to Haiti, they were all in boarding school, and they worried about leaving their friends and where they would spend their vacations. Larry asked them to choose a spot where they would like to have a home in the States, and they decided on Princeton. We found a lovely old farmhouse. When the time came to move in, I asked what day they would arrive for Easter. It turned out that each of them had other plans for most of the vacation. We never opened the house, and the furniture remained in storage. The farm was sold at an unexpected profit.

Larry and I began to make our dream a reality, standing alone, but together.

The architect, John Lord King, was a friend of mine from Phoenix horseback riding days. When we asked him to recommend an architect to design our tropical hospital, he said there was no one better than himself. During the war he had built a hospital in Okinawa. We could not have made a better choice. Jack spent the better part of each day perched in the *chèn* (oak) tree that today still stands between Wards II and III. He studied the elevations of this area, the angles of the sun, and direction of the wind. It is not by chance that we enjoy shade and cool breezes within the hospital. It was his care and precision that have provided the staff and patients with pleasant working and recovery areas. The hospital has survived forty years and continues to fill the needs of those who come here, despite the enormously increased demands that have been put upon it.

Groundbreaking Ceremonies. Left to right: Daniel Théard, Minister of
Protocol, me, President Paul Magloire and Larry.

Now that we had a contract, an architect, and blueprints, we were off to
Deschapelles for the laying of the cornerstone.

From Port-au-Prince to Deschapelles was a long trip over poor roads,
and we were lucky that so many made the effort to join us. Among the dig-
nitaries were President Magloire and his guard, the Chief of Protocol, the
Catholic and Episcopal Bishops of Haiti, the Sisters of Charity, Maître
Léger, and Emory Ross. Happily, local people came to make us seem like a
crowd.

The ceremonies began at high noon in a treeless, shadeless spot. First,
Dr. Ross spoke and then Larry gave a beautiful speech. Both were in French.
Larry spoke of his plans and hopes for Hôpital Albert Schweitzer and the
community:

EXCERPTS FROM AN ADDRESS DELIVERED
ON THE OCCASION OF THE DEDICATION EXERCISE FOR
HÔPITAL ALBERT SCHWEITZER
AT DESCHAPELLES, ARTIBONITE RIVER VALLEY, HAITI
BY WILLIAM LARIMER MELLON, JR., MD,
DECEMBER 11, 1954.

The aims of Hôpital Albert Schweitzer are essentially three.

First and most important is medical service to the community of Deschapelles and its vicinity. Second comes that of inviting recognized authorities in the medical specialties to visit Haiti, and of encouraging Haitian doctors and qualified students to attend demonstrations of operative techniques and to join in discussion groups. Finally, the hospital staff must seek to foster interest and a sense of responsibility in members of the community, especially among the young people, for solving public health problems and spreading information about hygiene and other aspects of disease prevention.

It will be a policy of Hôpital Albert Schweitzer to engage Haitians whose character and training show competence to perform a given job. If plans materialize, we hope to live to see Hôpital Albert Schweitzer owned and operated efficiently and on a sound financial basis by persons of Haitian nationality.

Without doctors, nurses, technicians and staff consecrated to the service of humanity, this hospital will fall short of our expectations. A modern building complete with diagnostic and therapeutic equipment is not a hospital although it may represent a useful tool. Even when staffed with trained medical personnel such an institution might be a dismal failure unworthy of the name "hospital." Unless medical care is practiced with care and concern, the hospital is but an empty shell.

Besides buildings and men and women, hospitals require food and medicine administered with insight and love, in fact all the qualities which make up *ethics*.

To this task my wife and I humbly dedicate ourselves. May the spark of *Reverence for Life* which came to us from across the Atlantic Ocean continue to burn until it has consumed us with a real and deep concern for every living creature.

(Note: this text is a translation from the French.)

After the ceremony, we headed for the United Fruit Company club-house for refreshments. We had prepared four trays, each holding about a cubic yard of sandwiches. As they were being carried to the party, the sandwiches passed through the soldiers of elite guard lined up on both sides of the path. The trays arrived safely at the clubhouse but not a single sandwich was left. Larry produced a bottle of Scotch, two olives, and a few potato chips for the President. The President did not even look at the olives or chips, but thought the Scotch was great. He was charming and affable and acted as if he had had a full meal.

I asked the President where he was posted during his military service, and he told me he had been at Saltrou, which meant dirty hole. I said it was a sad name for a beautiful place and he should change it. He asked, "What to?" Quick as a wink, I said, "Magloire." He did change it, but he changed it to Belle Anse, or beautiful cove.

During the two years of construction, Jack King, our architect, would fly from San Francisco to New Orleans every three or four weeks. He and Larry would discuss the plans and the schedules, and then Jack would fly on to Haiti where he and I would work together to carry out those plans.

Sometimes, after one of my trips to New Orleans, Jack and I would return to Haiti together. We had to change planes in Miami and then spend the night in Havana. Planes did not fly at night in those days, so we had no choice but to stay overnight in Cuba. Castro was only just beginning to show his beard, and the city was still gay and vital. On one occasion we went to the famous open-air night club that had a sliding glass roof in case it rained. But even more exciting was finding and ordering the louvered doors of Cuban cedar for the two houses that Jack designed. They traveled from Cuba to Saint Marc by boat. Jack's plans for our house were so detailed and exact that the louvered doors fit perfectly. Today the louvers still work and the wood is more beautiful than ever. More important, the doors have no termites.

When Jack and I came to Deschapelles, we would stay with Dr. Burns and his wife. He was the Knappen-Tippet engineer during the finishing stages of the Péligre Dam and the Caneau control point.

When I stayed in Saint Marc, I would stay with Bob and Alva Laws while I was waiting for our house there to be ready. They had a Delco generator, and once those motors are turned off for the evening, you do NOT automatically reactivate them by turning on a light in the middle of the night. I had been well-advised of this by my good host Bob, and since he was our job foreman, when he advised me of something, I stayed advised. One night, I got up, forgot about being advised, and turned on a light. I remembered his advisement immediately, and turned off the light almost as soon as it was on. I was barely back in bed when I heard the screen door slam shut. It was Laws on his way out to the pump house to undo what I had done. "Well, too bad," I thought, and was almost asleep again when he was back in the house and out again, slamming the door really hard this time. I wondered if I should get up to hold a flashlight for him as he repaired the damage I had done. Then I thought better of it and went back to sleep, but not for long. All through the night the screen door kept slamming shut, and with each slam it seemed to me Bob got madder and madder. Daylight brought the truth, and it was kind. Each time Bob slammed the screen door, it was not Bob. It was a green mango hitting the tin roof. But it was an unhappy night for me because Bob was always so good-natured, and the only thing he had asked of me during my stay at his house was to not turn on the electricity once it was off for the evening.

That first summer in Saint Marc, I was going daily to Deschapelles to monitor and evaluate the construction of the hospital, and the grading and planting of the land surrounding it. Only three big trees had survived the devastation of the early construction. I began to protect all of the remaining trees on the property.

When the kids came for the summer, we rented a house in Saint Marc. It was tiny: two rooms, a porch, and an open, concrete block garage. Jenny and I had one room and Ian and his friend Deanie had the other. Our little bedroom had real charm. It was whitewashed and had two beds with black spreads, and a Van Gogh-esque chair like the listing yellow one in his painting from Arles. But my chair out-listed Van Gogh's. We also had two toucan prints on the wall.

Life in Saint Marc was simple, full of nice surprises and things for us to learn. We lived and ate on the porch. We had an outdoor toilet and shower,

The house in Saint Marc. Bachelor's quarters.

and every morning at four a.m. we pumped enough water to fill our daily needs. I finally decided to buy a butane icebox for the purpose of keeping leftover food. However, it was difficult to refuse local requests for space in this very rare refrigerator.

Before Larry and Billy arrived, we turned the garage into bachelor's quarters. The four sides of the wooden icebox crate made a perfect front wall. The crate's top and bottom served as tables. All of the sheets, towels, and clothes were kept in *makout* (straw bags), like those used by everyone in the countryside.

Everyone in the town observed us, and assisted us in all ways possible. Gilberte, a cook, appeared under a big hat one day, and convinced us that we needed her help, which was true. Venturing to the market, and cooking in a pot balanced on three stones, did not make it easy to prepare early-morning breakfasts, or suppers after long days back and forth to Deschapelles, where I was working on the hospital and the kids were working with a group to build the chicken house.

On one of our first trips to the market, we passed a woman cooking a huge bowl of soup. As she stirred, a goat's jaw complete with teeth surfaced, and Ian's friend Deanie fainted. As he recovered, his first words were, "My mother would hate Haiti." Deanie became a doctor and visited us several times in later years, but although his mother remained a close friend from our days in New Orleans, she never made the trip.

In Port-au-Prince I saw a lovely chair in someone's house. I found out that it came from Marbial near Jacmel, and went there to to order more. One family, from the grandfather on down to the grandsons, worked on the chairs. The wood and rush had to be cut during the right seasons to elude termites and bugs. One day, unexpectedly, the sixty chairs arrived in Saint Marc. They were accomapnied by the entire family of chairmakers and almost everyone from the tiny town of Marbial. Seating was no problem. We just unpacked the sixty chairs.

We understood when we ordered that many chairs, that the price had to double from two dollars to four to cover their storage costs in Marbial. Our house in Saint Marc was just big enough to hold the chairs until we could get them to Deschapelles.

Our neighbor, the young handsome Captain Corvington, the chief of police, became a steady caller. One day, he appeared with a group of men carrying five gallon kerosene cans on their heads. Each can contained a beautiful plant for the new house in Deschapelles. As the men came closer, we saw they all wore striped clothes. Since we had the sixty chairs from Marbial, I did not hesitate to ask everyone in for coffee and cookies. The prisoners, the police chief, Jenny, and I all had a happy time. These plants were the beginning of the landscaping around our house in Deschapelles.

There was a much-loved doctor in Saint Marc, who cared for the sick and needy as well as the town leaders. When he died, the local residents took turns carrying the coffin round and round the town. They would not let him leave them. It was nightfall before they carried him to the cemetery and released him to stronger hands.

In church one day, I put a dollar in the collection. I saw that a friend next to me was pushing around the money in the plate. After church he handed me "my change," telling me I had given too much.

In Saint Marc I wanted to find a horse to ride. Over the front door of one of the buildings there was a beautiful copper horse's head, and I went in and asked if they rented or sold horses. The owner said, "Neither," and added that he was the butcher.

We did rent horses in Cap-Haïtien, where we went frequently, and usually we rode up the steep mountain to the Citadelle. The horses looked old enough to have known Henri Christophe, and apparently had not eaten since then. We hoped that some of the money from our ride would be used to feed them. Ian had trouble getting his steed up to speed. The rest of us went ahead, zigzagging up the slope, leaving Ian far behind. All of a sudden we saw Ian on foot coming straight up the mountain to reach us, shouting, "Wait for me!" His ancient horse had died under him. This was a terrible experience for a young cowboy.

While living in Saint Marc, the kids and I went to Grosse Roche each Saturday night, to dance the night away with our local friends. I never sat down all evening, except to take a sip of the rum, or grab a piece of the cake that was brought to us. When Billy and Larry arrived from their South American "R and R," life took on a faster beat in every spot but Grosse Roche. Jenny had said to Larry, "Wait until you see Mommy. Everyone dances with her." We arrived at the place, Larry sat with me, and not one person asked me to dance. A humbling experience, but was it humbling for me or for Larry?

Two of the few cars in Saint Marc were ours. One was Jenny's black Buick roadster with a canvas top and yellow-spoked wheels. It was used for the daily trip to Deschapelles. On one occasion an employee on the construction crew asked to borrow it. I said yes, thinking he meant for a trip to the market and back. Not at all. He returned in a week with a new wife in the front seat.

Ian had a DKW jeep with no doors and no roof. It seems that the primary purpose of this vehicle was for Ian and Deanie to impress Gladys, a beauty with long black hair. They picked her up one day to take her on a picnic. She brought a cake with green and yellow icing that immediately became quite melted and covered with ants. The boys were horrified. But Gladys picked up the cake, placed it in the sun, and the ants disappeared in moments. The icing began to melt more quickly than ever, but the cake was good.

Jenny had a friend, Pete Addison, who came to visit. The cook made a picnic for their trip to Cap-Haïtien. The fried chicken came complete with its two yellow feet, a local delicacy that neither of the young Americans appreciated at the time.

The son of Bob Laws, our engineer, came to Haiti, and he and Billy spent hours skin-diving at Montrouis. In those days, the sea and its beaches were open along the coast. One could stop anywhere and jump in. Later, when Larry and I were swimming, someone recognized our car and stopped to talk to the two heads out in the sea. Luckily, they couldn't see below the water. Our clothes were piled up on the rocks. Today, almost all the good spots for swimming between Saint Marc and Port-au-Prince are unavailable to those who pass, because they are behind high block walls with iron gates. There are four beach clubs where one can swim, eat, and sleep, but they are expensive.

The kids said Saint Marc was the best summer they ever had. They worked daily, danced all night long each Saturday night, and had a myriad of local friends. After returning from Deschapelles every day, we had time to go to the beach for a swim. And the Saturday night dancing at Grosse Roche was never surpassed.

During his internship, Larry found, on the steps of Charity Hospital, a little black dog with a white muzzle and no tail. He picked him up, took him home, and named him Peachie. He became a lovely friend. Larry would continually ask Peachie if he wanted to go to Haiti, and Peachie would wag the stub of his tail. When Larry finally came to Haiti for good, I went to the airport to meet him. What I saw was Larry and Peachie together, looking out of the plane's window, both happy to reach their new home at last.

Peachie's adjustment to his new country was easy and complete. And he was always the best dressed member of our family. When there was no water to do the laundry, he was still well dressed, sleek and black, with his white necktie. And even on the dusty roads to the farm, there was Peachie, looking divine in his well-tailored, double-breasted suit.

When Larry first saw our hospital he was truly surprised. He had never translated the blueprints into anything near the size of what was rising before him.

Construction.

After the children left for school, the months in Saint Marc continued to be pleasant. Larry and I went daily to Deschapelles where the hospital construction was in its finishing stages. I filled my leisure hours with a pedal sewing machine Larry gave me. One could get excellent local cloth in those days.

We had a Sailfish, a good harbor, and always a good breeze. Early one Sunday, Larry and I sailed out of Saint Marc. We had a plastic bag of sandwiches and a plastic bottle of water tied tightly to the mast. The breeze was fine, and we flew toward the north end of the harbor, about ten miles away. At this point Larry said we must begin to fight our way back. As we were coming about, the Sailfish turned completely upside down, with the mast straight down under us. We righted the boat fairly easily and prepared for the hard sail home. Much to our amazement, the wind was behind us all the way. Our sandwiches were dry and delicious and the water was good. We were back home in Saint Marc in no time, at the same speed we had sailed out. We have since noted that all local fishing boats leave early in the morning, and return at about the time we came about.

One day, we put the hull of the Sailfish in the canal at Caneau. We planned to float down to Liancourt. We amazed all of the people working in the fields when they saw us pass, sitting on the Sailfish and using the mast as a pole. It was a quick trip, but caused a lot of conversation along the way.

While we were living in Saint Marc, we were invited to have dinner with President and Madame Magloire at the residence in Port-au-Prince. Unable to refuse, we drove to the city. The table was set for twenty, with a pink tablecloth and napkins, wine glasses, and gold service plates. Behind each chair was a waiter wearing white gloves. After the soup was served, we noticed that each waiter had a bit of *soup joumou* (pumpkin soup) on the thumb of his right-hand glove.

Dinner had been delicious with lots of general conversation in French and in *kreyòl*. After dinner, the men and women were separated. Among the ladies, I was lost and uncomfortable in local gossip. Madame Magloire, tiny and short with hair piled high on her head to compensate, enjoyed it immensely. Among the gentlemen, Dr. Villard whispered to Larry, "Now we play poker. The President likes to win."

We were invited to a doctor's house in Saint Marc. It was a nice old gingerbread residence, with lots of cracks between the boards of the ceiling. As we sat at the dining room table, drinking warm red wine from red glasses, we were conscious of many eyes watching through the cracks above. In the middle of the table was a shiny brown artificial arm, wearing a glove. A truly macabre centerpiece! People do receive pensions for disability in Haiti, sometimes long after the person is no longer there to receive them. One pair of eyes from the room above us became, years later, those of our head nurse!

When we were still returning to Saint Marc each night, Larry had his first patient, a construction employee from Deschapelles. He showed up sick at our house one evening. Larry told him to go right home to bed, and not to eat, just to drink a lot of water. He realized that the man had measles, and told him so. Larry added that he would come to visit him in a couple of days. At the end of the week, the man appeared again in the driveway, very thin and very weak from lack of food. Larry had forgotten to go see him.

Living in Saint Marc was a happy time. We were the only foreigners. The Saint Marcoise were good to us. We learned *kreyòl* and so many of the niceties and essentials of the Haitian politeness and customs. This would stand us in good stead for the years to come. However, I still learn something new and something of value each day.

Supporting and financing our hospital in Haiti has been a constant challenge. In the very beginning, Addison Vestal, with his wisdom and foresight, established the Grant Foundation, and he was a member of the Board from the start. Larry chose to give it my family name. All contributions to the Foundation are tax deductible, and they are the life blood of the hospital.

From that day when I was introduced to him at Mormon Lake in Arizona, Addison Vestal had his arms around me. His very first job had been with Larry's father as a tax advisor. After Mr. Mellon died, he continued to work for all four of the Mellon children and their families.

I think it was Larry's choice in life that endeared him to Addison, and consequently made me close to him. For the next thirty-eight years he came to every Board meeting. Not infrequently, when his car would bog down, he walked the last mile or so on a treacherous and muddy road to Deschapelles. His briefcase was heavy, with information that was vital to the well-being of Hôpital Albert Schweitzer.

Cigars were an essential part of his life, but I never saw him with one. He smoked only in his room by the garage. We greatly miss his presence in our lives.

In New Orleans, the architect and Larry and I were discussing the plans for the hospital. Ian guessed that it must cost a lot of money to build a hospital, and asked who was going to pay for it. Larry replied that it would be paid for by friends and people who wished to help. Ian gave us his month's allowance, and for a young schoolboy it was a big gift. He was our first donor. Ian's second gift to the hospital was a wooden footstool he made at school. Today, it sits in my bedroom in Deschapelles. It was quite a turn around since the day in Fort Rock when Larry asked Ian what he thought about his going to medical school and building a hospital. Ian had said, "Well that's one thing I would never be, a doctor."

When it came to choosing the hospital farm, I had a great idea. I asked a former Fruit Company employee for advice. He recommended two farms: Ferme Cinque and Drouin. We chose Drouin for our beef farm, and later on we rented Ferme Cinque. When Jenny and I went out to Drouin to meet the officials who would be defining the borders, we learned that they wished to do so on horseback. Getting seven horses was not as hard as getting the gentlemen in their city clothes up on the horses! The seven officials rode the perimeter of the farm, and we signed the papers on the bonnet of the car. The transaction took place with Gilberte, our cook, in attendance. She said it wasn't fitting for two ladies to go alone, so she put on her hat and came with us.

The farm proved valuable to HAS. We upgraded native cattle by bringing in good quality bulls, like Charollais, white-faced Hereford, and Zebu. All of the cattle became fat and sleek from feeding on the pasture of Pongola grass that we had planted. Twenty-five years later, we had a herd of sixty head with the same color conformation, and to this day there is no comparable herd in Haiti. We raised these animals to feed the patients and the staff. Had we been left to the mercy of local farmers, the price of beef would have been astronomical. For the same reason, we raise chickens for meat and eggs, and pigs for local distribution.

We had a beautiful herd of milk cows, again the only one in Haiti. The pasture lay in front of our house, and as we sat on the porch, they would look at us over the *ha-ha* (retaining) wall. Despite their bucolic charm, we finally decided we could not keep them. The six cows gave a total of two gallons of milk each day. No one would buy the herd because it was too difficult to find the pasture to feed them. Sadly, we decided to take them to Drouin and consider them part of the herd. Then a miracle happened. Local farmers bought them up, one by one, to provide milk for their children. We could not have had a happier ending.

In later years, we needed and rented Ferme Cinque to grow feed for the cattle. The Fruit Company land was fertile and flat, and we plowed and planted a large piece of land. When we returned to hoe and weed, we found a deep cut across the road. We got out, filled it in, and went to the garden to work. When we came to work again, the cut was there again. Obviously, we were not wanted. Larry turned around and never went back to this piece of land.

Before the hospital was completed, Larry and I were stopped on the road to Drouin by a man who asked us to see his wife. She was thin and wasted and breathing badly as she lay on a straw mat. It was all too evident that she had TB. Without medicines and X-ray, there was little that Larry could do for her. But each day as we passed, Larry brought her an egg. At that point in her illness, his love, concern, and the daily egg were probably the very best medicines.

Also, during the construction, I used to visit the *Matènite* (Maternity Hospital) in Verrettes, bringing old sheets for the patients' beds. Several times, I saw a young boy on a board with a roller skate attached beneath. Using the backs of his hands to push, he was able to cover quite a lot of ground. My efforts to speak to him were not successful at first. Finally, I was able to tell him that when the hospital was finished, I thought we might help him. Sylvestre was among our first patients.

The results were not good. He had a spinal cord injury, and the only thing we could do was to provide him with a wheelchair. Each New Year's Day, to wish us well, he made a trip in the wheelchair from his home in Verrettes to Deschapelles. Needless to say, after the twelve-mile journey, he always needed a new chair.

Sylvestre married an *oksilye* (auxiliaire or nurses' aide), from our hospital and set up his own boutique where he was able to be an independent and useful citizen. And he did something a Haitian rarely does. He asked me to come to his house, and in the privacy of his bedroom, he whispered to me. He told me how hospital supplies were being taken, and who was responsible. I was grateful to him for making us aware of this fact and protected his confidence.

Transportation was excellent during our early years in Haiti. The port of Saint Marc was in good condition and could accommodate the large vessels that brought the heavy materials needed for the construction of the Péligre Dam high up on the Dominican border. The railway line could efficiently deliver bananas from the fruit farms of the Artibonite Valley to Port-au-Prince. The port and the railroad proved invaluable for the transportation of our own construction and hospital supplies.

Saint Marc used to have a big heavy dock, and what seemed to be a bottomless harbor. The wharf served as a loading depot for the supplies for the Péligre Dam. The bags of cement were unloaded by the thousands and sent up to Péligre on flatbed trucks. Although the road was dirt, it was kept in perfect shape to ensure regular deliveries by the big heavy trucks. Soon it was discovered that many bags were lost en route, and it became financially advisable to ship the cement in loose bulk and store it in three heavy iron silos at the Saint Marc dock. From there the cement would be delivered north in closed, metal trucks. Mute evidence of the enormous cement loss are the many concrete houses that sprang up along the road to the dam site.

Today, the harbor has become so filled with silt and debris that only a flat-bottom boat can approach the once excellent dock.

For the large landowners, delivering produce to Port-au-Prince was a problem that a two-wheeled bullock cart could not solve. The time came for a railroad. Although it was known as a national railroad, it was certainly subsidized by the sugar and banana companies. The engines, passenger cars, and freight cars were made by the H.C. Porter Company in Pittsburgh, the first business venture of Buddy Evans, Larry's boyhood friend.

The narrow gauge railroad ran to Port-au-Prince from Verrettes in the North and from Léogâne in the South. The round house was in Saint Marc. Depending on the season, it was fueled by either sisal or by *bagas,* (sugar cane pulp) that remains after the juice is extracted.

In the late 1950s, a hurricane tore up some of the tracks between Montrouis and Saint Marc and the line never was re-established. Not too many years ago a Japanese company came in and bought up every piece of iron: tracks, round house, trestles, and all. It might well be that those pieces provide the steel in the Mitsubishi vehicles that crowd the roads of Haiti these days.

Before the Japanese came, Larry used many rail sections in building bridges across canals. He also used pieces of iron leftover from the Péligre Dam construction.

We were fortunate to have these facilities during the building of our hospital. Supplies were easily transferred from boat to wharf to train. The train unloaded at Carrefour Alexandre, a quarter of a mile from the hospital site. The big generators, steam boilers, X-ray machines, OR tables, and other equipment reached Deschapelles by this route.

Once, while unloading our supplies in Saint Marc, we lost a crate of heavy slate between the boat and the dock. We could not grapple for it because the water was too deep. Our insurance company would not pay for this loss. We were covered on the boat and on the dock, but there was no coverage for the crack in between.

The American Marine occupation, from 1915 to 1934, warranted plenty of negative criticism. But there were also many positive contributions made during this era. The Marines built all of the harbors and port facilities, among them Saint Marc. Because of the Marines, every city has a building that can be used for a tropical hospital. Open and airy wards usually surround a large central courtyard. In addition, the Marines brought medical equipment and expertise. But by the time we arrived in Haiti, the functional part of the Saint

Marc hospital had fallen into disrepair, and the structure was usable only as bed space. Medical care was given by physicians in their own clinics.

Larry and I asked Jack Lord to design a compact unit that could be placed in the center courtyard of each of these hospitals. It would be locked and accessible only to the Catholic sister in charge. It would contain an OR, central supply, X-ray, and lab. But as the work at our hospital demanded more time and energy, these blueprints were laid aside.

We hired the Brun brothers, two Haitian engineers, to follow Jack King's detailed hospital plans. It was quickly evident that the job was too big for the Brun brothers, and they were glad to bow out. Jack's American engineer, Bob Laws, was placed in charge, and under him were Americans who supervised electricity, plumbing, carpentry, and tile-laying. Each of these men hired and trained a corps of local workers, and by the end of two years of construction, the workers had become highly-skilled tradesmen, capable of finding jobs anywhere. It was due to Bob Laws' supervision that the hospital was finished on time and according to Jack King's plans.

At times, between our trips down to Haiti, a lot seemed to have been accomplished, at other times nothing. The four foreign construction leaders often went to Miami for the weekend, leaving Friday and returning Monday. We didn't complain, since we were lucky that they were willing to work in such an isolated spot. I offered to set up a library to be used during their the evening hours. The "library" was hardly a library. The one time I made a quick visit, I was stunned at the literary choices. Thankfully, there was no brass plaque that said, "Kindness of Mrs. Mellon."

The first thing we needed for the construction of the hospital was a good water supply. A father and son team from the Chicago Bridge and Iron Company came down to build the water tower. They were great. They whistled as they welded the tower and the big tank up in the air. When I would meet them at lunch time, the father would say, "Mrs. Mellon, you are going to have a wonderful life here." None of the hospital foundations were in place, and there were piles of stone, cement, and iron everywhere, but he continued to say the same thing every time I saw him. Today, I often think of him and his son, and how wise and right they were.

Pouring the roof.

The time had come to paint the big HAS water tower. Someone produced for us two men fresh from working on the George Washington Bridge. We thought we were lucky. The job entailed completely painting both the inside and the outside of the tank, as well as the tower. The two men slept late in the morning and ended early in the afternoon. They did not seem to feel a need to communicate with anyone and were satisfied to be together. At their departure, three empty cases of Barbancourt rum were discovered in their room. They were asked how they could manage to drink and paint. They said they could not climb the water tower each morning without the reassurance of rum. A ten-day job and thirty-six bottles. Ten years later, when once again the need to paint came around, we discovered they had never painted the top of the tower, only up to the edge.

The sun and the breezes had been carefully considered in the designing of the hospital. The roofs with big overhangs provide shade from the hot tropical sun, and protection from the heavy seasonal rains. The hospital is made of stone walls, concrete blocks, and glass louvers. The only local supplies were the stone, the sand, the water, and the willing and eager labor. All other items had to be brought in.

The biggest and most exciting event was the construction of the roof.

Ward III had to be poured in one day. The roof was prepared by using the concrete columns and the sustaining wall. The original forms were corrugated Transite. One-quarter-inch iron rods were layed in both directions, four inches apart, on top of the Transite, and they had to be spot-welded to prevent the iron from creeping in the heat. There were two hoists, each large enough to hold a wheelbarrow and a worker. The cement mixer was at the base of the up-hoist. The worker with an empty wheelbarrow went down the down-hoist. This relay of four hundred men lasted twenty-four hours, nonstop, to complete the pour for Ward III.

The main part of the hospital had to be a continuous pour with no joints. For this job we had even more men and the added problem of using corrugated tin instead of Transite. The tin buckled in the heat, so it had to be spot-welded. The cement stuck to the corrugated tin, so it had to be oiled, which made treacherous footing for the barefoot men with wheelbarrows. The completed roofs were four inches thick and had no seams. The entire hospital construction is earthquake-proof, grade four.

Aerial view of the hospital.

Originally there were four open breezeways and two open courtyards. The breezeways and one courtyard were to be used for the relaxation and enjoyment of the doctors and nurses. These spaces soon became working parts of the hospital, with the moments of rest rare indeed in the busy day. The larger courtyard was originally built as a horseyard. The space has been now given over to hospital specialty clinics, and the horses have been moved to a swale just below the hospital building.

Larry asked Dr. Schweitzer what he should plant around the fountain and basin in the center courtyard of the hospital. Dr. Schweitzer suggested

140

trees that were fruitful. Today the courtyard is filled with avocados, mangoes, almonds, cherries, and breadfruit trees. On the back of the fountain wall is a bronze plaque that was given by Billy Mellon. It contains words of Dr. Schweitzer's philosophy. Below the plaque are benches where people can spend a quiet moment under the breadfruit tree. Today, this courtyard is the place where Dr. Mellon's birthday, June 26th, is celebrated. June 26th is also the hospital's birthday.

When we first came to Deschapelles, the village had only four *lakou* (courtyards). Each *lakou* had four or five *kay* (straw-roofed houses), filled by the extended family. Soon after we arrived in Deschapelles, the road between Carrefour Alexandre and the hospital became a desirable place to build a house and establish a residence. This was because the hospital presented many opportunities for work. The road was narrow and dusty, and the small houses that sprang up were no things of beauty. With my first grandchild Wendy in my arms, I walked the length of the road, offering bougainvillea plants to the residents along the way. Today, Wendy is thirty-four, and there are three places that are brightened by old and venerable bougainvillea plants.

Now, between HAS and Carrefour Alexandre, and also in the other direction up the mountain, houses stand one after another with almost no room for trees or gardens. Today you can hardly walk between the houses, not only on the borders of the road but also in the areas behind. Even in a community as tightly packed as this, a family is able to maintain its privacy.

With the land came the Fruit Company clubhouse, a swimming pool, and eight stone houses. Gradually, the Artibonite Valley Development Organization's (ODVA) temporary houses were turned over to us. Today, with the ones that we have added, we have forty housing units. Since arriving in Deschapelles, we built our house and a similar one for an administrator. We built a huge depot for storage. We have repaired, added to, and subtracted from the ODVA "temporary" houses, now forty-five years old but standing strong. Electric wiring, water distribution, and control of waste will be upgraded soon.

Hôpital Albert Schweitzer.

Today, with a medical staff of sixteen physicians, many with families, and a nursing staff of forty, we all fit in well but there are few empty beds.

Virtually finished, the hospital opened in two years, which is remarkable when one considers the obstacles that lay in our way.

They Came From Near,
They Came From Far

The staff arrived before the hospital was finished. They were in Port-au-Prince for a while and then we moved them to Deschapelles. It was a good group. Having no medical work to do, they made themselves a nest in Ward III and helped uncrate hospital supplies. The staff was made up of Dr. Yank Chandler, surgeon and medical director, Miss Walbourg Peterson, head nurse from Massachusetts General, Doctors Hy and Burma Nordstrom, Navy physician and anesthesiologist, Mary McVaney, lab technician, Dr. Alec Earle, pediatrician from Samoa, and Dr. Larry Mellon, internist.

Several of the construction people were still around to finish last-minute details. They were a tough group, and when they were joined by the Navy couple and the doctor from Samoa, the result was a lot of drinking and a lot of time spent in Port-au-Prince. Even though it was not paved, the road was excellent then, and everyone seemed to have a car.

Yank Chandler and his wife Alva held things together until the hospital opened and everyone had a full time job to do. Yank, head of the surgery service in a Palo Alto, California hospital, came to us for his sabbatical year. The Chandlers' presence proved to be as important for morale as for medicine.

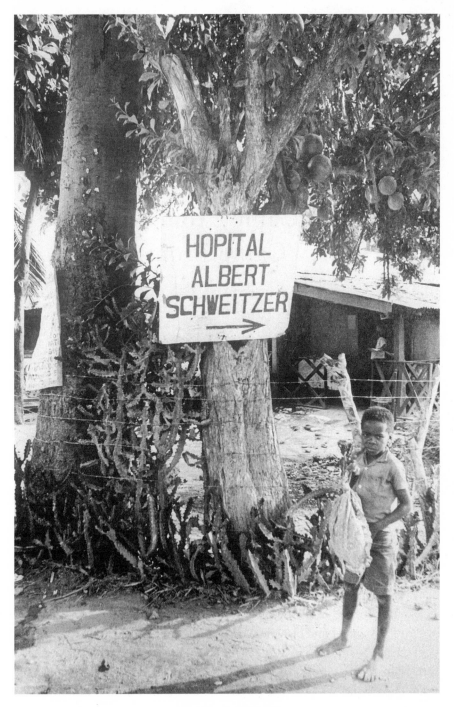

Carrefour Alexandre.

Yank kept a needed semblance of discipline. Alva was wonderful. She took care of all the wide-eyed visitors who came to the hospital, the first really modern hospital in Haiti. It was full of trash and rubbish left by the construction crew, but Alva would show the visitors around and bravely say, "This will be the surgery ward." The generators ran, the water was in the tower, and the people marveled at the electricity and the bathrooms.

Olga Ditterling was one such visitor who came to see the hospital. Her family owned and operated Shell Oil in the Dutch East Indies. Larry showed her around. As they were standing on the garage loading dock, the Shell truck drove up with a load of gasoline.

Dr. Schweitzer had understood why our hospital in Haiti wound be different from his. We would be associating with Haitian doctors and nurses who had been well trained, many in Germany and France. They were accustomed to first class equipment, therefore ours needed to be comparable or better than what they expected.

The year that we began building our hospital, the Dean of Tulane University made a survey of all the medical schools in Central and South America. He told us that we were lucky. The school in Port-au-Prince was one of the very best.

While the hospital was being built, we sent four Haitian nurses to the States for two years of training. The nurses were then expected to return to us and work in surgery, medicine, public health, and anesthesia. The anesthesia nurse never kept her appointment at the school. The other three nurses completed their courses and returned to Deschapelles. They became the backbone of our nursing staff, and stayed and worked with us for several years.

On the day of the cornerstone laying, the Bishop of Haiti told us there were four Catholic Sisters en route to Haiti. The work that had been arranged for them had fallen through, and he asked if we would be able to use them. Two were nurses, one was a lab technician, and the fourth was their housekeeper. We were happy to have them and they stayed about ten years. We already had the three Haitian nurses, and with the addition of the two Sisters, we began with a good nursing staff.

The beginnings were stormy. Early each morning, Larry and I were coming from our house in Saint Marc. The hospital courtyard was still piled with odds and ends of construction materials. Nothing was completely ready, and Larry could see that the opening might have to be postponed for quite some time. He decided to change the date, and set the opening of the hospital for June 26, 1956, his 46th birthday. This decision was a wise one. On that day we were ready, and off and running.

I used to have nightmares that the hospital would open its doors and no one would come. That was a needless worry. On the first day, the patients were mostly our own employees from the farm at Drouin. On the second day, we saw everyone who appeared, and finally closed the clinic doors at nightfall.

Long before the hospital was finished, Haitian doctors had strongly advised us to limit our medical responsibility to a defined area. Otherwise we would be overwhelmed. We did establish a district, even though we later added to it. From the beginning, we tried to limit the patients to our district and to make exceptions only for emergencies. There had been no census, so we had to determine each patient's eligibility with a series of questions. Since I spoke *kreyòl*, I was able to help with the screening. The job brought me in close contact with all who came to our door.

I also worked at the front desk, filling out cards and dossiers, and making change. Each patient pays for his dossier, not much, but enough to assure him that there is a value to the service and treatment he is receiving. The dossiers now number well over 350,000, and no dossier has ever been lost. These records provide priceless research material for anyone willing to go through them. Today patient information is on computers, and our present records are readily available.

In those days, country people had little money. Occasionally, old and valued Carolingian coins would surface, but for the most part, we saw only the small copper and silver coins that could survive burial or fire. Twenty small coins equalled one *goud* (Haitian monetary unit), or twenty cents in US money. Strangely, today we see almost no coins, only worn and torn, almost unrecognizable, paper coins. People hold their paper up to the light to make sure there are no holes as it. In the market it is unacceptable in such a state.

Front steps.

147

Front desk.

Once the hospital was fully functioning, the staff became a close-knit, coordinated group. An emergency, like a bus accident that caused lots of injuries, brought everyone running. One person would place identification bands on wrists. Another would find and fill out dossiers. Another would administer tetanus shots. Lab work and X-rays were ordered, and blood donors were found for surgery cases.

We survived the first year. The OR finally opened, and Yank had time to do one surgical procedure just before he left. It was a brain tumor, but it was easily removed and proved to be benign. The opening of the OR began on this positive note, and the hospital and all its departments were at last functioning.

Larry noticed one day that a Haitian physician had been absent for several days. He sent a note to the doctor, asking him to return to his duties in the clinic. When this note produced no result, Larry sent another one, relieving this doctor of his responsibilities at HAS. In the same mail, Larry received word from the doctor offering his excuse. He had been made Minister of Public Health of Haiti.

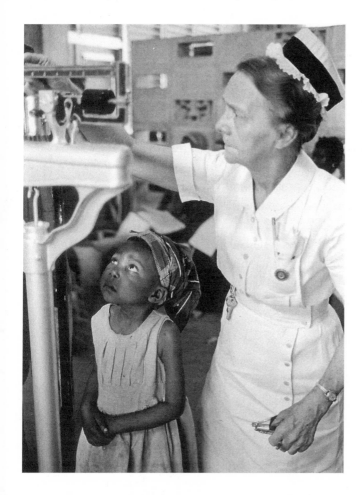

"Miss Pete."

Many people passed through the hospital, but the one who had the most impact was our first head nurse, Miss Walbourg Peterson. She came from Boston in 1955, and she arrived, wearing her brown tweed suit, brown felt hat, and brown shoes. Until the day she left Deschapelles in October, 1977, "Miss Pete" contributed far beyond her duties as head nurse. She could never learn *kreyòl*, but everyone understood what she meant, and loved her. There was no corner of the hospital that her bright eyes did not watch over.

Before dawn, Miss Pete would start down the path to the hospital, wearing her crisp white uniform and dirty old sneakers. Before she reached her destination, however, her dog, Spot, would meet her, and she would seldom arrive without muddy paw prints on her white skirt. She would go to her

149

office, put on her Massachusetts General Hospital (MGH) cap and her MGH pin, and change into clean, white shoes. She was then ready for whatever the day would bring. She was by our side for over twenty years, and could still fit into the same uniforms!

When we had finished picking up after the building was completed, Miss Pete announced that she and I would clean the bathrooms. We set to it on hands and knees, scrubbing what two years of construction had left. Right behind us was a self-appointed helper, tall and polite, who worked by our side throughout all forty washstands, showers, and bathrooms. When we were finished, the man asked if he could be the head of the bathrooms. We were delighted to fulfill his wish. Antoine Veus was with us until his retirement in 1996, at which time he was working with equipment, with oxygen, and in the morgue.

Antoine was a very valuable and loyal employee. He worked in the morgue at a time when we were doing surgical lung resections of TB patients. He contracted TB, and was first put on the isolation ward, then moved to our TB recovery village at L'Escale before being sent home to recuperate. It was a long illness, but he came back to work with a better resistance to TB than many of us have. Now his greatest worry seems to be what will happen to the hospital when I am no longer here.

Not one aspect of the hospital escaped Miss Pete's eyes, from the adhesive tape on the walls to the conductivity of the OR floor.

She saw that the nurses always wore their caps and that the *oksilyes* always had their uniforms buttoned.

The suction machines, the oxygen tanks, the Stryker frames, and the blood pressure apparatus, were all supervised by Miss Pete, and with Antoine's help, kept in perfect order.

Both the laundry and the Central Supply Room fell under her care. She was always trying to save money for the hospital, but never at the risk of letting supplies drop below an acceptable level.

She kept the narcotics count, and patients gave her their money for safekeeping.

Whenever orthopedic, pediatric, or eye patients arrived from St.

Vincent's school for handicapped children or Children's TB Hospital in Port-au-Prince, or from La Pointe, Miss Pete always had their records ready for the doctors.

On her own, she assumed responsibility for the eye clinic, the dental clinic, the library, and the staff's annual health exams, which were always up to date. For years, she posted *The Boston Globe* calendars in all the clinics and the wards.

Miss Pete insisted that I learn all about the workings of the hospital. This included quite a long education on the mechanics of the morgue, and how it should be supervised and used, as well as how to handle the deaths. Few Sundays went by that she was not called to the morgue to aid relatives.

Miss Pete's cozy home was a haven for many. She helped the Dutch, Swiss, and Mennonite nurses make the adjustment to Third World medical care, and although they were far from home, she tried to make their lives happy ones. Good music, cakes, cookies, National Geographic, and a warm welcome could always be found at her house. It was a great treat to be invited there for Sunday morning breakfast.

She fed not only her own dog and cat, but all of the others that came to her door.

Miss Pete always made the place cards for the Christmas dinner. At hospital parties, she was among the first to be asked onto the dance floor.

She was an HAS historian, able to answer any questions on past employees and past dates.

She was excited and prepared for each staff baby. The crib, the layette, and the OR pack were always ready and waiting. And she never let a staff member be sick at home without food, care, and concern, plus she could always find a warm jacket for guards on night duty.

"The headed nurse," was known by all who came to the hospital, and she was recognized throughout Haiti.

One of our early medical directors and a great friend, Frank Lepreau, said that Miss Pete was the jewel in the hospital's crown. No matter how long the day or how big the problem, she never failed to act in the spirit of Albert Schweitzer and his *Reverence for Life.*

The hospital very quickly attracted talented people from near and far. All were willing to contribute their work and knowledge.

Our second year began and stayed strong with Dr. Eugene Szutu as head surgeon. He was a graduate of Yale who had been living in China, and he brought two of his students with him. Tai and Sylvia Kong worked in medicine and in anesthesia.

Dr. Szutu insisted upon strict discipline in the OR. His surgery was basic and impeccable.

He and Larry had great respect for each other. Gene was wise, and told Larry never to make a final decision at a meeting. This was timely advice, as we were having quite a few stormy medical meetings in those days.

Dr. Szutu played the violin, and Tai the recorder. On one occasion, Larry insisted that I get the cello and join the group. I wheezed through, "Oh Sacred Head Now Wounded." When Gene said, "Gwen, that is terrible," I gave up music for fifteen years.

Deschapelles was full of vagabond dogs. On Sundays, Dr. Szutu and Larry would spay them in the emergency room of the OR. They would also X-ray horses' legs at the morgue entrance, with a portable X-ray machine.

I had a beautiful red leather Chinese trunk, and I asked Dr. Szutu to translate the mysterious, exotic writing inside the lid. He said it was a laundry list.

On a more meaningful note, in a junk yard in New Orleans, I had found two seven-foot red boards with lacquered gold Chinese letters carved on them. I had planned to make a headboard for our bed. Once the house was under way, I decided to install them on either side of the entrance to our bedroom and paint a matching door between them. Dr. Szutu asked me how I had known how to place them. It was by chance, but they were indeed placed correctly. Dr. Szutu translated the characters, "Those who pass through this door are a happily married couple."

Dr. Szutu stayed with us many years. He left us for the same reason he had left China, to become an American citizen. His wife and children were already in New York, where she worked in the Immigration Office. He and his family had left China together, on foot, from Nanking. To avoid suspicion, as Gene kept saying, "The only thing we carried with us was an extra pair of underpants."

I saw the Szutus, and Tai and Sylvia, a few years ago when I went to Hong Kong.

Our international group began to swell when Dr. Modi, an Indian ophthalmologist, and his wife and two boys came to Deschapelles. They frequently asked us to dinner. We would be seated at a table alone, and fed bright pink and bright green food. All four of them watched us eat, and at each mouthful, asked if it was good.

The family wore their Indian clothes. Mrs. Modi was skin and bones, thin like an Indian fakir. One day she called and asked me if it would be all right for her to swim in the pool without a bathing suit. I said I certainly did not care and nobody else would notice. A few days later I walked by the pool and saw her in her Indian sari, swimming, completely and modestly clothed.

One day, in church, our dear friend Dr. Ross said, "Christianity is the only and greatest religion." The Modis got up and left.

Midway into his two-year contract, Shanti Modi called Larry late one night to say goodbye, as he had decided to leave early the next morning. Larry asked what was the matter and offered to come up and try to solve the problem. Shanti said that nothing could be done. He would be gone when Larry got to work. Bewildered, Larry arrived the next morning to see Shanti in his office seeing patients as he always had. No explanation was asked for and none was given. Shanti not only finished his two-year contract, but stayed an extra year.

Dr. Hal May had just finished a year of recovery from conical eye surgery and had successfully regained his eyesight. He arrived just as Larry and I were packed and ready to depart for New York for my back surgery. When Dr. May asked if there was a good job for him, Larry answered that he could take his place. He came during the time when Dr. Szutu was medical director, and they became close friends, not only in the OR, but in the hospital community.

Hal was deeply religious and spent his Saturday nights preparing for Sunday service. As a highly educated student of the Bible, his sermons were always applicable and interesting. In church, Hal played the bugle, with Larry on the French horn and Eugene Szutu on the violin, while the the rest of us stood up and sang full-voiced. He organized choral groups and had much to do with the Christmas pageants on the tennis court.

Periodically, specialists volunteered to come to Deschapelles. Their time here was carefully scheduled so that not one minute was wasted. Appointments were set up well in advance. This wonderful service has included ophthalmology, urology, oncology, orthopedics, neurology, and, recently, even a pediatric psychologist.

Earliest among these doctors was Dr. John Golding of Jamaica who came three times a year for orthopedic clinics and surgery. Soon after, three orthopedic surgeons from Atlanta set up a rotation system. Every four months one of the doctors would come for a week. They found and screened orthopedic patients on both sides of Port-au-Prince, and included cases from La Pointe and St. Vincent's. Caroline Bradshaw from La Pointe would take care of long-term bed patients, like those who had Potts. Sister Joan would care for the handicapped, providing limbs and braces. It was a highly successful working relationship, with HAS providing OR facilities, and La Pointe and St. Vincent's taking on the long-term care.

As a young boy, Dr. Gérard Frédérique lived with his mother in a little house on the seaside of Petit-Gôave. His mother was a very simple but wise woman, who was extremely poor. One day, years later, she showed me the corner of the bedroom where Freddie's placenta had been buried under the dirt floor.

Freddie went to the local school wearing his mother's shoes with the heels removed. The school was taught by the Catholic brothers who encouraged his mother to make Freddie study, because he was unusually bright. With great effort, he was sent to Saint-Louis de Gonzagues School in Port-au-Prince, and from there he went to the University and graduated from the medical school with a degree in ophthalmology.

In Port-au-Prince, his survival as a medical student was extremely difficult. He was unable to afford textbooks and would borrow them one at a time. With fine Spencerian writing on foolscap, he would copy, and learn at the same time, each page of the medical books. I have seen these stacks of papers, now yellow with age but still very recognizable for what they are.

Such is the evidence of his strong will and perseverance, which would stand him in good stead for the rest of his life.

Dr. Norma Elles, a famous ophthalmologist, came to Deschapelles to instruct two brand new ophthalmology graduates from the University in Port-au-Prince. She had palsy, and was no longer able to operate. And although well beyond her retirement age, she was astute and able to give good instructions to the doctors without entering the operating field herself. Freddie was new and nervous. He hesitated and hesitated until finally, Dr. Elles ordered, "CUT!" At the end of her stay, she advised us to choose Dr. Frédérique for our staff, and she sent all her textbooks on ophthalmology to our library.

Freddie worked well and hard at HAS, but he also had time for a Mennonite nurse to teach him to drive a car. And he fell in love with her. When he was selected to go to Pittsburgh for further training, and for the opportunity to take the American Board Exams, he renewed his friendship with Esh, and they were married.

When Freddie and Esh returned to Haiti, the Catholic brothers from Petit-Gôave were on the same flight. There Freddie stood, with his Board Certificate in his hand, his new Mennonite wife on his arm, and a guaranteed job in Deschapelles. What a joyous reunion it was!

The couple returned to Deschapelles, Freddie as Haiti's first American Board-Certified ophthalmologist. His wife became my dearest friend, and their three children were welcomed in succession. All of the children went to the States for further education, and the older ones are still there. Anny, the youngest, is by my side in Deschapelles.

Dr. Jack Demlow, a pediatrician, admitted that the only reason he dressed like a cowboy was to please his young patients in Tucson. Nevertheless, Jenny and I decided to get horses and take him on a riding trip to Petite Rivière. We found that his hat and his boots were much better than his riding. As we were waiting at Coupon to take the *bak* (barge) across the Artibonite River, a woman who was cooking and selling food came shaking her fist at Jack. It seems that the horse belonging to the *blan* (white person) had put out her fire.

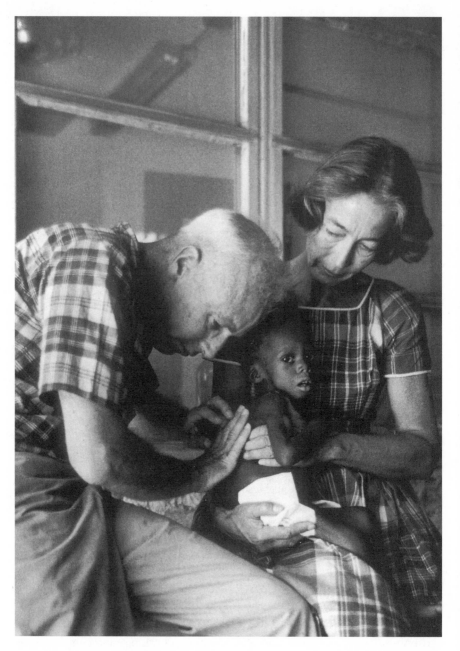

Pediatric Clinic.

Pediatric Ward.

Dr. Renée Bergner, another pediatrician, came to HAS for one summer. Her husband Arthur, a lawyer, accompanied her. In the clinic I translated for Renèe, and began to know her well and to admire her. Larry gave Art and Ian the task of rethreading four miles of used metal pipe. This was hard, hot, and dirty work, but it showed Art just how many different kinds of help were needed in this valley. At the end of the summer he gave up law and started medical school.

Each year brought Art and Renée closer to us, as they returned to work in Deschapelles. Today they play important roles in the success of the hospital. They screen potential medical and staff members, run the Alumni meetings in Burlington, and publish an Alumni Newsletter. Renée is also a member of the Board of the Grant Foundation. Both have the invaluable wisdom of time spent with Larry, and a deep understanding of the meaning of *Reverence for Life* and its application in Deschapelles. Their oldest daughter is named Gwen. If the second child had been a boy, I am sure he would have been named Larry. Instead, they have Kim, who now has a medical degree!

André Cassius is an incredible friend. As a young man he came to work in our maintenance department and today, he is head of the department and has chosen this to be his life. He leaves the garage area only once a day to eat, and once a week to have a haircut. His hair is now white, except when it seems to be a bit black.

I have yet to find anything that André has been unable to do. He has built water cisterns of concrete blocks, and installed fire hoses and outlets on both sides of our house. When I had cellulitis, and my foot swelled, he stretched my shoe so that I could wear it to New Haven.

André sharpens my woodworking and stone carving tools. He helps me assemble ceramic lamp bases. He sends me just the right people to knock down a wall inside a house, and by the end of the day, the debris has been hauled away, the ugly scars have been plastered and painted, and everyone marvels at my competence and wisdom! He is the keystone of the hospital, and everything surrounding it.

HAS lacked storage space, and I asked Larry to let me plan and build it. I thought I could solve the problem. With help from Larry and the transit, I set the uprights, and then André Cassius provided the labor and materials. The building fits right in with the existing architecture and does not look like a storeroom. It has a central second floor platform which adds a great deal to its capacity. I asked Larry how he dared to let me do it. He said, "It didn't fall down did it?"

At the same time, we constructed eight smaller buildings, each one suitable for housing four nurses.

Before he came to HAS, Andy Gallagher had been an engineer on a rich man's yacht. When he left that position, he hoped he was also leaving an alcoholic wife he had somehow inherited along with the job on the yacht. Unfortunately, she caught up with him in Deschapelles, and eventually lost him his job here.

Once, while still at HAS, Andy declared that he could jump from the water tower and land in nothing larger than a washtub full of water. The tower stood tall, the tub was in position, and a crowd was gathered to witness this feat. On a Saturday, at high noon, before the huge audience, Andy climbed up two rungs and jumped - about two feet from the rung to the tub!

There were occasions when patients died that no one came to claim them for burial. It fell upon HAS to see that they went to the potter's field in Verrettes, where the gravediggers always had a grave dug and ready. Pastor Bois, Larry and I would travel there together, and Maître Delinois would have made the coffin out of our waste strips of cardboard and wood. Once, we arrived and the grave was too short for the coffin. The gravediggers were asked to extend it, but refused unless paid more money. Larry jumped into the hole and started digging. The Magistrate appeared, and the gravediggers quickly took Larry's place. From that day on we never had a problem. The coffin was placed in the ground, and Larry played his accordion while he, Pastor Bois, and I sang, "Nearer My God to Thee."

Pastor Bois worked for HAS as a pastor, and played an important role in seeing that children who had been discharged were delivered home if their parents failed to come for them. It was a temptation for the families to leave their children with us for as long as possible, since they knew the children would be well fed, clothed and loved. At the requests of pediatricians, Pastor Bois and an *oksilye* would take a child to the local market places. There, they would hold up the child, and ask if anyone knew the parents. This met with a fair amount of success, but there always seemed to be one or two left in his hands. It was thus that he started an orphanage which received great support from our Dutch and Swiss nurses.

This took a somewhat ugly turn, when we visited the orphanage one day, and discovered that he had not tried to deliver all of the children to their families. Instead, hoping to encourage more support, he had kept those with the most appeal to show to visitors. We took the ones in question home.

Pastor Bois had another project, a bakery, which we subsidized, as it provided free bread for the local school children. It went well, until the children complained that he was using *lakrè* (chalk) in place of flour.

His biggest mistake, and the one that cost him his job, was selling raffle tickets in the market places. Pastor Bois said that since Dr. Mellon was very modest, he didn't like people to know when he gave things away. The raffle was Doc's way of helping his neighbors. The "pot" would be big. The people here are known to play games of chance, and the tickets sold like hotcakes. When no one won, Pastor Bois was chased out of the market. His car was turned over, and he barely escaped with his life.

Sympathetic Consultation.

One night, we got a call from an employee living in the B.Q., or bachelor's quarters. He denied parentage of a baby boy who had been left by his door, and asked us to put the child in the hospital. Larry answered that as long as he was not sick, he could not be admitted. We settled the impasse by taking the baby home and having him sleep between us in our bed. The next morning we looked at each other and said, "Now what?" We did not worry long. The mother was frantic, and when she was reunited with the child, she grabbed him to her bosom. Under her good care, this baby grew up to be a fine and able citizen, and has become an important member of our staff. He may or may not know of this incident, and we will never tell him.

There were many on our staff who went to serve in Lambaréné. And there were many who came from Lambaréné to work in our hospital in Haiti. Over the years, these people were to strengthen the bonds between our work in Haiti and that in Africa.

160

Davika Franchenbach was one of three Swiss nurses who came to HAS from Lambaréné. In Deschapelles, she made the tracking down of negligent TB patients her crusade. She followed the delinquents far and wide. She was concerned, not only that they took their medicines, but also that they had good food. She came to Larry to ask him for help in getting a young milk heifer up to Perodin, the farthest and highest spot in our medical district. Early one morning, we loaded the calf into the back of the Land Rover. Davika, Larry, and I sat up front. We traveled in this way, until the road became too narrow for the vehicle. Then we unloaded the calf, who was dizzy from trying to keep his footing on the slippery bed of the car, and we said goodbye to Davika, who would make the rest of the trip on foot. It turned out to be a two-day struggle for Davika and the calf to reach Perodin.

On our way back to Deschapelles, we stopped at the L'Estere River, borrowed a bucket, and made the Land Rover somewhat bearable. Even so, it took a lot of time and a lot of fresh air to let us forget that heifer calf.

Emma Fullerman, a Swiss dietician, also made the trip from Lambaréné to Deschapelles. She spoke only German, and with tears in her beautiful blue eyes, she would seek out Dr. Mellon, saying she could talk to no one. Soon, however, she learned to speak *kreyòl* and made good friends.

She convinced Dr. Mellon of the importance of using the plentiful cabbage. She said, "Sauerkraut, they would love it." Larry got four big, ten gallon, ceramic crocks with lids. Emma filled them with finely sliced cabbage, set the covers, and waited for the sauerkraut. The great day arrived when the sauerkraut was ready to be served to the staff and patients. It was eyed with suspicion by some and refused by all. Luckily we were raising pigs that year, and they seemed quite taken by it. But since then the crocks have stood empty and idle.

There was a German nurse who had bicycled from Lambaréné to the Mediterranean, and somehow or other, she appeared in Deschapelles. Uninvited, she said she would stay, and was hard to deny or discourage. In desperation, we suggested she go to the pool. She spoke only German and

Translations for foreign staff.

English, and in her black Annette Kellerman bathing suit, she asked a local person for directions. "Pool? Pool?" Of course, he led her to the *poul* (chickens). She did not stay long, and left on her bicycle.

Dr. Henrique Percy arrived in Lambaréné to work as a surgeon. He was a post-WWII Hungarian without identification papers or a passport. When we were with Dr. Schweitzer, he was married to a lovely French girl. Dr. Percy had a patient, a wood logger, who had a feisty wife. Soon, the logger's wife replaced the French wife in Dr. Percy's affection. With great tact and honesty, Dr. Schweitzer asked Larry if he could possibly take on this excellent surgeon and his new friend, since it was impossible for Dr. Percy to return to Hungary or any other place in Europe. They did come to Deschapelles, but soon proved to be a difficult addition to our staff. They both left voluntarily for Port-au-Prince, where Dr. Percy again changed wives. Larry assumed the responsibility of returning the second wife to her home in Europe. When last heard of, Dr. Percy was in Morocco, with a fourth wife.

Dorrien Venn, an eminent surgeon from South Africa, had spent time in Lambaréné. He had the highest recommendations and qualifications. With the hope that Dr. Venn might be available, Larry tried to phone him in South Africa. The call went through, which was amazing in the 1950s. Dorrien was sent a round trip ticket, so he could come and size up the job, but return to South Africa if Haiti did not suit him. Suit him it did, and he was our chief surgeon for seven years. Soon after his arrival, his pending divorce was finalized. Soon after that came a lovely woman who stayed at our house for a year, waiting for her own divorce to become official. Mina cooked dinner for Dorrien in his apartment, but as he said, there was no "hanky panky." They were married in our house, and her seven-year-old son Nicky flew from South Africa to join them.

A year later, Mina, with much detailed planning, gave an anniversary dinner in their home. She made a special dress, cooked very special food, and selected a truly special wine to celebrate. The dinner table was beautifully set and seated for eight, with Larry on her right and me next to Dorrien. As cocktails were being served, a big open-bed truck drove up and Dr. Mellon's presence was requested. Larry put down his drink, and went out to greet these unexpected friends who had come to see him. It was one of the four brass bands he had put together. Larry attempted to say that he was out for dinner, and that this was not a good time for their visit, but the issue was settled by allowing them to play one piece. They got out of the truck, sat on the front porch, tuned their instruments, and blasted all eight of the invited guests speechless. Unasked, they played a long encore. When Larry thanked them, he saw that their truck had gone, and nothing was to be done but for him to go to the garage, take out our truck, and drive them to Verrettes, an hour round trip! Dinner proceeded with a very empty chair next to Mina. I do not think she ever forgave Larry's gest to his local friends!

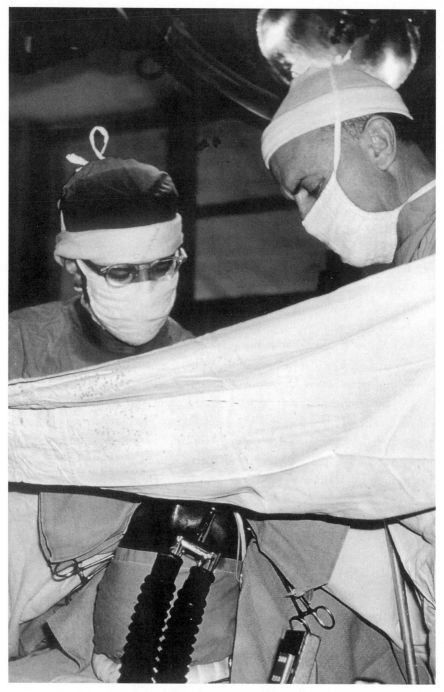

Dorrien Venn on the right.

Dorrien was a warm and lovely friend. He was happy to leave South Africa, with its apartheid laws, and to be in our community, where he endeared himself to the entire staff with his courtesy and consideration.

But even in Deschapelles, when facing a complicated surgery one day, he looked at the field and said, "I say, we really are in tiger country."

CHAPTER 8

Heritages Of Haiti

In the early days of HAS, most people arrived on foot or by horseback, so we have always had trained local men to help with the horses. When patients arrived, the horses were directed to the open courtyard within the hospital where there was a loading dock. There, people could descend easily and unload *makout* after *makout*. The horses were offered grass and water, and every saddle was lifted so the horses' backs could be examined and treated for sores. No horses were ever shod, but their hoofs were trimmed. If teeth were to be floated, Larry was the one who could do it. All animals received tetanus shots and a rest in the shade. At a minimum price, our vet, Julian Strauss, sold humane saddles that did not touch the backbone of the horse.

The horses became omnipresent around the clinic area, which was close to the courtyard. Finally we had to move them into an open corral in a swale below the hospital where, unfortunately, we did not have all the niceties of the watering trough and the loading dock. But the vet was there to care for the animals.

Now we have bicycle racks, and soon we will have motorcycle racks. One day, when the gas shortage was acute and one rarely saw a *taptap* (small passenger truck) or a bus, I found forty horses in the corral and sixty bicycles in the racks.

A farmer brought us a horse that had swallowed a mango pit. It acted

Veterinary care.

like a valve and kept the horse from eating or drinking. We tried to push the pit down with a hose. No luck. Then we got Ian with his long, skinny arms to try and reach it. Again no luck. We realized there was nothing we could do, and brought the horse to our garage. Larry wanted him to die in comfort, and he died in a few days. The yard boy left when he was asked to dig a hole to bury him.

Once, Larry stopped the car to help a woman's heavily laden horse whose legs had buckled under the load. He removed the load, took the horse by the tail, and yanked him to his feet. He then loaded up each *makout* again, got back in the car, and drove away.

Another four-legged friend who arrived shortly after we did was a Texas jackass said to throw good mules. As far as we know, he succeeded only once after coming to Haiti. We loved him anyway and he filled a certain need. He hauled the milk, carried the sugar cane to feed the cattle, and provided rides for the kids in his two-wheeled cart. We called him *"Anmwe"* (help me) from the sound of his bray, and he knew us and would come to us. One day, when he was very old and had stopped working, he disappeared. Everyone knew he was a great friend of ours and everyone looked for him. When he was younger, he was known to jump the fence to search for more attractive mares, and one time even went so far as Petite Rivière. But he was nowhere. Finally, we found him wedged in a narrow concrete ground silo we had made. It was three-sided, open at only one end. He had pushed his way in but could not back out. Neither could he make the awful jackass bray. When he had neither eaten nor drunk for three days, he had space to swell his lungs enough to yell for help. With much care, food, water, and grass near our house, he regained some of his strength.

We were sad when he died, quietly and peacefully one night in the pasture below our house. Early the next morning, André Cassius came from the garage to take him far away so I would not see and hear the dogs that appear so quickly after an animal dies. Dogs take the place of vultures, and we should be grateful to them both.

At the time of the buccaneers, Haiti had pigs. They were similar to boars, with tusks coming up and forward from the lower jaw. They had long skinny legs, stiff wiry hair, and a pandus of fat on the shoulders. The descendants of these pigs were the mainstay of a household and were like money in the bank. They were bred and raised to pay for a wedding, funeral, or the children's schooling. They lived in a pit by the family *kay* and survived on the daily refuse. They were never fat, but lean, tough, and tasty, and just right for *griyo* (spicy fried pork, a Haitian delicacy).

When the African swine fever appeared, the US offered to buy up all the existing pigs at a good price. A new breed was introduced. It was healthy and large, but without the pandus of fat. HAS, among others, built breeding pens. Boars of the new stock were imported, lots of piglets were raised, and sold at a very low price. The disadvantage was that they had to be kept on cement floors and fed a supplement. If both of these expenses could be handled, a good profit could be made. But soon the local market was saturated and there were too many pigs.

Our vet, Dr. Keith Flanagan, agreed to help the owners get their pigs to Port-au-Prince where they could be sold to a meat processing plant. To guard against faulty scales in town, each pig was weighed before transit, and had a number painted on it. Each number corresponded to an owner's name. The vet rented the truck himself so the owners could be paid in full before the trip. Dr. Keith loaded the pigs that were gathered, drove the truck, and was always en route to Port-au-Prince by midnight. In town, each pig was weighed again and the purchase price was recorded. The total was paid in a lump sum. Then Dr. Keith would stand in line at the bank to get the big bills changed into small denominations. Back home, the money was distributed. It was a full twenty-four hours of work, and always carried the risk of the truck breaking down and the pigs being held up in the heat of the day. Two or three pig owners always made the trip to report any unforeseen calamities and to witness weight loss. A load of pigs could reach a value as high as $7,000 US. The local people would not trust one of their own to do this job.

Keith stopped helping with this program because the local people would not keep the pigs and goats off of HAS property, where the animals do devastating damage. We have had to protect property with barbed wire fences and candelabra cactus. Now we have productive gardens, but not without great expense and continued upkeep.

All dogs are given rabies shots. Vagrant dogs, when they form dangerous packs, are mercifully done away with. Even so, periodically a case of rabies surfaces. It is hard to prove as the attacking animal is immediately bludgeoned to death and the only proof is a description of its behavior. But we accept such a report as a bona fide reason for treatment.

We have always had one or two dogs around the house, two of our most recent ones being *Lespwa* (hope) and *Melanj* (mix). *Lespwa,* as a puppy, was a hopeless looking ball of pale fur, but his name was apt, and he grew and thrived. *Melanj,* a brown, white, and black mixture, is a mouser and a ratter, and also chases goats, pigs, and other animals off the property.

When *Lespwa* recently passed away and *Melanj* seemed about to join him, we sought replacements. I chose a black puppy and called him *Li Chwa* (her choice). The owner said we should take another so each would not suffer *chagren* (heartbreak). We did choose another, and I called him *Degi* (bonus). The word *degi* is used to describe the extra orange a *machann* (vendor) sometimes gives you after the termination of a hard bargain. Along with *Li Chwa, Degi* is an extra dividend.

We never felt very close to cats, which is fortunate as they are considered a special delicacy here.

A local boy sold me a small injured green parrot. He fast became a pet, and hardly ever entered his cage. He loved Larry best and in the evening would sit on his shoulder and often put his head inside the front of Larry's shirt. We all loved him and called him "Bud." Suddenly Larry came down with a terrible itch and rash. We still loved the parrot but we did change his name to "Bug."

Birds are plentiful around our house. We have a flock of bright green parrots with rosy throats. They nest in the sugar mill and fly back and forth from there to our big ficus tree. We have a devoted pair of owls sitting on the telephone line. We have green crested herons, called *rele* (limkin). One night, in a full moon, I saw eight of them getting water from our garden pool.

Early one spring, I saw a great blue heron, legs extended, standing on top of the *mapou* tree. He may have had a nest there, but it was completely hidden by new foliage.

Recently, a fighting cock took up residence outside my living room. I knew he was there daily from four a.m. on. I could put up with that, but suddenly he entered the house and made himself completely at home. Later a second fighting cock appeared, and I learned that, by using food as an incentive, owners lure their birds to stay close to an important person to gain force for the *gagè* (cockfights). Cocks have small brains and are creatures of hard to break habits. I displayed my lack of hospitality by having the dogs drive them out of the house.

We have lots of cattle egrets, mosquito hawks, woodpeckers, black birds, and lizard cuckoos, and most endearing are the hummingbirds frequently seen at the hibiscus hedge.

The *Madanm* Sara are a threat as they travel in big organized flocks, and once installed in a tree are impossible to dislodge. Their hanging nests crowd, defoliate, and eventually kill the tree.

Once, on the floor of the valley near Desdunes, I saw a roseate spoon bill.

When tobacco was introduced as a new crop, heavy spraying became necessary as many insects thrived on the new plant. The result was a disaster for local wild birds who fed on these bugs. The birds on the north-south flyway now pass this area less frequently. The different types of *jako* (parrot) survived well as they eat corn. The cattle egrets were unharmed as they eat bugs that feed off cattle.

There are many, but no poisonous snakes in Haiti. We knew we had quite a few in the house when the electrician went up to the attic and found shed skins, then live snakes! There are sleepy, large, long boas, with no scales. One arrived and got into the toilet via the septic tank. Mr. Angus, head of housekeeping, said he could get rid of it. He poured in pine oil, and the snake shot out and escaped faster than Mr. Angus could run.

Snakes also like to coil around the louvers of our doors. One night we had a large snake under the bed. It didn't worry Larry, but I wanted it outside. Larry took a bath towel to get a grip on it but the snake locked itself around the bedpost, letting off an odor in close competition to that of an American skunk. Nothing could make it let go, so we left it and slept in another room. In the morning it was no longer there. Where had it gone? Where?

Another time we were trying to urge a snake out of the house, and it became so scared that it delivered a good dozen small and lively offspring.

Local people are very frightened of frogs and snakes. Both play important parts in the *Voodoo* religion. We have huge frogs with small, short legs. They are so big and heavy that they can hop only half an inch at a time. We have *toro lagon* (bull of the marsh). I have heard them, but have yet to see one.

Then there are the small, thin, almost white frogs. With suction cups, they can leap from one side of the bathroom wall to the other, climb a vertical tile wall, travel through water pipes, and end up in the bathtub. They can land in your hand when you turn on the spigot, and make you think for a moment that you're holding soap.

There are many lizards, beautiful and bright green, with red throats in mating season. They lay soft, white eggs. Like frogs, they easily travel up the wall with their webbed fingers. They seem to live behind all the pictures and come out particularly at night to eat mosquitoes and bugs.

There are two insects said to be poisonous but I have yet to hear of anyone being harmed. One is the *krab* (tarantula), and the other is the beetle-like *vennkat lè* (twenty-four hours).

We have scorpions, but they are non-poisonous. They do not hibernate in the winter and store up their venom like those in Arizona.

We were lucky that the most part of our life in Haiti was spent in the country. Time spent in the city was for a need, was short, and ended as soon

Soap?

as that need was met. It always began and ended with a long, three-and-a half-hour drive. Country life reveals the real heart of Haiti, and one that we grew to understand and love.

Haitians value highly their own privacy, and equally value the privacy of others. Traditionally, in the country an extended family lives in a *lakou*. A new house is added for each new generation, and each *lakou* ideally has one well and, at times, a privy. There is a deep pit that takes care of all refuse and is home for the courtyard pig. Surrounding this group is a fence of candelabra cactus and a gate that is firmly closed when entering or leaving. Someone who wishes to enter knocks on the gate and cries, *"Lonè"* ("Honor"), if the answer within is, *"Respè"* ("Respect"), it means he will be welcome.

No one in Haiti meets a friend, or even a stranger, without a *"Bonjou"* ("Good morning") or *"Bonswa"* ("Good afternoon or evening"). A man will raise his hat. It is a courteous and friendly greeting. On being introduced, one must always be ready to shake a new friend's hand. If the friend is a Haitian, he will never extend his hand until yours is already on its way.

A family *lakou*.

When walking at night, one learns never to shine a light on a passer-by's face. It is termed a *"flach"* (flash or flashlight) and is not only rude, but thought to be threatening.

Haitian markets in the countryside, especially on market days, are centers for many things. Besides the exchange of produce, there is an exchange of news. In the early days, even in larger towns like Petite Rivière, the market would be in the open. People would come the night before to be ready for business early in the morning, and leave for the mountains in time to arrive home before nightfall.

Mountain people from the Cahos were afraid to travel at night. They would, but at a high price: a *paspatou* (passport) written by a *bòkò (Voodoo* priest and traditional healer) that guaranteed safe passage. Once I was handed one of these passports at the front desk to serve as means of identification.

In these early days, with practically no transportation to Port-au-Prince, the market was the center for one's needs and dreams. On this open space

Shopping.

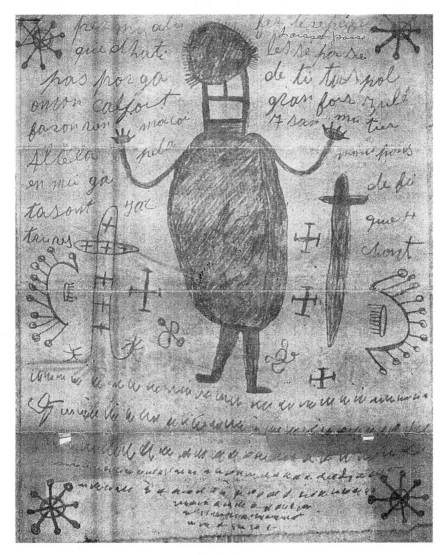

A *paspatou.*

were found all the necessities for life and death, from baptism clothes to coffins. There were wedding clothes for men and women, and material for sheets and for clothing. Most all clothes in those days were *gwo ble* (denim) and *siam* (muslin) or flour sacks that could be bleached white and used for clothing. Few people wore shoes but usually, if lucky, each household would have one pair. Even the poorest had to have a pair to enter the city of Port-

175

au-Prince. Wedding veils, wedding rings, voodoo charms and crosses, herbs and folk medicines, and hand-made tools, pots, and pans were in regular spots in the market.

On market days, the *Jij Lapè* (Justice of the Peace) would be available to officiate for land transferrals, legal marriages, birth certificates, and other transactions. He had a large government seal which, with a great flourish, he impressed on all papers, thereby making the documents official.

Unfortunately, also scattered around the market today is a very popular game of chance, called *"borlet"* (a numbers game), which attracts too many. Also available are card games and dominoes. The loser in dominoes wears a spring clothespin on his ear or his nose. This is serious and no one laughs at this man. Closing the market is a spontaneous affair. When the first merchant leaves, all the rest fold up their wares and the market is over. It is considered unacceptable for anyone to stay later and sell.

One of the imported tools is a heavy hoe from England, a *wou* (hoe). It is heated and shaped by a *fòjon* (blacksmith) to fit the owner's needs and it lasts for years. It has a very long wooden handle, and with the height from which the heavy blade drops, it is able to break hard ground. The older the man, the shorter the blade because it is sharpened every season.

Nan pwovens (in the country, anywhere outside of Port-au-Prince), every household has a *manchèt* (flat-bladed iron knife about two feet long including the handle), and every man with any importance carries one. They too are made in England and supplied to many parts of the Third World. The service life of a *manchèt* often begins at birth with the cutting of an umbilical cord. Next it is used to dig a hole in the corner of the house where the placenta is then buried. The *manchèt* is used to cut and pick up candelabra cactus, which must be handled carefully because of its lethal milky juice. It is used to harvest coconuts from the high trees and to cut the tops off the nuts to get the milk for drinking. It is used to prepare gardens before using the *wou*. It is used to plant young trees, prune branches, cut down trees, square up limbs to be used for construction of houses, and cut palmetto for roofing. It is used to pick teeth and to shave. Hurrah for old England; it gave a solid and useful gift to the era of colonialism!

Not as frequently, an important tool called the *"sèpèt"* (sickle), a smaller, curved *manchèt,* is used for cutting sugar cane.

The Haitian *wou.*

The *manchèt.*

Forty years ago, Haiti was reputed to have the largest and most disciplined cooperative work groups in the world. The arrangement was called a *"konbit"* (cooperative peasant work team), which was a group of farmers having neighboring fields. They rotated through their holdings until all were prepared for planting.

At the first rains, the leader called the group together by blowing a conch shell. Each worker brought his own tool. The work began at dawn, and no food was offered during the working day. The rhythm and pace was maintained by songs and a propitiously passed bottle of *kleren* (sugar cane juice for rum).

In recent years, there have been few working groups and none that are volunteer. The men expect to be paid either in money or in a portion of the crop they help to harvest.

A farmer chooses carefully the workers to pick the individual stalks of rice. If not done slowly and gently, the grains of rice fall uselessly to the ground. Rice is threshed on a smooth area either by flails, two sticks joined by a piece of leather, or by many feet keeping a fast rhythm. The mills are motorized and no longer use hand grinders. Often, an owner dumps his sack of rice into the hopper, remembers that he had coins in the sack, reaches for them, and not only loses the coins but also a finger or two.

When a new fast-yielding rice was introduced, the enthusiasm was greatly reduced when it was discovered that the old mills did not accept the new rice grains.

Sugar was a lucrative and major commodity of the island. Many landowners, small and large, planted this successful crop annually. In the country, sugar cane is milled today in two ways: by a water-driven wheel that grinds the cane, or by a horse walking in a circle, turning two big wooden logs that the cane passes between. The juice is caught and boiled in huge iron cauldrons and reduced mostly to *kleren* for Haiti's well-known rum. The residue of the squeezed cane is called *bagas* and is used as fuel when cooking the syrup for *kleren*.

Diri (rice), *pitimi* (millet), and *mayi* (corn) are dried on any flat cement slab, often a piece of the highway. Cars driving over it seem to do it no harm although some grains are lost depending on the speed of the vehicle.

It is a tradition that local farmers plant their gardens simultaneously. This avoids the birds devouring the first ripened field of grain. A little loss from each field is acceptable.

When somebody sells a piece of land, a young surveyor is hired to measure the property. When someone buys a piece of land, the older the surveyor, the better. Young surveyors have new chains, approximately six meters long. Older chains have worn links, the length of which increase with the age of their owner. No one can say that Haitians are not canny.

In the country, the decision to get married and to have a wedding was serious and complicated. It used to be that a man would not ask for someone's daughter unless he had a house, a garden, and basic furniture, including a bed, a table, and a dresser for dishes. The girl was to provide the sheets, towels, pots and pans, and spoons. The groom needed two suits, one for the wedding, and one for calling on friends after the marriage. He also needed two pairs of pajamas. The bride had to have a wedding dress and other clothes. They had a *marenn* (godmother) and a *parenn* (godfather), who helped get all this equipment together and stood ready to solve all marital arguments and difficulties that occurred over the years. The *marenn* daily brought the food and barred visitors from the house during the first days of marriage. The groom often relaxed on the porch in his pajamas.

There was another country custom called *plasaj* (common-law marriage), most often practiced among people from the mountains. A young man who had chosen a girl and wished to marry, but as yet had no house or garden, would go to the girl's parents and ask for her in *plasaj*. This was no casual relationship. The appeal to the family was written by a scribe on especially decorated paper. The union usually ended in marriage, after the young man had acquired a house and a garden. The couple often had two or three children by that time.

There was a Catholic priest who told all of the couples who were in *plasaj* that he would marry them if they would follow his lessons for ten Sundays. On the eighth Sunday, when they had all arrived, he married them, with rings for each couple. Thus they had avoided all the expenses that marriage traditionally involved. That day in Verrettes, I was lucky enough to see two hundred couples joined in marriage.

Today, the picture has changed radically. Liaisons are anything but permanent and are often complicated by three or four different spouses with no feeling of responsibility for resulting offspring. Another outcome is a child with one parent. With the economy so fragile, this takes a tremendous toll

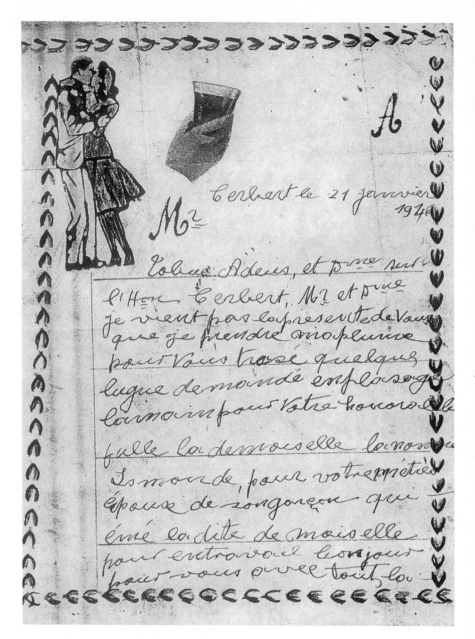

A letter of *plasaj.*

on the child. Often the mother is forced to leave daily to sell in the market, and the child is left to be cared for by others. All too frequently, the result is malnutrition. Our employees, the women with steady incomes, are especially desirable targets for liaisons. There can be much disappointment, bitterness, and jealousy.

The music of the *kontredans* (quadrille) and the *mereng* (popular dance rhythm) has an identical cadence with the French minuet. The steps of the kontredans, even though done barefooted, conjure up a vivid picture of the French court in the early 1800s.

Our loved and loyal pediatrician Dr. Skeets Marshall was due to leave after one of her triennial years with us. Wishing to do something very special for her, I tried to gather from the mountains four couples for a *kontredans* on our porch during pre-dinner drinks. They came with their own fife, drum, and tin horn for music. Three of the couples were in bare feet and real country clothes, but the fourth couple could not be found and was replaced by a local couple who insisted on doing all the latest disco steps. The country people performed their *kontredans* completely unconcerned by the strange addition of disco to the group. They all had such a grand time that we invited them for dinner.

In plantation days, just before Lent, an owner would have his slaves leave the plantation, with a group leader who carried a whip to keep them together. They traveled far and wide, making music and noise while visiting other plantations and encountering other groups. The owner's ulterior motive was to prevent inbreeding and bring new genes into next year's crop of beautiful babies. The event, the music, and the noise was known as *Ra-Ra* (noise-maker), from the early colonial dictum *Le roi ha dit*, or The king has said. The music and the bands still exist, with the group leader's whip acting to keep everyone together. The termination of *Ra-Ra* and Carnival marks the beginning of the forty days before Easter. The ultimate festival is on *Madi Gwa* (Fat Tuesday), and it is celebrated by dances and the blast of tin horns, drums, and gourds producing faster and faster rhythms. Everyone wears costumes and masks. In the country they dance as they travel on foot. In Port-au-Prince are big trucks made into floats, each with its own costumed revelers, and music.

There is a small sulphur seep on the way to Port-au-Prince. When illness threatened the life of a family member, relatives often bought a coffin in readiness. Should the patient survive, he often personally brought his coffin to the shallow sulphur stream and disposed of it with gratitude. When we stopped one day, we saw several coffins encrusted with sulphur, and one that was sulphur free and newly arrived. This was a bleak spot with hundreds of crabs that scuttled ahead of us as we entered. Several dolls were lying on the edge of the stream, along with the remains of a bath house dressing room that looked like a broken off, decayed tooth.

Before entering Port-au-Prince one comes upon a potter's field. Once, I saw a truck carrying its load to be buried in a mass grave. Obviously, their bodies had come from the city morgue. Port-au-Prince is a city of several million and full of poor and needy people. Consequently, the single city morgue is inadequate.

Funerals in Port-au-Prince are momentous events among the elite and the politically important. Occasionally, one sees in Port-au-Prince a tiny white hearse drawn by tiny white black-plumed horses walking slowly toward the cemetery. Most families have a large and imposing tomb in a cemetary plot. Beneath the tomb is a *kavo* (burial chamber), dug to receive the coffin of the deceased. After a burial, the *kavo* is sealed, and by law cannot be opened to receive any other member of the family for three months.

Recently a macabre situation has developed in Port-au-Prince. The well-off are often buried with gold jewelry. The jewelry is costly, the coffins can be recycled, and even the bones are valuable for *zonbi* detail. With the Haitian economy at rock bottom, the relatives of the newly deceased have to place guards at graves in cemeteries.

Family burials involve the whole family purchasing black clothes, and if it is a parent who dies, black is worn for two years. The poor country people settle for one black costume that they do not replace, but wear until it is threadbare. Before morgues and air conditioning, death necessitated quick burial. Today, relatives are brought from Europe and the United States to be present at the funeral service, with coffins often costing hundreds of dollars. One wonders if the addition of the morgue at HAS was a service or a disservice to our community.

Larry always respected each local doctor and *bòkò* and at times referred

A local *bòkò.*

his patients to them for what was termed a "natural" illness. The local healers respected Larry and told him they saw all his patients first. That explained why some arrived at HAS penniless.

A tiny piece of red cloth sewn onto a dress or shirt is mute evidence of concord with other healers beyond the hospital. It is reflective of their perceived need for further support, other than that of HAS and our doctors.

To aid the painful hours of a teething child, a dog's tooth is hung around the child's neck. There is also a hard circle at the end of a pumpkin stem that can be used as a teething ring.

Once, a local *bòkò* had a *kanzo (Voodoo* ceremony that involves fire). The child was burned and died. A group of angry local women then killed the *bòkò.* This is an example of righteous indignation where no other alternative is available.

Once, on his day off, our Dutch nurse Udo went to Saut D'Eau, a beautiful waterfall and significant site for voodoo ceremonies. There was a huge storm with thunder and lightning. People were hanging tokens and lighting candles on the tree near the waterfall's edge. Lightning struck the tree and two people were thrown to the ground unconscious. Udo rushed over and administered artificial respiration to the two. Seeming like a miracle to all who stood there, the men were revived and got up. No *bòkò* could have brought them back to life any faster. Thus, our Dutch nurse Udo strengthened the mystic force of Saut D'Eau.

In Petite Rivière, there is a colonial building with a rotunda and 365 tall wooden doors, supposedly one door for every day of the year. It seems the second floor was never finished. The building is used as a school, and the rotunda for government offices.

During the *fèt* (festival) of the town, I saw an upright piano unloaded for the ball to be held there that night. Placed above the keyboard was a carved figurehead of a woman with flowing hair and luscious bust, painted in brilliant colors. I never saw it again. I asked where it was and to whom it belonged, but no one knew.

The Catholic Church has always been important in Haiti's national education system. Most towns of any size have a boys' school directed by Catholic brothers and a girls' school directed by sisters. The quantity of sisters and brothers has dwindled, and instruction has often been turned over to lay people.

There are three large iron markets in Haiti: one in Jacmel, another in Jérémie, and the largest and best in Port-au-Prince. The cast iron pieces were shipped by boat from France and the structures were assembled here on arrival. The market in Port-au-Prince is large and soars high above the surrounding shops. From a distance, it resembles carved lace. The two large sections are open on all sides and covered with a high roof.

I was introduced to the Port-au-Prince Iron Market an hour or so before my departure for New York, so that I could pick up a wooden carving. I had been warned. Never removing my hand holding my money inside my pocket, I paid for the carving with my other hand. On the way to the airport I discovered my ticket and passport were with me but my American bills were not. Despite this experience, I often visited this market, always teeming with people and alive with exitement.

The grains and dry produce are displayed on large flat woven trays, piled high with cornmeal, millet, peanuts, rice, and all kinds of beans. The fresh fruits and vegetables are plentiful and beautiful. The elite often come personally with a yard boy, to make their choice and bargain.

Another side of the market contains household accessories, baskets of all kinds and uses, and carved wooden and iron items. One whole area contains secondhand articles. I have found hand-blown, pale green glass demijohns, and apothecary jars that are deep blue with gold, bearing white and black labels telling what they had once contained. The apothecary jars may once have been lined up on the shelves of a now deceased chemist, and put up for sale by a needy relative. These I made into lamp bases for the staff houses. I always avoided placing them in households with children, having once seen a demijohn shattered in a thousand pieces on the cement floor of a doctor's house.

A section of old books contained many treasures. I always looked for, but without success, *Le Livre de St. Marie*. It was a large folio, two by three feet, written in the late 1700's. It full of lithographs and maps and elevations of each important town with locations of the forts protecting them. One lithograph had a description of plantation life, with fields marked with crops, living facilities for owners and slaves, and water sources. There was a page of drawings of animals found at that time: wild boars, wild cats, alligators, caymans and birds, long since extinct. There are small reprints of this book, but only of the written part, with no lithographs or maps.

The Iron Market originally consisted of covered alcoves between the two main sections, but now extends into the streets that surround it. Facing the market on the opposite side of the street are blocks of family-owned stores. Each family had a section that was two, and sometimes three stories high. On the top floor were living quarters, and on the first floor was space for selling one of the groups of wares currently in demand: hardware, textiles, or household items. There was one small entrance on the street. All packages were checked at the door before entering. Inside, on a raised table and in a high chair, sat a family member who controlled all details of the transaction, be it the measurement of cloth, the weight of produce, or the listing of the quantity of items, and including all the counting and holding of the money involved. On the crowded sidewalks outside these stores are opportunists' stalls selling recently-available items.

Several churches were shipped in pieces from France. One of the smallest, but certainly the most beautiful, is a chapel in the courtyard of Haiti's earliest, and still the best, private school, Saint-Louis de Gonzages. Every detail was included: the slate floor, slate roof, and the lead gutters embossed with religious symbols.

In a little-known corner not far from the Iron Market, in a Catholic convent, I once saw a small chapel containing a figure of a black Madonna. I tried to find it later, but both chapel and sculpture had been replaced by a wide city street.

Another 19th century iron shipment from France was an unassembled bridge. The road between Cap-Haïtien and Port-au-Prince was a major artery, and crossing the Artibonite River as it crossed the road was proving to be a seasonal hazard to the increasing traffic. The bridge was reassembled to span this river. The market town that grew up quickly around this iron bridge was called Pont Sondé, or tested bridge. It was so named because of the difficultly of finding a solid base in the silt-filled Artibonite Delta. The bridge served well for over one hundred years, and only recently has been replaced by a cement structure.

There was a lot of European trade in the last half of the 19th century. Every port of any size had at least one fort placed at a strategic elevation above the town. They were solid constructions, with cannons and powder houses. People who lived in Jérémie said that in their grandparents' time a boat arrived from France each month. The captain had a catalog from which residents could order lace, buttons, silk, hats, and shoes. They would receive their goods when the ship returned.

At each port, the shores were piled high with *kanpèch* (logwood) for dye en route to Germany, and *sik* (sugar), *digo* (indigo), *koton* (cotton), and *kafe* (coffee) were standing ready to be loaded for Europe.

Kanpèch is a wonderful, useful wood even though Dupont Industry precludes its being used for dye. *Kanpèch* can be used ideally for local house construction. It does not rot easily and also is not susceptible to termites. It can be used again and again. *Kanpèch* does not ripen like *chèn, tavèno* (sabicu), *kajou* (mahogany), and other tropical woods. It doesn't need to be felled before the widest boards are divided into *planch* (planks) by the roots at the base of the tree.

In Port-au-Prince, in earlier days, French Catholic sisters established an outstanding school for young girls. To this day, the girls still produce embroidery and sewing of the finest quality. At the same time, the Salesien brothers established an excellent school for young boys from the country. Here the young men learned ironwork, carpentry, tailoring, and shoemaking. Boys were given a two-year course with pension, and could return to their homes with a viable profession. These were valuable and useful trades before shiploads of second hand clothes and sneakers began to turn up in piles in all the local markets. The day has long since passed when suits were made to an individual's height and stance.

Two local friends, veterans of the Salesien brothers, still sew well. Both use pedal machines. Joe is a good tailor who can exactly copy any model you bring him. I taught Willy to upholster furniture, and to make beautiful pocketbooks faced with my own needlepoint Haitian houses and lined with bright Thai silks. Both of these men live on the very edge of survival. They spend their lives in one-room, thatched roof houses, surrounded by lots of children. All of their children have received a basic education with the help of our school fund, which is composed of contributions made by short-term employees of HAS.

Soon after I arrived in Deschapelles, I found myself surrounded by a wonderful group of boys who helped me and have stayed my loyal friends throughout the years. When they were very young we had peanut hunts, croquet, and volleyball, and they often came to our house for a bath and swim in the shallow pool. They shared a community bicycle which was kept in our depot. Almost every Sunday they joined us for lunch on the porch.

In those days, there was no school in Deschapelles. I taught the boys many things, and then got together a blackboard, chalk, paper, pencils, benches, and a local teacher. Parents and students alike were happy with the school under the big ficus tree, but one morning, everything was gone. The teacher had left.

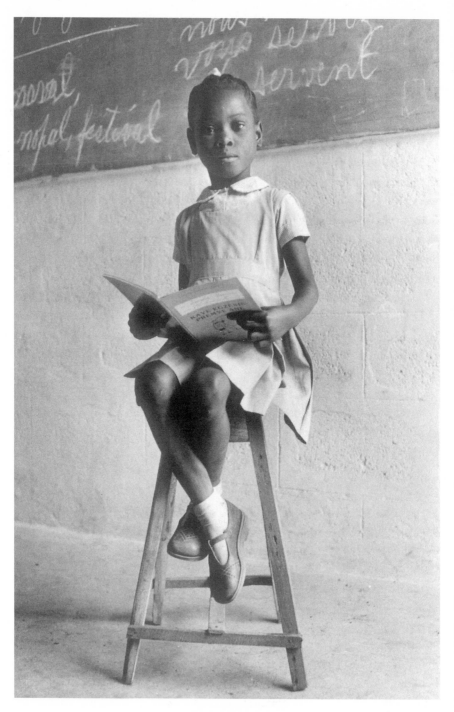

The future.

In a few years time, these boys were ready for secondary school, which meant moving to Port-au-Prince. Sister Joan offered each boy bed and board in exchange for his helping with the deaf and blind students at St. Vincent's. The boys from Deschapelles would bath, dress, fed, and walk Sister Joan's students to and from school. Many filled this job for four or five years and had the time and opportunity for their own educations. Sister Joan could always apply for, and was always granted, scholarships for our boys as they were residents of École St. Vincent.

During one summer vacation, these boys had time on their hands, so I hired a stone mason and a carpenter who taught them to cut rocks and lay stone walls, to make doors and shutters, and to put up a scaffold for a tile roof. The result was a two-room house with a breezeway in the middle. The privy and shower needed no walls as they were on the far side of the trunk of a big *mapou* tree. Each boy was permitted to live in the finished house as long as he was a *selibatè* (bachelor). I never had to question them. Each one thanked me when the time came to move on.

When their lives took on more serious dimensions, I was able to give each of them a running start. Luquece Belizaire was given a piece of the meadow by our house and the use of the cow barn for his iron work. Leon Belizaire and his two brothers received an irrigated farm near Verrettes. When Frédérique Pierre Jules got married, I helped him build a house.

Today, all of the young men are good citizens, all with different talents. One has a very responsible job with our wells and water projects, repairing pipe lines and pumps. He often worked with Larry so he knows all the trouble spots. Another is a generator operator, and his brother rotates an eight-hour duty at the electric plant in Saint Marc. Still another is head of the hospital kitchen. Three boys left the country and are doing well in the States.

Aristomene Jacques, known as "Ti Blan," was sent to school like the others, but could not learn to read and write. He tried French instead of *kreyòl*, but this was no better. All the others went on through school but he did not. Still he remained in the group, coming to the house, sharing the bicycle and working on the bachelors' quarters.

On his left hand Ti Blan had a sixth finger, which he seemed to be quite proud of. When Larry tried to start Ti Blan in the broom business, the machine operator saw the dangling sixth finger and said, "No way." Losing it was a big decision for Ti Blan, but a thread tied tightly around it did the job. Finally, my gift to Ti Blan was a beautiful sub-irrigated rice field. Three

The "boys."

times a year, he brings me a big bag of rice, one-third of his harvest. Ti Blan also works in the hospital as the most responsible custodian on the surgical ward.

Luquece Belizaire is my most trusted and valued neighbor. When Larry became ill, Luquece would sit in the bedroom, unseen at the side of the red Korean chest, always within hearing distance and available to help when needed. He traveled to Miami with us before Larry had nurses. He picked up the demanding part of the cotton business that Larry had established by carrying the raw and spun cotton in sacks to and from Petite Rivière.

Today I am able to ask him for advice about what community reaction might be to a prospective HAS decision. He always has thoughtful suggestions or wise answers.

He is a first-class welder and worked in maintenance at HAS until he lost his job, most likely because he was good enough to replace the chief. Now he has his his own successful iron works, plus he has established a popular restaurant in Deschapelles. Recently he was hired to oversee the ceramic, carpentry, and weaving shops, plus the Boutique.

Each month Luquece travels to Miami and back, carrying cassette tapes. Words spoken on tape are the medium of communication for those who can't read and write, and tapes are not incriminating. He returns with large sums of money that relatives in the US send to their families back in Haiti. It speaks well of his reputation for reliability and honesty.

Frédérique Pierre Jules has been a close friend for years. He went through the local school and graduated in mechanics at St. Trinité. He had a chance to work in the HAS garage but chose not to stay there. He soon became indispensable to our household. Now he is in charge of the household.

Frédérique is the first up in the morning and the last to bed at night. He opens the house at dawn, seeing that my hanging chair and cushions are in place when I come to await the rising sun. He washes the car and runs the lawn mower and helps with dinner party dishes. He is always ready to head to the market for necessary items. He tightens faucets and waters the plants. He changes the electric bulbs, keeps the pool fountain clean, and the leaves out of the gutters. He has trained our dog *Melanj* to chase goats and pigs out of the yard. When I return from the States, he helps me unpack my clothes. Twice a year, he takes down and cleans all of the screens, and oils all the many louvers in the house. In the evening, he is always prepared to play a mean game of Rummikub.

Although Frédérique now has a house of his own, and a wife and two beautiful children, he still has ample time to show care and concern for me. This does so much to make my life the happy one that it is. And we have the tremendous bond of having known Larry well.

It is a comfort to know that each one of these long-time friends will stand by me whenever and wherever I need them.

A Life Of Privacy
With No Secrets

arry was neat. The top was always on the toothpaste, and his shaving brush hung up to dry by a wire hook he made on the inside of his medicine cabinet. His hair was cut regularly by a local barber. He shaved with two razors, a Gillette and a Schick. When his shaving mug broke, he continued to use the soap by putting it in a teacup. When Larry was too weak to scrub himself, his Belgian nurse put him in his bathing trunks and scrubbed him in the shower.

He had a false tooth with gold prongs on each side. It was a miracle of workmanship and fit. The dentist who made it conceived his work much as a jeweler would, and probably demanded a jeweler's price. Larry would remove and replace it each evening and morning. It was an important part of him and his daily life.

When Larry was a most eligible bachelor, the father of a highly available girl brought his daughter to Breezy Bench in Arizona to visit. Larry was not tempted, but he did stop to see them on his next visit to California to see Billy. He was leaving their house at his usual early hour, when he dropped his gold tooth down an old fashioned sink which had a straight ceramic pipe with no goose neck. He took the sink apart and retrieved the tooth. Putting the sink back together, however, was beyond his ability, so he left the pieces scattered on the floor and departed. Later he received a large plumber's bill from the father.

Over the years, the tooth disappeared many times down the wash basin drain, but it was always recovered by Larry's ever available Stillson wrench. Having gone through these moments, I suggested he have a duplicate tooth made. He would have none of it.

He never left anything on the floor. He always hung up his towel and bath mat, and always put away his shoes. He washed his dark blue socks inside and out. He would close the faucets tight and slightly jiggle the handle of the toilet tank to keep the water from continuing to run.

Larry's wardrobe was insignificant. He returned from Europe with my father's tweed-lined raincoat that I had given him when he left. Years later, when it became really threadbare, I had a copy made at Dunhill.

His dress suits went to Port-au-Prince graduates or local grooms. He kept a dark suit (Alfred Dunhill), khaki pants and tweed jacket (Brooks Brothers), a lined raincoat, and his always shined, heavy shoes from Milton's Clothing Closet. All of this latter group was for trips away from Haiti and, I might add, seldom used.

Larry kept his supply of shirts and pants to a minimum by frequent distributions to his friends. He carefully chose the recipients, and the "gift" was always neatly wrapped in a piece of brown paper tied with string.

For years, Larry wore Sonny Miller's old scrub suits in the HAS clinics.

Larry did have a lot of hats, and all were easily recognizable as his. He had a straw cowboy hat, but with no wild turkey feather, and a big, heavy Stetson hat with a tiny American flag. He had bought the Stetson in Salt Lake City one July fourth. It was wide-brimmed so he could duck his head through the Jack Pines.

In Haiti he wore a straw hat, and later, a cork hat, to which he attached a washrag on the left side for protecton from the sun when driving his Land Rover. When traveling, he wore a broad-brimmed felt hat. When he went to Choate to receive the Pine Prize, he ended his speech by putting on his fifty-year-old band hat. Jenny gave him his last hat, a baseball cap. He could lean back in the car and the brim would not bother him.

Hats.

His writing was clear and neat. The daily entries of his five year diary seldom went beyond the allotted four lines. He wrote very few, and extremely short letters. The exceptions were the careful and beautiful French letters he sent to Dr. Schweitzer. Donors were often thanked on an Albert Schweitzer postcard, always signed "Larimer Mellon." Letters to me when he was for two years in Europe were all too few and much too brief.

Larry wrote on a black clipboard that had a silver clip with his initials, "W.L.M." He would sit in the bedroom at the sewing table, or in the living room on the sofa near his record player, preferring these spots to his office.

His financial statements came and went with Addison Vestal's visits. Bank papers that were no longer needed were torn into tiny shreds before being discarded. When the La Providence school closed, we no longer needed to shred the documents. We just threw them into the small privy hole designed to accommodate four hundred students.

Larry was left-handed, but he trained himself to write with his right hand. Maybe that is why he wrote so neatly and with such care. I'm sure his governess had insisted he learn to use his knife and fork like the rest of the family. Probably because one mounts the horse on the left side, he used his rope with his right hand. Out of necessity, he adjusted the microscope and transit with his right hand. He had left-handed scissors, but he could use his Swiss knife in either hand.

Larry's gift of choice to others was a Swiss Army knife. André Cassius, Gesner the plumber, Luquece, Art, Jenny, Mike, Ian, LeGrand, Frédérique, and I were all honored to receive them. Larry always carried one, along with his small jeweler's magnifying glass.

Larry's hands were not large. They were square, used and abused, with the nails pared short. They reflected all the heavy physical work he was so often doing. Looking at them, it was hard to conceive of his being able to slice and pare fine oboe reeds and tie and glue them together.

Larry had a box of mini-tools with tiny screwdrivers, files, wrenches, pliers, and even a tiny vice. He could repair everything from leather straps on sandals to earpieces on eyeglasses. These tools are for Mike, who left them for me to keep. They are in Dr. Schweitzer's wooden box covered with a solid, fitted, wooden lid in Larry's bureau.

He had fine French drafting tools fitted in leather-covered cases.

We had a telescope made by a Mr. Brasheer in Pittsburgh. Whenever we set it up, all the kids fought to be the first to look through it. As Larry removed the leather cover from the lens, you would almost always see a frog looking at you.

There were three British Land Rovers. Larry seemed to spend as much time in his as in his home. It carried friends, old and new, and patients, sick and well. He always got out and opened the back door to let people in or out.

Larry's car still rolls. The other two have been cannibalized and provide a continuous supply of parts for Larry's car. It seems right that the daily trips to the well rigs are now made by Larry's old friend and well supervisor Bòs Murat, driving Larry's car and wearing Larry's hard hat.

When the rains began and the road became muddy, Larry bought a steel tow cable for my car. It is used and borrowed by many, and so far has always been returned.

Larry's collection of dictionaries, and textbooks in foreign languages were always in order, as were his many books on different religions, and his numerous folios of music. He was always studying a new language, and learning more about societies of the present and civilizations of the past. I remember his reading Salvador Madariaga's *El Corazón Verde* about the Aztecs, Mexico, and Christopher Columbus. *The Source,* by James Michener, lured him into our trip to Israel.

Larry once told me that he found many parts of the Bible difficult to understand. To make the meaning clearer, he would often translate a chosen part into another language. I include here a verse he kept close to his heart:

"It is easier for a camel to go through the
eye of a needle than for a rich man to enter
the kingdom of God." *Mark 10:17-25*

He had made a beautiful Arabic translation of this, his favorite verse. At the end of this book I also include Christmas prayers and an Easter sermon, both originally given in *kreyòl.*

Larry's religion was a practicing one, an essence of all religions. Our devoted internist Marcella Scalcini once asked Larry if he built the hospital out of philanthropy. She said his reply had been, "I built it to follow Christ." I thought his reply had been, "to follow in the footsteps of Jesus." Marcella and I were equally certain of his reply. Maybe he replied differently to each of us, but the philosophy is the same.

We seldom talked about religion. Larry felt everyone's faith was a private matter, not to be questioned. The hospital was built on this belief and all who came were free to follow the way they chose. There was rarely any conflict.

Dr. Emory Ross was a dear and valued friend who provided us with our first close contacts with Dr. Schweitzer. We were about to embark for Haiti; Larry was in his last year of medical school and I was preparing to live in Saint Marc. Dr. Ross spoke of his concern that we had no formal religious connections, and he emphasized its importance. He was so anxious, that we agreed to join his church. "Jesus Christ is My Personal Savior" was a tenet not difficult for us to accept, but little did we know that the commitment included baptism with total immersion.

We were led to a large tank where Dr. Ross baptized us one after the other. We assumed that the wall separating us from the congregation was opaque as we could not see them. It was only afterwards that I learned the special glass permitted the entire congregation to watch us. We returned to the hotel to find Mike and Billy, who had categorically refused to take part in the ceremony, playing cards.

Dr. Ross felt strongly about the importance of a pastoral position on our staff. Park Avenue Christian Church sent Lloyd Shirer, Dr. Ross' friend from African missionary days, to fill this position. In the early years of the hospital we often held church, together with members of the staff, in our living room with the doors wide open and the beautiful view surrounding us. Gene Szutu, Tai Kong, and Larry all played the hymns and took turns giving a very short service. With Pastor Shirer and the arrival of the Mennonites, church had to be moved to the school building. My brother Glen built the church pews, the lectern, and the beautiful wood cross. It made the dingy classroom into a suitable church.

Incidentally, Glen never went to church. At the Quaker meeting service we had, Dr. Lepreau said that we had someone in our midst who never went to church but was the greatest Christian of us all: Glen Grant.

I usually went to church. Staff members took turns leading the service. At times I could train myself not to listen when necessary.

Easter service is held at daybreak, either on the hill above the hospital or on the lawn in front of our house. On Christmas Eve, the entire community comes to the tennis court for the Nativity Play. The pageant includes a very pregnant Mary on the donkey led by Joseph, the rude innkeeper, the barn with a cradle ready for the baby Jesus, the wise men, and the shepherds with their sheep, and goats, and always some curious pets.

The Mennonites sang hymns and had a short prayer in the hospital before going to work each morning at seven a.m. All too soon, Larry saw a Catholic crucifix in the hall and realized the inference. He took the crucifix down and respectfully handed it to the head sister. There was no need for

Ecumenical service in our living room.

words. On the other hand, the Catholic priest was able to wheel a small table to patients who asked for their last rites.

In Ligonier, Larry's grandfather had a chapel with a rotating altar for Catholic, Jewish, and Protestant services. Larry tried to build a similar ecumenical church here, and asked Dr. Schweitzer to help us have the Catholic and Apostolic leaders in Europe to come to some agreement. Dr. Schweitzer replied that we should abandon all hope of doing so. Once again, Larry was a man ahead of his time.

Larry fought hard to keep HAS ecumenical. He felt strongly that all sects and all religions should work side by side. We have had, over the years, many nationalities: Haitian, American, Indian, Chinese, Israeli, Polish, Swiss, Dutch, Italian, Spanish, Belgian, and others. And many religions: Jewish, Catholic, Protestant, including Mennonite, Jehovah's Witnesses, and Mormon. All have been able to follow their own faiths and all have been able to live in peace and accord in Deschapelles.

We have had Catholic priests and Protestant ministers. Today we have valuable Haitian chaplains. We have had Catholic sisters who served as nurses, teachers, and lab chiefs.

More recently, some staff choose to go to one of the other local churches of Deschapelles. The minister is usually an employee of the hospital.

Larry and I often went to a local country church high in the hills where we were announced, greeted, and kissed on arrival. It was so warm, so genuine, that it was more acceptable than the welcome from the huge Park Avenue Christian Church in New York with its expectation that we be at the coffee hour. We stopped attending despite our friendship with Emory Ross.

In these country churches we were always offered seats close to the speaker. We preferred the bench near an open door where the sun would not hit us, and like many others, we slept but did not snore. The service was periodically broken up by whole-hearted singing of *kreyòl* hymns. The morning usually ended with a trip to a spring, or talk of a well project.

Each small community seems to have at least one formal church, often used as a school on weekdays. With luck, an itinerant pastor appears periodically to perform baptisms and weddings. On these two occasions women used to always cover their heads and they usually wore white.

These days, church seems to be a real source of strength to the local people. It is an eagerly anticipated removal from the daily routines and responsibilities, and emphasizes the need of stability in all aspects of personal life and the importance of cooperation.

During Dr. Schweitzer's and Dr. Mellon's lives, music gave them the strength and solace both needed. It played a large part in their fulfillment of life. Dr. Schweitzer survived better in Africa because of the tropical piano which all too soon gave no musical sound. Organs were not only his profession, but the music they produced also provided a source of support for his hospital in Lambaréné.

Larry's love of music started when his brother Matthew gave him his first guitar and taught him how to play it. Two songs Larry often played on his guitar were "Mon Pays C'est Haiti," and "I'm Just Wild About Gwennie and Gwennie's Wild About Me."

Clarinet on the beach.

While Larry really enjoyed music, he did not enjoy dancing. Early classes in Pittsburgh did not inspire him. In the middle of a dance floor, he was completely removed from anything that had to do with his feet. He was looking at the band and thinking of the arrangements, but his feet were not moving.

Out West, when he could, Larry square-danced well, but there were more demands for his accordion, his guitar, and his dance calling talent. Over the years I have also seen him play French horn, oboe, cello, bass, clarinet, viola, guitar, slide trombone, and violin.

When I was flat on my back recovering from surgery at Presbyterian Hospital, Larry was flat on his back at the Julliard School of Music playing the oboe. Larry went to see a famous oboe teacher at Julliard. Another student was there with a slide trombone. The teacher told the trombone student to play out of the window and turned to listen to Larry. Then she told him to lie down on the floor and she put her foot on his chest, telling him he had better tone and use of air that way. She told Larry to remember how he breathed lying flat, and to breathe that way when he played sitting up, and then she sent him on his way.

Band practice.

Larry used to practice in Central Park. I worried about him even though he was playing upright.

One week, Larry had a string quartet play in our living room. Joe Stein from Belmont came with his wife and a friend. The four of them would play for hours. These were happy moments for Larry.

On every trip to the States, we carried musical instruments. Larry would visit Charlie Ponte, who had a music store on 42nd Street where the big barter and exchange took place. Larry always returned with reed-making supplies for his clarinet and oboe, and a new choice of instruments.

Charlie became a close, good friend, and visited frequently, bringing suitcases full of discarded instruments. He trained a local craftsman, Sewing Machine Joe, to do the repairs and provided him with a small welding machine and pads to make the instruments usable. Before long, there were four marching bands and a music master. To be a member of the marching band and have an instrument, one had to read music. This was a major step for people who could not read or write. All eventually got their instruments.

Duets.

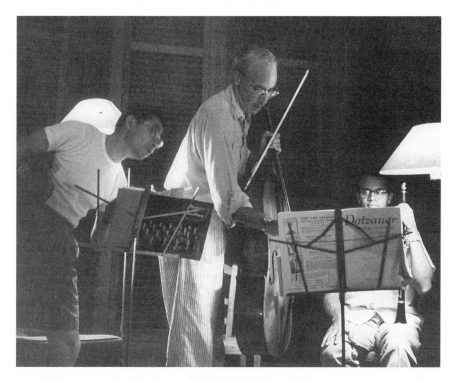

String quartet.

The bands played at weddings, funerals, town events, and gave concerts in the park at Saint Marc. All with great success.

Then we lost the repair man to *kleren*, and the musicians wandered off to Port-au-Prince to play in jazz bands and discos, or to other towns and cities to play in carnival bands. One marching band remains with Maître Delinois in Petite Rivière. On the twenty-sixth of June, Larry's and the hospital's birthday, the band marches into Deschapelles, playing as it enters the hospital courtyard for the annual celebration.

Until Ponte's instruments, the Music Master, and the marching bands appeared in Deschapelles, music was limited and improvised, consisting mainly of *Ra-Ra* (Carnival) bands with tin horns and drums.

Once, while staying at the Savoy Plaza, Larry returned to the hotel room to discover his things had been thrown around and his beloved oboe stolen. He reported this loss to the hotel detective. The next day, he set out to search for another oboe to replace it. At the first music store he visited, in a glass cabinet he thought he saw his oboe. He asked to try it and discovered it really was his. Delighted to have his oboe back in his own hands, the cost of buying it a second time did not bother him.

Larry's greatest and most difficult accomplishment was to teach me not only to read music, but to play the flute. I was an avid pupil as I was trying hard to stop smoking, and with hands and mouth busy, I was able to overcome temptation. Larry bought me a Haynes flute and a Powell flute. He thought I played well, but I was sensible enough to realize that is was wishful thinking on his part. This teaching assignment reveals, as much as anything, Larry's patience and kindness. I have not played since Larry no longer sits on the other side of the music stand. I gave my Haynes flute to my granddaughter Nicole. My Powell flute is in the coffee table drawer unopened, along with the big blue book of music scores.

When we went to Scotland, Larry took his cello and I my flute. On the train, the cello had to be in the baggage car, and Larry just had time to get the cello before the train pulled out. I was left to get the baggage. The guests at the castle at Oban did not appreciate our music, so we went down by the pond and played to the swans.

One day back in Haiti, Larry and I took our flute and oboe to a picnic at Saut D'Eau, a *Voodoo* shrine with a beautiful waterfall. It attracts many people all year round, but especially during August. Before swimming, we clipped our music on a branch with a clothespin and sat down to play. A small green snake appeared, reaching toward us. We finished our piece, and the snake hung from the branch, motionless. We picked up our music and went swimming, ate our lunch and returned to another spot to try to finish our piece. In no time at all, a black snake appeared. Having seen cobras in India lured and lulled by oboe-like music, we figured it was not a picnic instrument for Haiti.

Although the double-sided music stand has been put away, and the big blue music book with the dates of the evenings we played our duets together rests in the drawer, I like to think the pleasure we had in playing the music of our house still reaches the ears of many others.

I, and all family members on both sides — sisters and brothers, nephews and nieces, children and grandchildren, supported and loved Larry. All respected his sense of privacy and modesty. All would have been happy to see him go a bit public; he had so much to offer. I am the lucky one to have been by his side for almost half a century. He asked and allowed me to help him and still he encouraged my own projects.

Larry truly loved me, but seldom said so. He discussed things with me and asked my advice. He delegated me to do important things for him. We never argued, luckily, because our decisions were almost always the same.

Once, I mentioned to Larry that over the years we got on pretty well and did not have arguments. He said, "Yes, but I was mad at you once." I asked what I had done. He replied that he could not remember.

Larry always told me to be careful not to fall. He urged me to take a shower instead of a bath. But one Valentine's Day, I was hanging our big double mosquito net and I did fall. I knew I was hurt, but Larry refused to admit it and told me to get on the bed to rest. Célicia was the one who ran to get Dr. Eustache. My knee was broken, and required a long leg cast. Happily, there was no sequela and my leg is still as good as new.

In Guatemala, I slipped and broke my arm, and we had one of our first lessons in medical ingenuity. We continued our trip up the mountain to Chichicastenango. Larry bought me a red, woven sash and made a sling for my arm. Our chauffeur said I should see a doctor, and drove us to the doctor's house. The doctor came out to the car and said we must go on to Guatemala City. He called a doctor for us to see. My sling appeared to be covered with dried blood, and I was seen immediately. The doctor had me hold a pail, and as he filled it slowly with water, the bone slipped back into place, and a cast was put on. This was a beautiful result with no X-ray. Larry refused to believe anything could happen to me; he also did not want a timid wife!

Larry always championed those who needed help. Besides Jack Beau and Lola Flores, there were many more.

In Haiti, one who needed help was Arthur O'Neill. Arthur had been the director and nucleus of the Princeton Triangle Club Show and loved by all who fell under his charm. He rode on his college days' success for years, and drank and danced his health away. His visit to Haiti extended to a permanent life in Port-au-Prince as rum was easily and cheaply attainable. Larry's sister Peggy asked him to call on Arthur. Larry found him in a house above the city. Once a month he descended the mountain in his Ford coupe and collected his allowance at the American embassy.

Larry remembered Arthur had been a very good musician, and he found and delivered a piano to Arthur's home. By our next trip the piano had been sold, but Larry did not give up. He knew Arthur had also been a good photographer. He gave Arthur his Leica and some money, and asked him to make a photographic documentary of the hospital in Deschapelles. Then the Leica and the money were gone. In the end, Arthur's sister came for him, took him back to the States, and put him in an institution. In spite of Larry's help, this popular and able person was lost.

In so many ways, Larry tried to make his friends' lives more productive, more interesting, and more pleasant. He tried to teach some to play the accordion. A balloon and an orange were valiant but unsuccessful models in explaining astronomy. He tried to teach members of his sewing group to drive the jeep, but for ones used to traveling by foot, velocity and speed were never understandable concepts. He held French classes, but most of his students remained adept solely in *kreyòl*.

Larry always worked *with* people. They never worked *for* him. But rarely did anyone call Larry, "Larry." Never when they were staff members, and seldom afterwards. Many of those closest to him, like Addison Vestal, Bill Dunn, Dr. Frank Lepreau, Dr. Skeets Marshall, or Gérard de Vastey always called him "Dr. Mellon." When speaking to me, they called him "Larry."

To local friends and neighbors, he was "Doc", an endearing title of respect and love.

In Arizona, many may not have known his last name. To one and all he was "Larry." He was Larry to me and I was Gwennie to him.

My name is consistently "Madame Mellon", words hard to say together in *kreyòl*. I am often called *"Madanm* Bellond" or *"Madanm* Bay."

Larry did live for almost fourscore years, but not many given the same amount of time could have done what he was able to do.

CHAPTER 10

A House For Many, But A Home For Us

It was Jack Lord King, the hospital architect, who persuaded Larry that if we were going to spend our lives in Haiti, we deserved a home of our own, slightly removed from the hospital. Larry agreed, as long as a house for the administrator was built at the same time. The Beaus moved into the administrator's house, but not for long as Jack and Annie felt it too lonely. Neither Larry nor I regretted our somewhat isolated location.

The two houses are a joy to look at and live in. When Jack and I rode in Arizona, we often went across the desert to Taliesin West, and he explained to me Frank Lloyd Wright's theory of living and why he designed as he did. Outdoors is indoors and your life synchronizes the two. Jack's admiration for Wright is reflected in the hospital and house designs. The climate of Haiti made this concept easy to work with.

We chose to build the house on a light rise surrounded by land that was eventually to be used as pasture, gardens, and an area for hauling soil and planting trees. This surrounding open and useful space, with a view of the mountains beyond, quickly became a part of our daily lives and added peace and tranquility to our home.

The house I live in is the most beautiful I have ever seen. There are four free-standing stone walls, and the rest is seven-foot-high Cuban cedar lou-

Our living room.

vers. At dawn the doors are opened wide, and in the evening they are closed before the mosquitos come up from the wet lowlands and the bats are attracted by the inside lights.

When the rains come, the Transite roof with the broad overhang prevents the water from entering the house so the louvers may be kept open. The only time water enters is when the rain is so torrential that it fills the courtyard at the front door, enters the hall, makes a waterfall down the steps into the living room, and another waterfall down the porch steps and into the garden. At times like this a spring bubbles up under the sofa, but by morning the living room is clean and dry.

The house is simple and comfortable. There are no rugs and no curtains. Most of the floors are large slate squares that were once ballast for ships from Europe. Larry really enjoyed our home, especially our bedroom and the living room, both with views of the beautiful Cahos Mountains. At one time the front door was almost hidden by a huge flamboyant tree with a crown of red blossoms.

The living room is large, open, and welcoming, and is filled with easy furniture. I have sent most of my furniture back to the States for my children, but not until copies were made in our shop to replace them. The coffee table, dining room table, and courtyard tool bench that Glen made have not been replaced. Two large sofas and three comfortable chairs are reupholstered when necessary. Benches with seat cushions fill the rest of the seating space. It is understated, and attractive.

In the living room is a photo of an island in the Ogowe River. It is the island that Albert Schweitzer was looking at when his succinct and all-inclusive ethic came to him. He followed it daily from then on. On top of the photo sits an ivory canoe with paddlers, a gift from Dr. Schweitzer. The stone mask that Dr. Schweitzer sent us hangs at the other end of the wall. On the stone wall over the sofa hang two Audubon prints. A double-faced music stand is at the end of the sofa.

The living room has been used for many things. It was a joyous place for the Venn, de Vastey, Burnette, and Gèrard Charles weddings and receptions. And sadly, it has been a dignified place for funeral services.

In the hallway between the front door and the living room are wood masks from Liberia, alternating with the best of our Haitian paintings.

Many of the paintings were chosen early upon my arrival in Haiti. El Saieh, or Issa, as he is known to all his friends, offered me a painting every month for one year, to be put in the hospital or in my house. He said he would choose them himself or I could make the choices. I thanked him and wondered if that was all I would hear about it. The first two paintings arrived, and after that, I went to Port-au-Prince to choose the next ten paintings together with Issa. They form the nucleus of a large and unique collection of early Haitian art.

Also holding a place of honor are recent paintings by Saincilus Ismaël from Petite Rivière. The ones I love best are a Madonna and a scene depicting a creche.

There is a squat Aztec stone figure with eagle headdress. It was bought from a local farmer who had dug it up in his field north of Mexico City. Nearby is a life-size wooden swan my brother Glen made for me.

In the living room and front hall are my nicest plants. They bring the outside indoors. Two great boxes of antherium and hanging baskets of staghorn ferns fill the living and dining areas.

The dining room is separated from the living room by three steps, hanging plants, and a Chinese screen standing behind one of the sofas. The din-

By Ismaël.

ing room table was supposed to be made with two facing boards, totaling four by eight feet. A third board was to be used for the side table. These boards were chosen in Cuba when we ordered the cedar louvers. In my absence, all three boards were used, destroying the mirrored grain effect formed by the two facing boards.

Adjacent to the dining room is the part of the house most lived-in: the large porch shaded by the giant ficus tree. Its table serves for breakfast and lunch, and it is used for small meetings of the administrative staff and other matters requiring privacy away from the hospital.

The shortest route to the opposite side of the house is through the center courtyard with its bubbling fountain. It is the passage of choice between the busy kitchen and the corridor to the library and our bedroom.

Entering the corridor, the first room on the left is Larry's office and library. He never enjoyed it, and it was used mainly for the semi-annual visits of Mr. Vestal who cornered him there for hours at a time.

The room does contain Larry's best-loved books, his many dictionaries, and his wonderful collection of musical scores. The desk his mother gave him was placed below the wide, open louvers. On the wall is a photograph of his mother's portrait, a needlepoint of the Galapagos Islands given to him by his mother, and a color photograph of Dr. Schweitzer. Also on the wall is the honorary degree from the University of Miami, accepted at the request of his good friend Dr. Harrington. A most appealing sight is the trunk of the big flamboyant tree just outside the room's open, louvered window.

My dressing room has all of my favorite photographs.

The bedroom is at the end of the wing. It is filled with special long-time friends: my huge mosquito net, drawn back during the day, over Jenny's four-poster bed with its pale pink sheets. Here you will find Mother's French desk, the red leather Chinese box, and my Korean red chest. There is the sewing table that Glen made for me, where Larry and I so often sat to eat and to play Scrabble and cribbage, and to translate the letters from Dr. Schweitzer.

By my bedside are my talking clock from Mike, my notebook and pen, and my tape deck which brings me my always available friends, books on tape.

On the other side of the bed is the dark red cashmere throw that Mr. Mellon used when I last saw him in Pittsburgh. Larry used it when he was so sick, and now I finally can use it without nightmares.

The Ismaël painting of Erzulie, his round creche painting, and three beautiful birds give color and warmth to the room. Two china boxes, my two Chinese lions, and two yellow jade bowls are on top of the desk and Korean chest.

Outside my bedroom.

Over the *ha-ha* wall

The porch.

Three sides of the room are louvered. Two of these sides are doors that can easily be opened. One side opens onto a small terrace shaded by grenadia vines, which provide us all year with fruit, and by bougainvillea, which give us daily shade and beauty.

On the other side, the doors open onto the pool under the *mapou* tree. The small shallow pool is a haven on hot days. One day, in the mango season, it became the scene of a Bacchanalian orgy. I sat in the pool with my friends Anny, Gene McGovern, and Jenny Miller, eating mangoes with the juice running down our chins and elbows. Everyone laughed at the others' orange faces. Jenny saved the day by running up for dental floss. Larry always used to say he felt like a sheep dog after eating a mango!

From the foot of my bed, I can see the stone arch and ruins of the colonial aqueduct that once served a sugar mill, and the remnants of the old stone storage buildings beyond.

Between the bedroom and the mill is the larger part of the pasture. A handful of beef cattle from Drouin have taken the place of the milk cows, and we miss those beautiful, bovine heads looking over the *ha-ha* wall in front of our porch.

Below the wall, the smaller piece of pasture has been turned into a productive vegetable garden with seasonal crops of beans, peppers, peanuts, potatoes, and cabbage. On the house side of the Walmé Canal I have built a holding cistern for irrigation water. This assures sufficient water for the garden during the dry season.

The adjacent garden belongs to Sabael Paul, head of medical records in the hospital. On moonlit nights an *abitan* (farmer) works there with his *wou*. Beyond the garden, one can see the fort of Petite Rivière, and still farther beyond, to the east and to the west, are the Cahos mountains, full of strong people just surviving on dying land.

The arch from the old mill holds *siwo myèl* (honey). The bees are a menace and a danger, and we pay heavily to remove both the honey and its manufacturers. Ti Me says no bees will sting him if he smears his own juice on himself. We never have gotten any honey, so we never have had to worry about what "juice" he has in mind. Ti Me also cleans out the *pwa grate* (pea scrapings), an evil pollen which can be carried by the wind for miles. It grows luxuriantly in the old mill and each year Ti Me removes the vine, but I am certain he leaves the roots intact. He is a good neighbor who originally came from Ternette. His first job was to sleep in a neighbor's rice fields and keep the birds away.

On Sunday mornings I often say that there is no need for me to go to church. The view in front of the house is like a cathedral. Our prayers are better said right here.

The small house built by and for the bachelors is now a workshop, where the artist De Louis paints lovely things to be sold in the boutique.

Forty years ago, we planted a stick. It had no roots and no leaves. The agronomist very carefully put it into the ground, and made me place it ten feet farther from the house than I had planned. Today that stick is a ficus tree of enormous proportions. One branch is over sixty feet long, and many others are almost that long. The wood of the tree contains a tremendous amount of sticky, milky sap. As the branches stretch out, threads are squeezed out from their undersides and reach down for the ground. The minute they touch the earth, their character changes. They are no longer limp threads that wave in the breeze but almost immediately grow bark along their whole length. These threads become fast and strong and support the weight of the long branches above. The supports balance the tree since its root structure, while equally long, is very superficial. The tree produces tiny green berries enjoyed by the birds, a whole flock of whom can be hidden in the dark green foliage.

The stick was planted as we began our life in our new house, and the enormous tree it has become shades our kitchen and our porch. As the stick rooted, and began to produce branches and leaves, it exemplified the growth of the hospital. The trunk is the hospital and each branch could represent some aspect of the hospital's growth. The longest and strongest could be community health. Equally strong branches represent community development, maternal and child care, TB care and follow-up, and our eight satellite dispensaries. The entire tree is filled with that flock of birds eating the berries, showing that there is always a busy community life going on.

From Lambaréné came a single seed in a match box. Dr. Schweitzer wished us to have a Caiman cherry bush in front of our house. Quickly it grew and every year it gives us wonderful jelly.

We had twelve big *flanbwayan* (flamboyant or royal poinciana) trees close to our house, and many others on the hospital property. But I remember the year of the caterpillars, who arrived with the fresh, lovely, new green leaves of the *flanbwayan*. We began to hear the chewing, then we noticed the leaves were disappearing. We found the caterpillars climbing the trunks of the trees in organized phalanxes, up and down, and up and down, all night. A soaked rag around the trunk of a tree discouraged the traffic somewhat, but then we found they chose to come into the house. They are small and dark green and can enter cracks easily. If you chance to step on one, they are very slippery. We ended up putting the four legs of our bed in pans of water, and then slept fairly well.

215

The ficus tree.

The mill arch.

No one had ever seen these caterpillars before in Haiti. After the leaves were gone, they were gone too. We do not know where they went or if they will return. The miracle was that within a month after their departure the leaves had grown back on the trees. Unfortunately, the growth of green leaves did not always mean the survival of the tree. Four of the biggest ones around our house died and had to be cut down, including the largest which hid the front door and covered half of the open front courtyard.

In the center courtyard we replaced the *flanbwayan* with *grenadin* (grenadia, passion fruit) vines strung on wires. The vine changes the court-yard radically but once again we have shade and fruit. A trellis of *bougenvil* (bougainvillea) and *grenadin* now provides the lost shade outside our bed-room. Each year the vine and fruit become heavier and the wires that hold them must be reinforced.

Fig (banana) and *bannann* (plantain) plants were gifts from a friend from Montrouis, and we quickly placed them across the front of the house to fill in the bare spots with luscious greenery. Each day a plant will produce a new crisp, green leaf. And this year they grew beautiful *rejim* (regimes, or stalks) of fruit that ripened gradually and yielded *fig* and *bannann* for weeks.

Lots of new things have come to the house: an electric fountain, an ice cream machine, and this year a bread machine, all gifts from my children. I also have a blender. I told my cook Célicia never to put a spoon in the blender when it was running. She did once, and it was a disaster. On her next day off, she went to town and bought me a new spoon. Surely it cost better than a month's wages. The gift was hard to accept, but impossible to refuse.

The driveway to the house begins at the Deschapelles road, continues past the cowbarns and the banana plants, under the mill arch, up a slight rise, through the iron gate that is closed only at night, and into the front courtyard of the house. I usually go farther and enter through the garage, where all the daily activity and life in the household seem to begin and end.

It would be hard to number the friends who have passed under the stone mill arch to visit us. They have come from every part of the world. The house was built with room for Larry and me, the four children, and with one guest room, but even though the children have long since moved on to their

217

own homes, we never have a spare bed for long. So many of our visitors are reflected in the lists of our contributors. Familiar names, like old friends, return.

Even though our life and our hearts are in Haiti, the necessity to return to the United States would periodically arise. Through the years, these trips sometimes involved serious occasions, but for the most part they were series of happy events. Still, we always tried to make the time away from our life and work in Haiti as short as possible.

Larry and I were really equipped to lead a life almost anywhere. Rather than keeping our New York clothes in Haiti, we stored them at the Savoy Plaza in New York. Everything would be brought up from the hotel cellar when we arrived.

One time, Glen and I dined together downstairs in the hotel's elegant dining room. It was truly fancy, and had great music. I entered wearing the new coat that "Big Pa" had given me, and a hat with a rose on the front. As we sat down at the table, there was a big clank, as a small white ball dropped and rolled round and round on the dinner plate: a mothball.

On a short trip to New York, I needed just one outfit. The baggage master took me to the storage room and left me with my wardrobe trunk. I selected a dress and started to leave, but found that the door was locked. Luckily the room had a telephone, and I called the front desk. When the clerk answered and learned it was me, he exclaimed how happy he was that I had returned and asked me how I was. I replied, "Plenty mad as I am locked in the baggage room!"

Fewer and fewer things made it out of the wardrobe trunks and suitcases. Before too long, we asked the baggage man to discreetly get rid of everything, except for the fur coat. At the last minute, we grabbed the top hat for Haiti. It is the perfect hat for a Baron Samedi's costume.

Besides visiting Charlie Ponte's music store on 42nd Street, we would go to Brooks Brothers for dark blue leather bedroom slippers, blue underpants, long-sleeved blue shirts, and navy blue rib socks. Once, Larry took a long time choosing a lovely powder blue sweater for Marcella.

Larry usually got his thick-soled, blucher-toed, heavy leather shoes at Milton's Clothing Closet. It was hidden on a side street opposite Bloomingdale's back entrance.

I am crazy about shoes and have them in all colors, with embroidery, and with flowers. They are all flat. With my enormous feet, who knows why I insisted on paying attention to them. Although I have a closet full of shoes, I am almost always barefoot at home, both alone and with my good friends. My everyday footwear is an old pair of my daughter Jenny's sneakers, just recently replaced after a year of devoted service. In Boston for the *Konbit* Clinic event, Jenny, her friend Ron, and my companion, Jenny Miller, and I shopped for shoes. My son Mike shopped for shoes with me in Bal Harbor. Even today, my granddaughter Susannah has her eyes out for snappy, flat-heeled shoes for me.

There have been some hats that have been important in my life; the ten-gallon hat that Larry bought in Salt Lake City and gave to me when he left for Europe; the New York hat that the mothball fell out of at dinner with Glen at the Savoy Plaza; a white straw hat with small, white flowers that I wore at the cornerstone-laying of the hospital, the same white straw which has served me for weddings and funerals over the past forty years; the gondolier's hat Charlie Ponte brought me from Venice, a straw hat with a flat brim and a short red streamer; and the hat that I was holding in my lap when my portrait was painted. I sawed off the bottom half of the portrait which included the hat, to make my portrait the same size as Larry's.

On the day I was eighty-two, I sported a special hat to lunch at Mary's Restaurant in Petite Rivière. It was white straw with a red band and two big roses on the front. Everyone in Petite Rivière knew that it was my birthday, that I was eighty-two, and that I had just come home after hip surgery. Why else would anyone wear a hat like that?

From my earliest years, I had a sewing machine and I used it continually to make my own clothes. I began for reasons of economy and continued out of choice. I always felt well-dressed and was proud to wear what I had made.

While dining at the US Embassy in Paris, I was asked twice by Parisians where I had bought my dress. To be sure, it was made from French material bought in Port-au-Prince, but the dress came forth from my Featherweight portable Singer sewing machine.

219

Once, in New York, in Bonwit Teller I saw a small cabinet containing Greek jewelry. I ran back to the hotel and asked Larry to please come, there was something I would like very much for him to see. As soon as Larry looked, it was mine and it is still my favorite piece of jewelry: a ram's head bracelet. It was the Greek jeweler's first chance at display. He later became firmly established in New York.

A special New York treat was the oyster stew at the Plaza Hotel. Having seen the movie *Crocodile Dundee* three times, Larry always hoped to find, but never saw, that great doorman. We also enjoyed the Sign of the Dove with its hanging flowers, but our real choice was the hot dog wagon at the corner of Gracie Square. Peggy would usually join us and not infrequently we would eat two apiece.

We met our friends Dr. and Mrs. Kee for dinner at a small restaurant in Chinatown. We were seated at a small table for four. One by one, large and happy men in somewhat worn and definitely tight-fitting Air Force uniforms entered. There were many joyful reunions, and finally the General entered. It was then we realized that we were dining in the same room with Claire Chennault and his Flying Tigers.

Norman Cousins was a good friend and wrote a beautiful article about us in *The Saturday Review*. He suggested that the next time I was in New York, I stop by his office and select books for the foreign staff's library in Deschapelles. The books were review copies that didn't have to be returned. I was in Norman's office choosing books while Larry and the kids waited in another room. A man came in and sat down. He did not speak and neither did I. Norman came to pick us up and take us to the Lamb's Club for dinner, and we walked to the club, the single man included. Dinner conversation was solely and completely a diatribe by this man against atomic energy while everyone else listened politely. Leaving the restaurant, Norman asked me if the man was my brother. I said I had never seen him before.

We often met LeGrand in New York. Once, Larry asked her to meet him at 7 a.m. to go shopping. There was no persuading him that the business world would not open either its eyes or its doors at that hour. After an hour of walking around, and an hour more on stools in a 24-hour coffee shop, he was convinced. Then they set forth. This time with success.

On another trip to New York, to have the pleasure and privacy of eating alone, we asked LeGrand and her husband, Herb Sargent, to book a room with a kitchenette at the Westbury for us. On our arrival, we expectantly looked in the kitchenette; it was completely bare except for a stove and small refridgerator. Before we could express our disappointment, LeGrand and Herb appeared at the door with huge picnic baskets, holding plates, cups, silver, pots, a coffeepot, and groceries. We were equipped for a stay with meals in privacy, far from restaurants' reservations and headwaiters. The day we left, the baskets were repacked to await our next visit.

I had heavy Louis Vuitton baggage, bought in our early years of European trips. Later, the large, square hatbox proved invaluable to carry Thomas' English muffins to Haiti in packages of six. Also packed were sliced honey-cured ham, frozen raspberries, Portuguese muffins, red currant jelly, and oven cleaner.

One time, my granddaughters Susannah and Wendy offered to drive Larry and me to the airport for our return to Haiti. They arrived in their little blue Renault Le Car. We were in the front of the Hotel Westbury with our usual twelve pieces of luggage. Quite close, but not embarrassingly so, was a big limousine with a chauffeur who had already asked us if we wanted a trip to Kennedy. The girls optimistically started putting, and finally pushing, the suitcases into their tiny car. It finally became evident to all five of us, the watching limousine chauffeur included, that the Renault was inadequate. We hugged and kissed Susannah and Wendy, sent them into the Polo Bar for their breakfast, and waved goodbye as we left in the limousine.

At the University of North Carolina in Wilmington, Larry received an award at the same time as André Segovia, who was close to retirement. He and Segovia had plenty of time to talk together and enjoy each other. With Segovia was a small boy in a black velvet suit with gold buttons and a lace collar. Larry referred to him as a grandson, but it was not a grandson at all: it was Segovia's son.

Larry, his sisters, his niece Louise, Jenny, and I all went to Larry's alma mater, Choate, on the day Larry was to receive the Pine Award. The week

With Larry and Jenny at Choate. No one would notice a tooth was missing.

before, he had been to the dentist, who had removed two of Larry's front teeth. No replacement was ready for the great day on which he was to give his acceptance speech, but Larry was not concerned. He said that no one would notice.

The Carnegie Museum in Pittsburgh was opening the Ailsa Mellon Bruce Gallery with a big gala dinner and Larry was persuaded to go. We went to store after store, forgetting it was June graduation time, and dress suits were scarce. The stores were filled with high school and college students being measured and fitted. The suit of choice was pale blue, followed by pink, mauve, green, or yellow. It suddenly became evident that black in all sizes and plain white dress shirts were available, and of course just what Larry wanted. It was a lovely evening. The room had green marble columns and the tables were set with pink cloths. We were far removed from Deschapelles that night.

As I look back, I've really had more than my share of medical problems, which took me to the States often. But each time, I have sprung back to good health and enthusiasm with such spectacular speed that all my doctors and surgeons have become my close friends.

My X-ray for a chest difficulty was sent up to New York's Roosevelt Hospital, where Jenny's husband, Jerry, was then a resident in surgery. The X-ray was shown, a doctor looked at the name, and said to Jerry, "This is your wife's mother. She'd better go to Haiti and bring her here." Jenny, a good seven-and-a-half months pregnant, was the one to come and get me.

Local people were upset when I left for New York on a stretcher. They said the big *mapou* tree died when I left. A young new one now grows in its place.

Jenny and Dr. Bob Hollister traveled with me on the plane, and had the stretcher laid across two seats. At a stop in Jamaica, Dr. Hollister, a confirmed teetotaler, insisted I have a gin and tonic. The emboli in my lungs were diagnosed as being related to medication I had been taking and I eventually got well.

One Sunday, when I was in Presbyterian Hospital for a back operation, the minister sent word that he and his wife were coming to call on me. I implored Peggy to stay until they left. They brought some wilted flowers from the church, and the three of them played the waiting game. Peggy finally had to leave and, lying in bed, I became the recipient of a complete church service.

After weeks in the hospital, I was ready to go home. As I put on the fur coat given to me by Father Mellon, my ninety-eight-pound frame melted to the ground.

Air traffic was irregular those days and no planes flew at night, so because of my recent surgery, we returned to Port-au-Prince via the Panama Line. It consisted of two small white ocean-going boats. Their raison d'être was bananas, but a few passenger quarters helped defray expenses. The Panama Canal had many American employees who took advantage of the easy and peaceful four-day trip to the States. The boats plied the route between Panama and New York, greeting each other as they passed at the halfway mark. The one stop on the voyage was Port-au-Prince, to pick up the Standard Fruit Company's shipment of bananas.

I had bought a beautiful Chinese folding lacquer screen for the house. Glen had given me a huge weather vane he had made, a cow that had just fit under my hospital bed in New York. The screen and the cow were put on the floor of our Panama Line stateroom, and we stepped around and over them on the two-and-a-half-day trip to Port-au-Prince. A station wagon met us and the screen and cow were safely put on the bed of the car. Both arrived at our front door unscratched. We put the screen up between the dining room and living room. That night a big wind knocked it flat. It bears the scars but is still beautiful.

Wherever we traveled and for however long, our roots and the center of our life's orbit was Deschapelles, where we fulfilled our dream: to improve the quality of life of those with whom we came to live.

CHAPTER 11

"Go To The People, Live Among Them"

Dr. Mellon, as HAS's Medical Director, worked long and demanding hours in the daily clinic, and he finished each day with the impression that everyone in Haiti was ill. It was then that he decided to leave the clinic and work in the community which was our part of the Artibonite Valley. He wanted to try to reduce the causes of so many of the illnesses he had been seeing in the clinic. By now, the local people had respect and faith in what HAS was able to do for them, and he was welcomed and encouraged to work in their community life. He continued to earn the respect of the Haitians. He worked along with them to broaden their bases of livelihood by teaching adult education, better livestock breeding, improved agricultural techniques, and by teaching the younger generation increased skills such as sewing, weaving, carpentry, and brickmaking.

Larry understood the need for a steady clean water supply for drinking as well as irrigation. Water is abundant. It is the most valuable, readily available resource that Haiti possesses, but until Larry's arrival no one had thought in terms of distribution. People expected to walk to the spring, or to draw water from the all too infrequent shallow, polluted, hand dug wells. He introduced, with the understanding and cooperation of communities, the capping of springs. Boxing and covering the source prevents the water from being fouled. A two-inch pipe is then inserted in the box, and a length of pipe is extended to the first fountain. Care is always taken that the clean water is maintained at the source. With each community's agreement Larry supplied the pipe, and the communities supplied the volunteer workers. As the pipeline lengthened, new communities became interested.

We had brought our transit, so well used in Arizona, to Haiti. It was used on all of the pipelines, irrigation projects, dams, and bridges that Larry built in the Artibonite. Larry would always carry the transit himself, often over long distances. He would never trust anyone else with it. Each time we went to New York, he would go downtown to Kuffel and Esser to have the blade sharpened. The last time he went they told him not to bring it back. The blade was ground down and sharpened as far as it would go.

The care and pride he took with the transit was lovely to see. He would replace the black cap on top of the tripod with the transit screwed in the box. The black cap, that had been on top of the tripod, was screwed into the place where the transit had been. He would undo the leather straps and extend the legs of the tripod. With great care he would level the instrument, being sure that the brass plumb bob hung true. He would put the sun-shield onto the eyepiece, and was then ready to read the stadia rod ahead of him.

He always carried his green canvas survey book in his hip pocket. On every survey each point was carefully documented in his book, and a strip of white cloth was tied to the tree or the bush that marked the position of the stadia rod. If he ran out of cloth for the tell-tales he would cut a strip off his shirt tail with his Swiss Army knife. This book is a marvel of neatness and accuracy, considering the heat and the dust and the sweat with which it competed. Today, with the tell-tales long gone, one can still locate any buried pipeline by following the bench marks recorded in the book.

Surveying, at least by Larry, was done in the dry season after the corn had been picked but when the stalks were still standing. Nothing is more itching on a hot day. We would cut and tramp through the fields sweating and itching, but no crop was damaged. I never saw Larry scratch or complain or stop in the middle. But I admit that I often had tears in my eyes. Larry would never bring a sandwich because no one else ate. He did keep a gin bottle of very warm water under his seat in the Land Rover, however. When we went to La Chapelle to work, we would pass Desarmes and Ti Blanc's bou-

Larry in his Land Rover.

tique. I would give Ti Blanc a signal, which meant put a beer in the ice box, I'd be back. On our return trip Larry would drive by fast with no chance for me to pick up my cold beer!

Larry taught the Community Development workers how to survey with an angle A and a flat-sided Gordon's gin bottle half full of water. This is a simple technique of acquiring true elevations without the benefit of a transit. The evening gin and tonic took on added value, as the empty flat-sided bottle frequently served unforeseen importance in aspects of community development work.

For the pipeline into the city of Petite Rivière, Larry wanted to cap a spring five miles north, and then run the water into town. He was promised the cooperation of the residents of Petite Rivière. Next, he approached the residents close to the beautiful spring and secured their approval plus volunteer help for the first section of the pipeline. As this spring was ill-defined, Larry had the government SNEP man, Engineer Poult, place the cap.

Larry and his "rod man."

Larry and the volunteer laborers began digging a ditch that was to be a quarter mile long and three feet deep. He laid in place a five inch plastic pipe, 20 feet long, joined with glue, and held by a collar. The plastic pipe was buried deep under hard and rocky soil to ensure that it would not be damaged by hoes and machetes. This would also discourage anyone from cutting into and siphoning water from the pipe.

When clean water flowed at the end of the first quarter mile and a fountain was put in place, there was no trouble getting enthusiasm to dig the next length. Each new volunteer group dug a quarter mile segment until the

Volunteers laying water lines.

Clean, potable water
from mountain springs.

A line of fountains.

line reached into Petite Rivière. Larry directed the line daily with his transit, and worked side by side with the men. Five miles later, when he arrived in Petite Rivière, he put in three fountains, one at each end of town and one in the marketplace in the center of town. Everyone was asking for a private outlet, or *ti branch* (little branch), but wisely, Larry made no decision. He let the town fathers decide on additional outlets.

Just below the fort he also built a huge cistern to be filled during the night with water from the pipeline. This was to guarantee the town a steady water supply no matter how heavy the demand during the day. When it was finished the town leader said it was dangerous and people could drown in the cistern, so Larry erected a high chain link fence around it. Even so, the cistern was never used. We still wonder if they were afraid someone would throw poison into the town water supply or if there was some other reason. Why it was never used remains a mystery.

Several more public fountains were put in strategic spots by the city government, and the people of Petite Rivière were very happy. For years, there was a steady supply of free potable water. But a travesty has occurred. Two influential people closed the valve into the town and built cisterns within their own courtyards. At night the valve is opened and the cisterns are filled. Then the water is sold by the bucket from these private cisterns, and at a high price. Free running water no longer exists. There is neither a recourse nor a way to re-establish the fountains. The result is that once again those who cannot afford to pay for water rely on the muddy canal, or a low seep in the middle of town where people and cars are washed, and cattle and goats drink. I am glad Larry never had to know about this.

Larry put in another remarkable pipeline in Valeureux, a small town high above the river, where there was growth only in the rainy season. Larry's four inch steel pipe made it possible to have water and gardens during the dry season as well. The spring for Valeureux was at the end of a ravine outside of town. The elevation of the spring was higher than the top of the ravine but a considerable distance away. From the cap, a sealed pipe descended down the dry creek bed to the foot of the ravine, and then it continued straight up for a good thirty-five feet to the plateau above. People shook their heads, certain that the water would never arrive. Larry went home with complete confidence. Three days later the water poured into the

The Tapion Dam.

town from the pipe at the top of the ravine. The plateau became a veritable Eden of beans during the dry season.

During the rainy season the creek ran big, and Larry warned the community that they should take the collars off the pipe joints, and move the easily lifted plastic pipe high enough to be safe from the torrential waters. The first year, Larry worked with them and showed them how to remove the collars off the joints and place the pipe on high ground. In the dry season the collars were all replaced and water ran again on the plateau. The next rainy season the community did not take the pipe up, and they lost many collars and sections of pipe when the creek ran. Larry replaced them and the gardens were green again. The following rainy season there was again pipe loss as the *abitans* (farmers) had not disconnected it. This time Larry said they must pay for the lost pipe, and he would order more. They never got the money together, and the water was not to run again for many dry seasons. One must get used to the fact that in Haiti, for a slash in a water pipe, or for the lack of a bolt or a pipe collar, an entire working system can fail.

A few years ago, a Mennonite community settled in Valeureux. They completed a project to re-establish the water supply at the top of the plateau.

New cultivation made possible by the Tapion Dam.

They chose to support and run a lighter pipe from the spring to the high plateau, along the top edge of the river, high above the rushing water of the rainy season. During the dry season the same bean fields are once again green.

An unusual incident happened in Valeureux one rainy season. Ten local men were working cooperatively in the lower field close to the Artibonite River. They uncovered a big cache of old Carolingean coins, often called doubloons. The group leader was a strong and good man, admired and trusted by the community. In the middle of the night he came galloping up to our house. He had brought some of the coins, and wanted me to take them to Puerto Rico where we were going for the weekend to hear a Pablo Casals concert. I said I would take a few to get a price, but I also said he should report his discovery to the police, since it is the law of the land to report all colonial treasures immediately. I warned him that ten men working in a field together could never keep such information confidential, and to protect them all it must be reported. My advice may not have been wise because when we returned to Haiti all ten men were in jail, and the coins were in the hands of the police. The men stayed in jail until the authorities were convinced they hadn't held any back coins. The leader, Marcel Charlorin, lost a lot of his prestige in the community due to this incident.

Now, twenty years later, Marcel's son is a leader in Valeureux. With the pipeline now re-established, the community is working together to keep this important system in good repair. One hopes they will remember the dry years and will work to keep the bean fields green on the top of the plateau.

The summer we were in Italy visiting my son Mike, he drove us to Tarquinia. We saw ancient Roman irrigation systems that carried water in masonry troughs from the water source to the fields. Larry wrote the measurements of the troughs in his little blue book, and when we returned to Haiti one of his first trips was to the headwater of the Tapion River. He took on the monumental task of planning an irrigation system using dalles similar to those in Tarquinia. He designed a dam some 40 feet high and 60 feet across which would provide a steady source of water to the dalles.

Larry supervised local volunteers in the building of the dam. Concurrently, dalles ten feet long matching the measurements of those in Italy were poured in the schoolyard in Deschapelles. They were strengthened with heavy iron reinforcing rods. Two of the huge dalles would just fit on the bed of our big truck. During the dry season twenty of them were made and transferred to the dam site. With his transit, Larry calculated the distance and height, and supervised the building of the masonry pillars on which the dalles would be set. The heavy concrete troughs were carried down the steep bank and placed end to end on top of the evenly spaced pillars. The water from the dam descended along the dalles down a gentle slope to fields which had never before received irrigation.

The dalles ended at a hill that was twenty-five feet high. It had to be excavated for the water to reach the other side. Slicing through this hill was a monumental but necessary task, if the water were to continue its gradual slope. It took two levels of workmen to remove the dirt. One level of workmen started at the bottom and threw the dirt up to a second level where it was thrown over the top. Once the path was cut through the hill Larry's job was finished. From then on it was the community's job to determine the distribution of the water.

The job was fraught with danger, with the heavy work of placing the dalles, but the only accident was a pinched finger of one of the Mennonite workers. Everyone rejoiced when the dam was finished and the dalles carried water. The river continued to flow even though the dalles were full.

Larry decided to celebrate the success with a barbecue for all the people who had been involved in the project. The hospital staff was transported to the site for the event. Larry brought a choice steer from the farm at Drouin, and our *agwonòm* (agronomist), Gustav Menager, began cooking it the evening before. The odors of the roasting meat reached the top of the surrounding hillsides, far beyond the homes of the expected guests. By noon time, the outlying area was crowded with curious onlookers, pressing closer as the cooking continued.

At the first stroke of the knife, the invited and uninvited rushed to be first. All of the hospital staff, and many of our loyal workers, left the barbeque with only the odor of roasted meat to satisfy their appetites. It was a disappointment to the hardworking participants, but we had the satisfaction of knowing that many hungry people had a good meal.

Twenty years of spring floods damaged the masonry pillars that hold the dalles. The area behind the dam filled with silt and rocks. The first dalles were cracked and damaged. The system worked, but precariously.

With a grant from the International Rotary Club we repaired and reestablished the Tapion project according to Dr. Mellon's original plan. The cost of this project was sizeable. Laborers were paid, and sand, cement, and gasoline were bought at inflated prices.

A new dimension has been added to this program. Farmers near the dam have learned the importance of conserving soil by terracing and planting trees. They have also learned to maintain the repaired system.

Anse Rouge, a small coastal town half way from Gonaïves to Môle St. Nicholas, had no potable water. A boat would go up the coast to a spring by the edge of the sea and bring back drinking water. Larry drilled a well and put up a fifty-foot windmill to pump the water. It worked well, but we had to go back each year with our strong and fearless plumber, who would climb up and grease the moving parts. Today the well has a hand pump and, ungreased, the windmill no longer turns.

Larry wished to bring potable water to the town park in the middle of Saint Marc, and he decided to use an old French colonial cannon as the fountain. The barrel was longer and thinner than most, with a small bore at the end. He planned to place the cannon at the end of a pipeline, and the flowing water would be perfectly safe to drink. He did not understand my lack of enthusiasm until I suggested he visualize it in his mind before installing it. He did, and the cannon was left where it was found.

The Péligre dam, and its irrigation system, built in the 1950's, included many canals. It became necessary for people to cross the canal to reach their homes or their gardens. Yet the canals had few bridges. A man wishing to reach home put his clothes on his head, piled his shoes and his hat on top, and then swam across.

Larry and Bòs André designed a cantilever bridge from two-foot pieces of metal ship pilings, and placed it across the canal at a strategic spot. Horses and families were then able to reach home easily.

Haiti is suited to drilling for water, as few wells have to be deeper than one hundred feet. Larry had a man from Texas build a sputter drill, and it has produced over four hundred wells. We provide Gould pumps at cost. This well rig is still in use throughout the valley, but with the increase in population around Deschapelles a source for additional water became crucial. We hired a large four-inch bore rotary rig to dig a two hundred-foot deep well adjacent to the garage side of the hospital. We were hoping to reach a lower stratum of water, thus ensuring a steady emergency water supply for the hospital's enormous demands. Unfortunately, this never produced water.

Two years later, the men who drilled this well returned to see if they could reestablish the first hole. It was not possible. But while the rig was still here, I said we must try again in a different spot. Before paying the $2000 for the drilling to begin, the business office asked me for a guarantee that water would be found. I explained that there is never a guarantee on a well. Many times on the ranch in Arizona we drilled five hundred feet, and if no water was found we capped the hole and moved on. But this time, in Deschapelles, we did find water. We discovered a source that would produce sixty-four gallons a minute!

Now local people are beginning to realize the importance of potable water for disease prevention. They are ready to work on a project, but no longer on a volunteer basis. When Larry began his water line projects, he had no trouble getting volunteer workers who would carry and dig and lay pipe, sometimes for a meal, but often for nothing. Now they demand a daily wage, or food. This is Haiti, and times are hard.

There are three sites where we are trying to get the local people to help restore their water supply. We now ask that people pay for the pumps and for the upkeep. The investment inspires better maintenance. There are some rare oases of hope and cooperation, and we continue to work hard to encourage our *konfrès* (colleagues) to shoulder their own responsibilities.

During the international embargo that followed the ouster of President Aristide by a military junta, the United Nations Development Project gave us a wonderful grant to reestablish the wells and water lines that badly needed repair. This was not an easy job. One must work with the community and have its support. Despite the embargo, the U.N.D.P. was able to give us this

Larry beside the
Artibonite River.

With his neighbors.

grant as it was termed a humanitarian action; secure clean potable water for communities.

Larry once said he wondered why he made all the effort to go to medical school when so much of his work ended up in Community Development. But he never would have gotten the permission to build the hospital, or the respect of the Haitian doctors, if he had not had a medical degree. This degree had enormous importance in Haiti. And it does to this day. Furthermore, his medical knowledge gave him a special understanding of the Haitian people. He saw that their well-being was intertwined with systems that promote good health. His medical degree took him beyond the skills of treating the sick.

Wells, pipelines, fountains, and dams need constant repairs. With extra pieces of pipe, pipe threaders, and Stillson wrenches, Larry was always ready to cure water ills. Those who love and know him best think of him not as Dr. Mellon, but as WaterMellon.

Two men who were leaders in international community development were Jimmy Yen and Lloyd Shirer.

We met Dr. Jimmy Yen in New York, and even before the hospital was finished he gave us good advice on how to begin community development. A wise man who headed the Chinese mercenaries employed to build railroads in Western Europe during World War I, Jimmy Yen was asked to write their letters home. It was then he started the literacy project, "Each one teach one." After he left China he worked in the Philippines on community and educational projects. When we met him he had left the Philippines and was in New York. Four sons had stayed in China, and four daughters had left with him and Mrs. Yen for the States.

When the hospital opened Jimmy Yen sent his assistant down to help us with the initial stages of our Community Development project. She told us not to begin near Deschapelles, but to establish a spot somewhat removed from the hospital. We chose our beef farm at Drouin as the site of our first project.

Pastor Shirer contributed a great deal to the Community Development program. Rammed earth was introduced for house construction and cement slabs for privy bases. His literacy projects were popular among adults.

The Ternette Road.

In the 1960's, young Mennonites, who are conscientious objectors, were able to work at HAS instead of serving in Vietnam. We had close contact with, and wonderful contributions from, many nurses and young men. They usually came from farms where they were used to hard work, and they were glad to volunteer in Haiti. Larry would meet with the young men and their Haitian counterparts each Saturday morning in his "office", a dingy depot full of wire, pipe, nails, chains, shovels, hand tools, and a blackboard. The workers and the vet sat on benches and discussed the accomplishments of the past week and the plans for the next.

On the wall of this office hung a piece of cardboard. On it, written by Larry in blue crayon, were the words given to him by Jimmy Yen:

Go to the people.
Live among them.
Learn from them.
Love them.
Serve them.
Plan with them.
Start with what they know.
Build on what they have.

Larry listened to the people to learn what they wanted and needed. He did not make decisions for them. Gandhi, too, expressed this important aspect of servant leadership. When watching a lot of people running down the road, Gandhi excused himself and said, "I must follow my people to find out where they are going." Larry worked with the community to find out where they wanted to go.

Once a project was decided upon, Larry would turn it over to a Mennonite volunteer who could always come to Larry for advice, but was otherwise entirely responsible for the project. The Mennonites usually stayed for three years, and were able to complete many projects including numerous wells, the road to Ternette, and the *azil* (asylum or home for the aged) in Petite Rivière. Edgar Stoesz, a Mennonite leader, once said the Mennonite boys arrived as ponies and left as work horses.

In the 1960's, Larry handed Randy, a young Mennonite, the keys to a small caterpillar tractor and told him to build the road to Ternette, an area high in the mountains. The result was a road that was wild but usable for many years with a four-wheel drive car. One day I asked Randy if he wasn't nervous about choosing where to climb higher each day in the Caterpillar tractor. He said no, that he never began a day without a prayer.

After years of heavy rain and neglect, the road has narrowed to the width of a footpath but is still heavily used, especially on market days in Verrettes.

Larry was always on time. If a community meeting was called, he arrived at the appointed hour. The meeting would usually take place under a big shady tree, near surrounding houses. Larry's and my arrival seemed to be a signal for local members to bathe and change their clothes for the meeting. An hour delay was not unusual, but Larry still continued to be on time.

One day, I was late in joining him for the trip. Larry left without me. I was never late again.

Childbirth in Haiti is a normal and all too frequent occurrence, often taking place nine months after the week of *Madi Gwa*. Traditionally, a family member or a midwife assists at the delivery, usually at home. If the procedure lags and the midwife wants to go home, she whistles for the recalcitrant placenta. In the past the cord was cut with a knife or machete, and often ashes, dung, or muscat were placed on the umbilical cord stump. Too often the result was neonatal tetanus.

When we began to see more and more cases of neonatal tetanus, our anesthesiologist, Dr. Lucien Rousseau, and his wife Renée, started courses for midwives. Graduates were given small aluminum suitcases for their cord tying kits. A kit contained Gillette blades, four-by-four gauze, a cord tie, a belly band, and an appointment at HAS for tetanus vaccinations for the child and mother. Each kit was wrapped in a large square of brown paper which unfolded to provide a clean spot for the delivery. At the same time, women of childbearing age were urged to have the three tetanus shots that would protect them and their subsequent newborns.

Over time, with the hard work of Drs. Warren and Gretchen Berggren in our Community Health Department, neonatal tetanus admissions were

Courses for midwives.

reduced from as high as almost five hundred in one year to zero. We still receive an occasional tetanus case, but only from outside our district. It is interesting that the babies who survive neonatal tetanus become strong and healthy children, with the head start of weeks of nutritional six-times-a-day feeding at the hospital, sometimes for as long as six to eight weeks. This was the Berggrens' initial project, and they have remained involved with public health at HAS. They have many international commitments which they fulfill well but always seem glad to return to us.

Malnutrition among children has always been an enormous problem. During the first years we distributed food, but later we started to give classes at daily nutrition centers. Here parents were taught how to choose from the foods available in the markets, and how to best cook these foods. At the same time, the parents would be taking advantage of these lessons in feeding their children. In the past fifteen years, part of the work of the nutrition

243

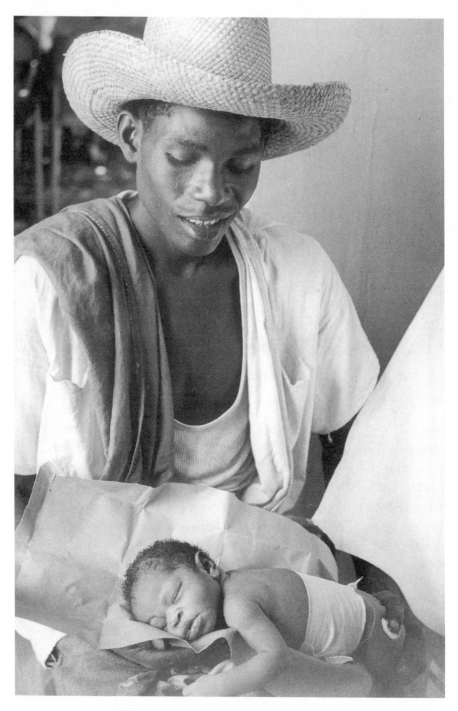

A father brings his newborn to the hospital.

centers was taken over by our dispensaries, with hospital-trained *oksilyes* teaching nutrition education.

A new program that is proving successful is one that continues this fight against malnutrition. In small local centers, mothers of malnourished children are learning by example from mothers of healthy children. These neighbors aid in the wise and economic marketing, and in the cooking and feeding of the daily meal. Each child is weighed after two weeks of supervision. At this point they often show little weight gain because, even with good food, they have lost only their edema. During the subsequent two weeks, however, these children show significant weight gain, although the mothers are no longer under daily supervision.

Our intention, after saving those who are malnourished, is to keep them healthy with proper diet and vaccinations, and to emphasize the importance of fewer and more widely-spaced births. A comprehensive choice of birth control methods is available but rarely accepted. There is pressure from the man or husband to have children, and a temptation for a woman to hold onto her man by bearing them.

Today the dispensaries provide many new services, like family planning with maternal and child care. They can handle TB screening and medication, as well as the treatment of syphilis and gonorrhea. Also, some simple lab procedures are being instituted in several of the dispensaries. More serious health cases are referred to the hospital.

The connecting link between a dispensary and an individual in his home is the *ajan sante* (health agent), who is a member of the same community. This is the beginning of a process of making health care the responsibility of the local communities. The *ajan sante* directs those in need to dispensaries and keeps track of appointments and follow-ups. He also finds delinquents and sees that they keep their appointments. All too frequently in Haiti, if people are not actively ill it is hard to convince them that booster shots for tetanus are all-important, or that breast-feeding is life's blood for babies, or that TB treatment must continue, and that TB and syphilis contacts must be screened and treated if necessary. The *ajan sante* also keeps records of all births and deaths.

Crises occur that involve the total area covered by HAS. Malnutrition, measles, TB, AIDS, rabies, and typhoid all require immediate action. The

Mothers of malnourished children learn by example.

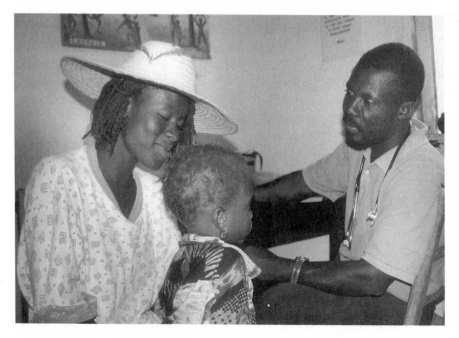

Care in dispensaries.

ajan sante is the key to covering the 216,000 residents within the 610 square miles of the hospital district.

In small communities removed from the dispensaries, health and education care are implemented by local residents called *animatris*. These volunteers carry great prestige and are able to oversee hospital programs.

Education plays an increasingly important part in Community Health. It is the key we hold to success. The Community Health Department continues to grow in importance as well as in size. The staff is close to approaching one half of the total number of HAS employees.

Larry always wished to improve the quality of life of local friends. To this end much was taught, and much was learned. The aim was to recognize the things that were simple and useful in this rural life.

Joseph Bernard and his wife Junie contributed greatly to the community development work. Mr. Bernard was an educator with clear and strong diction. People, especially adults, were anxious to read and write. He held night classes, going into the communities carrying a Coleman lamp, a large blackboard, and chalk. The thrill that these country people displayed when they could write their own names was unbelievable. A signature took the place of a thumb print, and to them had the value of a university degree.

Local girls, if lucky, went through the first two classes of primary school. With Mr. and Mme. Bernard, Larry established centers for young girls, where they could learn to read and write, to sew, to cook, and prepare to be good wives. The basic aim, especially on Mme. Bernard's part, was for them to avoid pregnancy, at least until just before marriage. With their newly acquired skills, they became the most attractive and eligible young women in the community, but still their pregnancies seldom ended in marriage. These babies, while absolutely no disgrace, were a big responsibility. The girls often brought their children to our little pool to swim.

Sultane, of the sewing group, was especially appealing, and soon became pregnant. The father refused to take the responsibility, but Sultane and her new baby were cared for and well looked after.

In Haiti, if a child is born fatherless no local priest will baptize it. A baptism certificate is an essential piece of identity in Haiti, and has become increasingly important. It ensures the right to property and a share of family inheritance. One priest in Port-au-Prince overlooks the need for dual parentage to obtain a certificate, but the trip to Port-au-Prince is long and expensive. Sultane made the trip, and her child was baptized.

Eventually both child and mother went to Sister Joan's school in Port-au-Prince. The daughter, Susie, later went to Jamaica to learn English. A few years ago, during a visit to Haiti, she rented a car in Port-au-Prince and drove to Deschapelles to thank me for our help. She is now doing well as a physical therapist in Brooklyn.

I think Larry wanted his sewing girls to look like me. I was fond of saris, and he bought one for each of them. They had no idea what to do with them, and on Saturdays they washed and scrubbed them with yellow bar soap in the river, and then put them in the sun to dry. My dress, ordered and made in Port-au-Prince, with butterflies embroidered all over it, was duplicated. I wore my Venice gondolier hat with its red ribbon. They all put red ribbons on their straw hats. I had a ball-shaped Swiss watch on a chain, and before I knew it, I was not the only one.

One season, wigs became a stylish trend in America, and local animals began to suffer from flies and gnats, as they lost their tails with which to swat. All of the tails, along with their manes, had been stolen or sold and shipped to the States. Around this time, I went on a trip to New York and returned with a dozen wigs, black and straight. The sewing girls were pleased but, like everything else they owned, the wigs ended up in the stream to be washed and scrubbed each Saturday. The result was twelve beautiful young women looking like Zulu warriors.

Larry took one of the girls, Ilora, on her first trip to Port-au-Prince. He left her in the Iron Market and said, "I will meet you right here at 3:00 p.m." He waited for her until 4:30 p.m., then figured she had made it home alone. When he passed through Payen, a few miles from Deschapelles, Ilora's parents stopped him in the road and said the radio had announced that Dr. Mellon had brought the girl to town and left her there. Larry returned to Port-au-Prince with the parents, found Ilora at the police station, and brought them all back home to Payen. The radio had told the story to all of Haiti.

Cotton for sale.

On a trip to Guatemala we were fascinated by the weaving on small hand looms. Haiti had the cotton and the thread, and we were already dyeing. We asked a Guatemalan man if he would come back to Deschapelles with us and train some of our girls to work on the hand looms. When we heard that the man was an alcoholic, we asked his daughter instead. We spent days getting her a passport, a visa for Haiti, and even clothes to wear. On the day of departure, the man brought his daughter to the airport, but said that he had decided not to let his daughter come with us!

Not discouraged, Larry started the girls weaving on large looms using local spun cotton thread. Raw cotton came from the Cahos mountains, and it also grew wild in local fields where our neighbors could gather it and sell it to us directly. Soon this was not enough to fill our orders, and we went as far as Gonaïves to purchase more.

The first step in the process was to clean the cotton. Thirty old, needy, and sometimes mentally handicapped people were chosen and divided into two groups. Every other Tuesday, fifteen of them would bring us cleaned cotton and were given an equal quantity of cotton from which to remove the seeds. Larry personally served them. The groups still come on alternate

Weighing and paying.

Tuesdays. Thirty-five years ago they were paid one dollar. Today each person receives seven dollars.

From the beginning the seeds were replanted. The cleaned cotton was taken to the Cahos Mountains by Maître Delinois who distributed it to people who spun it into thread. Then Larry bought the thread from Maître Delinois, as well as from local people who would sell it to him directly. Larry was ready to weigh and pay for raw cotton or thread wherever it was available. He carried a clock-faced scale, and a scoop with three chains to hang from a rafter or the branch of a tree. He always carried a Mellon Bank canvas bag containing small change, and he would weigh the cotton and pay for it from this bag. One woman made Larry weigh her thread inside her house with the door and window closed. She didn't want her neighbors to know how much she had been paid.

More was paid for fine thread, and we found many a *boul* (ball) had fine thread on the outside, but heavy thread on the inside. And sometimes we found stones hidden deep in the centers.

All of the thread was brought back to Deschapelles, usually in Larry's jeep. Then it was woven into cloth and rugs, to be sold in our boutique. Quality was hard to maintain outside of Deschapelles, so all dyeing and weaving was done here.

There are steam pipes available at the back of the garage. Every few weeks we would disappear for half a day. To anyone looking for us, it would be explained, "Dr. and Mrs. Mellon are dyeing behind the hospital."

We still make rugs, placemats, and cloth, and the quality is good.

These days cotton is rare, as the goats have destroyed almost all the plants. I have had to scurry far to get raw cotton to give out to our old friends. This was not the case during the embargo. We were unable to ship a five hundred rug order, causing some of our former clients to lose interest in the rugs. So we had piles of raw cotton and sack after sack of cotton thread. Our friends in the mountains kept spinning, and each Tuesday a group arrived to clean cotton. We were trapped in a web we could not untangle without destroying for many the means of a dignified livelihood.

A fantastic solution presented itself. Someone from Port-au-Prince was looking for cotton thread. Did we have any? Did we have any! It was counted, weighed, put into crates and delivered on the next truck into town. We are now left with very usable fine cotton yarn, and a stock of heavy loose woven thread. Instead of buying more cotton and delivering it cleaned to

Dyeing behind
the hospital.

Maître Delinois for the mountain people to spin, we are now handing over *bouls* of the heavy yarn to our Tuesday groups to be unwound. This cotton will then be re-spun into fine thread by the people in the mountains. This does not cancel our losses, but our huge inventory is not growing bigger. Using the natural-colored soft thread, we are producing and selling high quality items, even though we have had to raise the prices due to the many hours of work now involved.

A resident cat, very small in size, discourages the rats from attacking our fine cotton, now hung in sacks from wires in the ceiling of the weaving shop.

When we were building the hospital, I would go frequently to Bois Dehors to see the ceramic shop where an American gentleman, Glen

Bouls.

Ceramics.

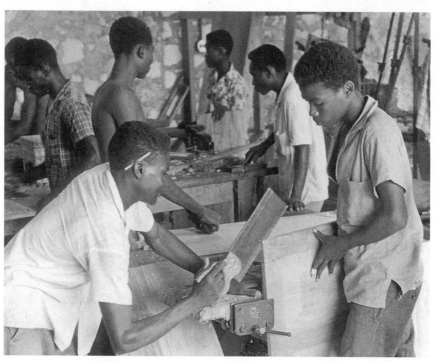

Carpentry.

Lukens, was training young local students. To encourage them, I bought everything they made. Soon after we opened HAS I established the ceramic shop here, and I had one of Glen's students come to work with us. Today our ceramic shop is a busy and successful industry, with three electric kilns and plenty of local and foreign orders. Larry Peabody's expertise and good taste added much to the variety of the items.

Our carpentry venture started slowly, turning out a few reproductions of furniture I had brought with me. Next, we began making some small original items. Then my brother Glen came and gave it great impetus.

Next to Larry, Glen was perhaps my dearest friend. He was married to Jane Cowdrey, and in their forties both worked in Honduras with the Peace Corps. Returning to Andover, Massachusetts, his farm and his carpentry shop did not hold the same allure. They were about to reapply to the Peace Corps when Larry sent a telegram asking them to join us. Glen came down to see what our woodworking shop had been doing under my supervision, which was not too much.

After a few days, Glen said he wanted to talk to us. He would join us, but had a couple of demands. First, he wanted power tools for the shop. This was a hard decision for Larry, as he wanted students trained with hand tools, so they could open their own businesses when they returned to their homes that had no electricity. Second and most important, Glen wanted it to be clear that Larry, not I, was his boss. I said, "There would be no trouble there, Larry is my boss too." In the end we agreed to his requests.

All was decided. Jane would teach at La Providence school. Glen would bring his truck and all his tools and we would be off and running. The years he was here were happy ones for them and also for me. Glen soon learned that Larry was off and unavailable once the sun had risen. But he never did learn *kreyòl*, and found he could not do what he wanted without leaning heavily on his little sister. He did, and I enjoyed it, and he liked my helping him. He set up the shop, gave carpentry training and filled the boutique with attractive items. He was full of enthusiasm, and would call me and say, "Come and see what I plan to do." He always had good new ideas. From his Honduras days he had brought his hanging bed. Here we reduced its width to make a hanging sofa, still a big seller for the boutique.

Glen, I must say, was a rascal. Twice he sold Larry the old van he had brought from the States. I am sure Larry knew this, but I also know Larry knew that Glen needed the money.

Glen, never having been sick in his life, suddenly became ill and had to leave. After many happy years in Deschapelles, he wanted to return to the States to fix up the farmhouse in Andover for Jane. I implored them to return and stay with us. No, he was afraid I would put him in the hospital, even though I promised him I would not. He said that I had taken care of Father, then Larry and I had taken care of Mother, and he would not let me take care of him as well. So he did go back to the farm and fixed up the house for Jane.

Several years later we saw where he had passed his last days, in a lovely old inn in Southern Mexico, surrounded by the pre-Columbian ruins of Mitla. In Oaxaca, Glen and Jane had a small cottage with a ceramic stove that was shaped like a man's head. Wood went in the mouth and smoke came out the top. I am sure Jane tried valiantly to feed him things he could swallow. One night she must have become frightened. She put Glen in the bed in the camper and drove north. Halfway to Mexico City he died. Luckily she knew people in the Embassy who helped her.

Shortly before Jane's death I wrote the history of my youth, and sent it to her. So much of it was about Glen. She said that it was beautiful, and to not change a thing.

The boutique was begun to provide an outlet for our products and means of livelihood for young men and women, and it easily produces good financial aid to at least one hundred local families. The success continued even through the embargo, since the boutique receives many orders from Port-au-Prince.

From the beginning, we welcomed paintings of good quality by local artists, and we hung them for sale on the boutique walls.

I first knew Ismaël as a tall, slight boy from Petite Rivière. Soon I had him decorating boxes and trays and ceramic items to be sold in the boutique. He really wanted to paint and not decorate, but he chose a good candidate to replace him in decorating, De Louis Jean Louis. I often bought Ismaël's paintings, and now I buy and sell all the works that he brings to me. Each year he brings about fifteen paintings of Erzulie, the Voodoo Goddess of Love. These are painted on wood and have been sold from the boutique for over ten years.

Ismaël was put in jail for writing political tracts. I would visit him and bring him paints and hardboard. He was released, but quickly put back in jail for the same reason. This time I brought not only supplies, but also one of the wonderful art books from the National Gallery in Washington. This book radically changed his style of painting. He was greatly moved by Byzantine. Today, Ismaël's paintings, with the Byzantine influence combined with voodoo themes, bring fantastic prices. He still sells to me and my family, and his are the prized items at the Haitian art auctions organized by my children in Pittsburgh and New Haven for the benefit of HAS.

Ismaël was among several chosen to go to Israel for a trip of artistic exposure. All expenses were paid, but he needed a suitcase and a jacket. I easily saw to that.

Ismaël was also invited to Colombia for a similar reason. I told him to wear no clothes offered to him in Colombia, or carry any packages, however small, on leaving that South American country. Others were not advised so wisely and got into difficulty. Both trips made him happy to be in Haiti, and even happier to be in his own house with his own boys and students in Petite Rivière.

Nemours was another Petite Rivière artist whose work sold well at the boutique and among the staff. With his success, he added a jazz band to his list of accomplishments, and soon disappeared into the maelstrom of Port-au-Prince. There he had a "school" where his pupils painted the backgrounds and he filled in the details. These mediocre paintings soon lost him his clientele. When last heard of he was driving a *taptap*.

Sadly, Ismaël has followed the same route. He has an *atelye* (studio) with about ten or twelve young aspiring artists. Unfortunately each one is taught to do a certain aspect of the background, and Ismaël puts in the details, making them a saleable item for the not-so-discriminating buyers of Port-au-Prince.

Alix Dorleus of Petite Rivière paints well and with fine detail, but very slowly. He had the courage to accept my idea to paint murals in the hospital. The walls were twelve feet high, and he began by making banana plants the length of my arm. I got a step ladder and told him to begin close to the ceiling. I then drew the spine of a banana leaf some five feet long, the size I thought it should be. Alix took the cue and now, around the pharmacy window stand two high green plants, one with a *rejim* of bananas. He was given license to express his love of detail and added a life-size rooster and chicken. Best of all, this mural hides the hand marks of the hundreds who stand and wait for their prescriptions.

There are three other murals in the wards, mostly tropical trees, but also *taptaps* full of people, and big roosters, hens and chicks for the pediatric wards. These touches of levity and color were added to take the place of the toys, clothes, and crayons that always seemed to disappear in a matter of hours.

De Louis Jean Louis, Ismaël's recommended replacement, does all of the painting on the furniture and birds and other small items sold in the boutique. He paints in one of the rooms of the bachelors' quarters by my house, unless he is painting mangoes and other fruits and flowers on headboards and dressers in the residence houses.

In Petite Rivière, I found Paul, a man who showed me a carved wooden duck. I bought it, suggested some alterations, and ordered two more. That year ducks were my Christmas presents to the resident staff. The following year they were sold in the boutique and in Port-au-Prince. Some have even been sent overseas. All were painted with feathered details by De Louis. I am sure that by now this one man has carved over two thousand ducks, all beautifully painted by De Louis.

In this country, it is a fact that when anyone produces a highly saleable object, every artist seeks to replicate it. With the success of our product, Haiti, in no time at all, seemed overrun by wooden ducks. But the ones that are carved by Paul and painted by De Louis are by far the most exquisite.

We have made concerted efforts to introduce productive means of livelihood within the local area. Some projects, such as ceramics, carpentry and weaving, continue to be successful. For the others, Dr. Mellon was able to acknowledge their failure and to close them. He was not one to beat a dead horse, but chose to bury it. This willingness is an illustration of Dr. Mellon's wisdom.

Larry was concerned about the price people had to pay for tin roofing in Haiti. Tin was expensive, but local thatch had three main disadvantages. Thatch had to be replaced each year, it provided no protection from rain, and it was a haven for rats. Tile roofing seemed a perfect answer.

When in Mexico we had seen a whole family sitting and molding roofing tiles from wet clay. They were using their knees as molds to make one end wider than the other. The tiles were fired in their simple jet-Diesel oven. We stayed in this town in Mexico for some days. Studying the roofing industry in depth, we saw that one family, with their own kiln, could make it a viable and successful venture.

We returned to Haiti well informed. We knew our local clay was good. We built the kiln, having bought the jet nozzles in Mexico, and were ready to fire. Instead of forming tiles on our knees, we made cement molds for roofing and floor tile.

Having trained Gérald Charles to run the project, Larry turned it over to him once it was a growing success. Along with a truck to haul the clay and make deliveries, Gérald was given a stock of Diesel and some sizeable orders to fill. He was on his own, but from day one things began to fall apart. The Diesel was expensive, and he would shorten the cooking time to save money. The resulting tiles melted in the rain. When he was paid for an order, he bought a motorcycle rather than more Diesel.

In the hospital area we have successful examples of the tile that was made when Larry was supervising the project. A perfect example is the tile on the floor of the hospital library.

We learned all too late that our friends in Haiti did not trust tile roofing. They were afraid that the wooden rafters would give way under the weight, and they also feared that robbers could lift two or three roofing tiles and enter their houses.

Two large classrooms of La Providence school were filled with undercooked tiles. Recently, with the addition of French to the curriculum for staff children, we needed one of those rooms. The tile was hauled down to

The bakery. Two hundred loaves each week.

the road, broken into pieces and used to grade and fill holes. This discarded tile was also used for the road itself. Larry would have appreciated that the tile failure had been turned into something useful.

The local palm leaf brooms were ineffective cleaning tools and so we were importing expensive brooms from the States, paying five dollars apiece. Larry decided we should economize by making our own, and he imported a broom machine, enough broom corn to get us started, and a man to teach this craft. He assigned Ti Blanc to learn the business. We cut the handles and planed them round to fit the machine. But the seeds that we planted never produced broom corn, so we had to continue to import it. The end result was excellent, but the cost was well above five dollars. And, even though we reused the handles, it was all too evident that the project would not support itself.

The bakery was a huge success for years. Larry would provide the flour and the wood for the oven, and twice a week he would bring back to Deschapelles one hundred loaves of bread in the back of his Land Rover. The baker, Thercilia, was a good friend. She had been one of the sewing girls who really made good, and never in any way did she disappoint us. She made good quality bread, and by carefully using her profits she was able to send all of her children to secondary school. And she built an attractive house which she surrounded with trees and filled with furniture that she bought from our boutique.

Senator Barry Goldwater, an old Arizona friend, arrived by Haitian government helicopter to visit HAS. We kept hearing the motor and occasionally seeing the helicopter, and then both would disappear. For a marker we had covered the football field with white sheets. Larry waited nearby. Finally after several circles and considerable time, Barry landed. He saw the hospital, had lunch and returned to Port- au-Prince.

Later, Larry told Thercilia at the bakery about the visit. She said the helicopter had landed in her yard and asked for directions to Deschapelles. The event brought no thrill to her, only unneeded dust all over the bread.

When we closed the cafeteria, and needed only fifty loaves of bread twice a week, Thercilia said we would need to pay the same price as if it were one hundred loaves, because the job required the same amount of wood. We continued to order two hundred loaves each week, putting one hundred into the deep freeze. But freezing the bread had poor results, and we had to look for a better solution.

In Verrettes, we found a baker who could provide the needed amount of good quality bread. He arrives daily on foot, delivering the basket of bread on his head. The cost is half the former price, but we truly regretted ending our business relationship with our Liancourt friend.

In the cafeteria, meals were served for the hospital staff during hours of employment. Also, ten minute coffee breaks were begun, staggering the staff from the clinic. The ten minutes became an hour of rest and gossip. We really wanted to stop the coffee hour, but found it difficult to do. No Haitian drinks coffee unless it is laced with sugar, and each morning ten to fifteen pounds of sugar were put out, and always consumed. Suddenly, no sugar was available in Haiti, and the coffee hour died a natural death. It was never asked to be revived. Today foreign staff bring their own morning coffee in thermos jugs.

Every Christmas all staff residents, and those on duty, were invited to dinner in the hospital dining room. It was a festive turkey dinner served at a long U-shaped table, with candles and placecards. Everyone looked forward to it. A special recognition of appreciation was to be seated between Larry and me.

When we decided to close the dining room and serve meals only to the bed patients, it meant giving compensatory pay to each employee for the meals that they missed. Also, we had the added expense of building kitchenettes in the nurses' residences. Even so, a savings was realized within a matter of months.

Larry liked ice cream. Someone found out about this, and sent down an ice cream machine which was set up near the hospital. It produced a hundred ice cream cones and Dixie cups each day. Larry would bring the sewing girls up for cones. For patients and neighbors, it was a special treat. People even came from Port-au-Prince, to see HAS of course, but often just for the ice cream. Most of all it was Larry who found great delight in this shop.

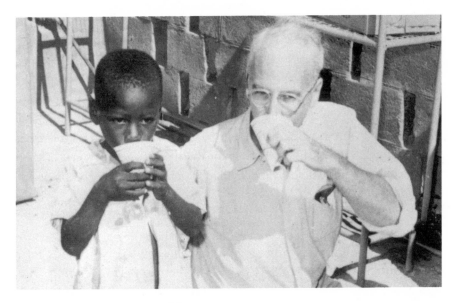

The ice cream event.

One Christmas day we sent word that each small child would be given a cup of ice cream. When we saw the number that arrived we had to find some sort of standard for limitation. We set up a board to measure the height of each child, and only those who could walk under the board received ice cream. Down from the mountains came an old man, a two-and-a-half foot dwarf. He walked under the board and got ice cream. As the crowd grew and the supply diminished, we lowered the board. Even so, hundreds of children got ice cream that Christmas Day.

Clovis ran the machine with great success, but one day we were faced with the decision to close. The ice cream had become thinner and thinner, while Clovis had become fatter and fatter. He was selling twice the number of cones at the same price, but with one-half the quality. Larry closed the shop, but we do still have the ice cream machine in the hospital kitchen.

The problem of HAS staff schooling began early, being faced with the McGovern, Berggren, Dowell, Frédérique, Strauss, Lepreau, Bergner, Szutu, Modi and May children all living in Deschapelles. The first teachers, Penny Potter and Louisa Stude, had been Jenny's schoolmates. Parents saw that the school was well equipped with good desks, chairs, maps, and the other classroom necessities. We still find large colored pieces of construction paper from this original stock. It was our first veterinarian, Julian Strauss, and his wife Katie, who found a wonderful teacher, Mary Jane Tiefault. She gave each and every one of these children a running start into their education. Deschapelles and L'École Flamboyant played a big part in these children's early lives. Speaking with them today, all married and with degrees and worthwhile lives, they look back on those early years as some of their very happiest. Almost all have returned to Deschapelles, some to work, some to visit.

L'École La Providence began with kitchen employees' requests for a kindergarten, as four-year-olds' legs are too short to walk to Verrettes. Dr. Hal May picked up the challenge. The school started small, with one room, then grew to two rooms with two teachers. Not too much later, L'École La Providence had become a Christian school with nine classrooms, fourteen teachers, and almost four hundred students.

Larry, after much soul searching, decided this school should not be a part of HAS. We were not equipped to be in the school business. The school program terminated with Larry having calculated every expense involved: land, buildings, salaries, donations, and equipment. He then matched the amount and offered it to any taker. We were lucky. The Protestant mission in Verrettes picked it up. The same students could attend, and the school became a much better one than ours. Dr. May is on the board of the new school and has continued his interest and support in its success.

Today several graduates of this school are now some of our most respected and able employees. One graduate, now a teacher in Canada, wrote a book about the hospital and the school, and how much they meant to his early education.

Children now have a chance to go to one of fourteen crowded and, for today's economy, expensive schools in the local area. The hospital has a school fund to which short term staff members donate, helping to satisfy children's year long demands for *kreyon* (pencils), *gonm* (erasers), or *tenis* (tennis shoes). The funds are distributed only on two days before each trimester. Many children take part in this opportunity.

Early on, the Catholic Sisters wished to train *oksilyes* for HAS. We built a classroom and dormitory for thirty local girls. This was financed by Larry's school friend, George Lockhart. The building, now a storeroom, still carries his name. Sister Alphonse chose well her candidates and the first year's results were good. Then a new class was added, and the pressure in the classroom and dormitory was doubled. The results were only half as good, and because of certain levity and loss of religious discipline, the community of Sisters became divided over the school. With Miss Pete's advice, Larry discontinued the school, but three graduates of the successful first class continue to work at HAS today.

Even while active in the countryside, Dr. Mellon was not isolated from the hospital. He continued to be involved in the routine and daily solutions.

Gérard de Vastey was one of our longest and most valued employees. He held the important position of *kontwolè* (controller) in the business office. Suddenly and swiftly, he was picked up, taken to Port-au-Prince, and thrown into prison, a veritable death sentence in those days. It involved fear, neglect, abuse, and, all too often, torture. Many people were abandoned and forgotten in the depths of Fort Dimanche.

No one knew why Gérard had been jailed. His life was at Deschapelles, where few secrets are possible. We thought he would quickly be released. When this did not happen, Larry wrote to President Duvalier, explaining de Vastey's fragile health. Sometime prior to this, we had sent him to New Orleans for a lung decortication. Larry also spoke of de Vastey's importance in running the hospital. When Gérard was still not released, Larry went to town to appeal personally to President Duvalier on de Vastey's behalf. I sat in the car and watched Larry in his white linen suit as he climbed the steps to the entrance of the Presidential Palace. He was stopped halfway by a military guard, but not for long as he said he was a man of peace on his way to see the President.

Larry told President Duvalier that de Vastey was so valuable to HAS, that he would prefer de Vastey be released, and he, Larry, be placed in jail in his place. Dr. Duvalier showed Larry an X-ray he had taken of de Vastey and said he had received good care.

Gérard was released that day with the admonition that he was a dangerous man. Highly sensitive and frail, Gérard paid an enormous health price, even for this short sojourn in Fort Dimanche. But he returned to Deschapelles to retake his place as head of the business office. Later it was proven that he had been picked up by mistake.

Gérard had the important responsibility of choosing his office staff. He was from Saint Marc, and he filled the slots in his department with men he had known since his youth. Considerable pressure was put on him by candidates from Verrettes and Liancourt. He always said to us that he did not know them and that the Business Office was a sensitive place. And indeed it is.

The Business Office is the power center of the hospital. It is here that loans are given and the large payroll is met. It is also an unrecognized center of information. The Business Office employees know of debts, of losses, of salaries, of raises, of pensions. These are important pieces of information and should be kept confidential.

Only the paymaster has the safe combination, and his position is autonomous. Once, a rumor reached Larry that there was irregularity in the bookkeeping. Larry, who had all of the safe combinations, asked de Vastey to be present when he opened the safe. According to the books, $18,000 should have been there. Instead, the safe was empty.

Larry accepted the loss and, as they say when firing someone, thanked the two employees. Typically, he did not press charges. We see these two men occasionally at weddings and funerals in Saint Marc, and they greet us like long-lost friends. One has built a big house, and the other has a first class supermarket, the only one in Saint Marc. Even though it is one of the rare places that stocks Gordon's gin, there is no question of my buying it there.

The two employees were replaced once again by Saint Marcoise. Local feeling ran high. How hard these feelings were was soon revealed. A band of machete-carrying, barefooted men arrived at the hospital garage. There was lots of noise, the gate was quickly closed, and since Larry was ill at the time, I raced up to ask what they wished. They quieted down and said their demand was only for air. We had closed off the air pump, as it was among the things we could do without during the Diesel shortage. It was quickly connected and the men left. I had no sooner returned to tell Larry what had happened, when I heard the same noise, louder and closer. This time they were on the far side of the fence by the business office. Again I went to face the group, but this time with Bill Dunn, our newly arrived administrator, standing with me. Bill, who did not yet know *kreyòl*, was unable to understand their demands. We stood alone until Ti Blanc came and stood by my side, refusing to be sent away. They started to climb the fence and I said, "Don't do that." They stopped and said that they wanted de Vastey. I said that they could not have him, he was mine. One of them said, "Leave. This is not your affair, Mme. Mellon." I said that it was. It was as if I were a mother hen protecting her chickens.

Miraculously they backed away. It was an angry group, and we had to protect Gertie and Gérard. They stayed in the operating room two nights and a day. All the nurses were frightened and slept in the library. Martha, the head nurse, and I took turns with them. Bill Dunn spent the night in his office. We were finally able to alert the police in Verrettes, and early in the morning, our three Land Rovers left the garage, each with armed police. On the bed of one, on stretchers, and dressed in OR gowns, lay the two de Vasteys. Once in Saint Marc they were safely out of the Artibonite district. They were then picked up by their family and driven to Port-au-Prince. Gertrude came back only to pack their things. Gérard has never returned, but continues to be a devoted legal advisor from Port-au-Prince.

The angry group had gone to *dechouke* (uproot, pillage) de Vastey's house, but stopped when someone said it was Mme. Mellon's house. The crowd then left, and instead went to *dechouke* Bòs André's house. Bòs André, the garage chief, and also a Saint Marcoise, hired only his boyhood friends whom he knew well. They took his clothes, shoes, icebox, bed, mattresses, light bulbs, electric wiring, doors, windows and roof in a matter of half an hour. Only four concrete block walls were left. Bòs André now sleeps within the hospital and uses his apartment only for meals and a weekly haircut.

Within the same year, two of our most respected nurses were seriously threatened. Discipline is strict in the nursing area but it had begun to be a problem, especially among the hospital trained *oksilyes*. Twice, the firing of someone from this group resulted in a hired accomplice entering the head nurse's house at night. It was a frightening experience, but none of the nurses left. They stayed and received the respect of the entire hospital staff.

We must never forget that we are visitors in this country. The Haitian interpretation of rightful indignation is different from ours and legal recourse is rarely available to them.

The clinics at HAS provide many poignant tales, some sad and some humorous.

A friend in Liancourt climbed a tree to get a coconut. When he reached up for the coconut, he saw a snake and dropped to the ground, breaking his back. He was on a Stryker frame for several weeks. When we took him home, we found he lived in a house with two doors, and a dirt floor covered by two mats. One mat had a hole and a basin, and he would roll from one mat to the other.

One day he complained of a stiff neck. I realized that his friends who came to visit stood in the open doorway to talk. We turned him around to face that door, and his stiff neck was cured.

Not too many months later I saw him going off to his garden with a *wou* over his shoulder. Hopefully not to get coconuts again.

A patient's family member was asked to give blood. His blood was not "strong" enough. The patient brought in his brother to be a donor. His blood was not "strong" enough. The patient came back a few hours later with a third donor. It was his horse.

Larry asked me to take a large pregnant woman home, down the small canal road and then inland from there. When the car could go no further, I found two men to help me. I showed them the four-handed fireman's carry. They were fascinated with the hold and delighted to help. But each time we put the woman in front of the fireman's carry, just as she started to sit, their hands would separate and lift her instead. She reached her house with the two men carrying her in a neighbor's chair.

A man, old and feeble, sent word for me to come and see him. He was lying on his bed with a shoe by each ear and a coffin resting in the rafters overhead. Before he died, he wished to thank me for the care he had received at the hospital.

Statistics and our clinic records showed there was no leprosy in Haiti but Larry did find a case. Scrapings confirmed the diagnosis, and the man was put on treatment. When the patient did not return, Larry followed up. In his courtyard in Marchand, we found four other family members who tested positive for leprosy. We treated them all for years, but when Father Olivier opened his clinic in Gonaïves, care for this family was transferred there. The Gonaïves clinic has uncovered many cases, most very benign and easily treatable. A patient may have a local white patch of insensitivity, but very little neural damage.

TB was a dreaded disease and almost a passport to early death. It was called *maladi ti kay* (sickness of the little house). As people realized it had a contact risk, they learned to isolate the sick family member.

Larry tried to eliminate the fear that was always present at a positive diagnosis. He gave a demonstration in the TB clinic, describing the case of a young healthy man with the accompanying X-ray showing a TB lesion. Did the patient die? He said that the X-ray was his own, of twenty years ago, and it was evident that he was healthy and strong and very much alive. Larry's infection possibly came from the Japanese butler who used to take Larry fishing on Sundays, under the bridge over the Monongahela in Pittsburgh, at a place called Panther Hollow.

Our Haitian physicians saw the necessity of housing our TB patients to ensure that they took their daily dose of medications, and that they were well fed. The doctors designed and had built the first house at L'Escale. It was complete with a privy and a kitchen. A Catholic sister was in charge. Often the patients were kept for four or five months, time enough to plant and enjoy a garden.

The four Haitian physicians financed L'Escale for as long as they stayed in Deschapelles. Soon the need for more houses and their upkeep fell on the hospital's shoulders. My children gave the second house in memory of Billy Mellon. Today there are six houses. One is a foyer for children. Even though the exacting treatment is shortened to three months, the forty-nine beds, nine of them for children, are always filled.

Once, several people walked from Jacmel to HAS. They had bad TB.

Even though they were out-district patients, we accepted them, and they settled in nearby Payen. Family members would send them hats they could sell to support themselves. Today, they are the hat merchants of choice in the local markets. Our roadway has a cactus fence that is covered daily by these hats. The hat man here has a little round compact mirror, and he offers the customer a look.

Another time, Larry sent a delinquent TB patient home without treating him. He later sent me after the patient to bring him back. Larry could get mad, but not often.

The cycle of fear is once again repeated. The relationship of HIV positivity and TB is so close with its powerful interactions and contagion. Today we are able to give respite for the TB aspect of this combination, but the core disease marches uninterruptedly onward. Luckily, the patient is not rejected, and families accept and include AIDS patients in their lives and their homes. The need of discipline and the dangers of the disease are public knowledge, but there is still much work to be done. This illness all too often is described as mystical rather than contagious. Thus, treatment for AIDS is frequently put in the expensive care of the *bòkò.*

CHAPTER 12

"Learn From Them"

Our life has not been limited to Deschapelles. Since coming here we have continued to visit many corners of Haiti that hold friends and interest for us.

Père Saget was the priest appointed for the staff at Deschapelles. He conducted mass in the Catholic chapel, officiated at weddings and funerals, and filled his role for our five Catholic sisters. He daily gave solace and comfort to our staff and to our patients.

Twice a year Père Saget invited our nurse Louise Remy and Larry and me for Sunday lunch in Dodard. Somehow or other, Père Saget always produced ice. Ice meant cold rum cocktails, which even Nurse Remy could not resist.

Dinner was a wonderful French country meal, with wine from Alsace. Père Saget's table was set under a tree on the very edge of a high bluff overlooking the Artibonite River. Larry was always nervous the bluff might fall in, because of the river's continually gnawing into the bottom of the bank. One forgot for the moment that the river was brown with mud from the uplands of Central Haiti.

It was Père Saget who introduced us to Maître Delinois, who had fourteen schools high in the Cahos mountains. The faculties were made up of volunteer teachers. Every fifteen days, Maître made the trip on foot to each school, bringing books, paper, and encouragement. The schools were free and they were full. Gradually, the teachers asked for transport: first a horse or a mule, and, all too soon, a bicycle and then a motorcycle. The volunteer aspect ended and, one by one the schools closed.

Today, children from the same area are brought down to Petite Rivière to stay in a *pansyon* (dormitory) that has been chosen by the parents as living quarters for the school year. Parents take turns supervising the care and feeding of the children.

Maître Delinois also had a very small *azil*, and he accepted Floyd, a disturbed but fairly docile candidate. Our patients began to swell the numbers, so soon, with a Mennonite volunteer, two dormitories of six rooms each were built. With help, Maître fed and cared for these destitute people. Today, the *azil* is full, plus a school for very young children keeps him busy.

Maître is a coffee, honey, peanut butter, and cotton merchant, and we buy all of these for the hospital and weaving shop. He also makes us coffins for the poor and we always have one or two in our depot for anyone unclaimed. Each week, for materials, he sends a two-wheeled cart and horse to Deschapelles to pick up pieces of carton and wood from the crates that brought in hospital supplies.

Maître had one of the four marching bands, and now his is the only one still intact. Every year this band comes on foot from Petite Rivière to Deschapelles to celebrate the HAS-WLM birthdays.

One day, we found he had made a carousel for the children from an old truck differential. It was strong enough for Larry and me to take a ride.

There was the time when a twice-daily, post-operative, hot bath was prescribed for him. He became our guest for six weeks, since our house was the only place that had hot water. His love and consideration for all with whom he came in contact endeared him to us.

He is my age and talks about dying. He wants to be buried beside Larry. I told him that was my place. Everyone knows that should I die somewhere other than Haiti, my ashes must be returned to that place in the cemetery in Deschapelles.

Lately, I have seen less of our good friend because the road between Deschapelles and Petite Rivière is often impassable, and the barge on the swollen Artibonite River is often broken down. Even so, cotton and coffee still make their way back and forth, and our friendship remains stronger than ever.

A long-planned trip to Medor and Perodin finally began. Maître was on foot, Père Saget and Larry had good horses, and I rode a mule. It was a long, uphill trip to the top of the Cahos mountains. At the halfway point, Père Saget produced ice-cold rum cocktails before the picnic lunch. The last half of the trip, though steeper, seemed to go much faster.

Our trip coincided with the dedication of the church, a huge building, completely built by volunteer labor with Père LeRoi as the self appointed engineer. It was made of rock with a tall steeple, and a bell tower with a bell that began ringing early and steadily that Sunday morning. Medor is in a basin surrounded by tall hills. As the bell began to toll, the surrounding hillsides filled with men, women, and children, all in white, starched clothes, running down the winding mountain trails. They formed long lines to the doors of the new church and filed into the building. There were benches, but many carried their own chairs from home.

Larry and I were seated with the priests and Maître Delinois on the raised front platform, precluding any chance of an early departure. There were several sermons, and the *kreyòl* hymns surged out and echoed through the surrounding mountains. It was a happy and festive end to our trip. Later in the day, as we departed, many of our new friends were along the trail down the mountain, standing on rocks to be able to kiss those on horseback goodbye.

In the history of the farm at Drouin, we once rode to Savanne Roche with Marcellus Brutus, our first agronomist. What a nice day it was. It began early: up at five, off at six, and at the farm at Drouin by seven sharp. After coffee with *Madanm* Brutus, Marcellus, his daughter Jeannette, Larry, and I started off. We were all very well mounted, and no stirrups broke the entire day. My horse was known as *"Mal Elèv"* (Bad Student) and kicked anything that came up close behind him. We left the farm and followed the river to a point about six miles away where there was a crossing of the Artibonite. All along the trail we passed, or were passed by, people on their way to the market at Savanne Roche. It is amazing how many people knew us or how many we had seen before at markets in Verrettes, Liancourt, Desarmes, and Deschapelles. One man came running up to us and said he was a painter at the hospital and that it was our paint on his shoes. And it was, too. It was the green paint of our pharmacy.

At the crossing there was a huge *boumba,* large enough for ten people. Water was only belly-high on the horses so we did not need the boat. Men took off their pants and shoes and women hiked up their dresses and, placing all their market goods on their heads, walked across on foot. Once across, we were in Savanne Roche. Savanne Roche, or Rocky Plain, is well named; every inch of land is covered by rocks. The town is scattered out for over a mile from the river bed, and as we rode up the trail and neared the square, we heard the voices and chatter of the market. We left our horses under palm leaf shade at the *Biwo Chèf Seksyon* (Office of the Section Chief) *Madanm* Philip. Everybody then got us chairs and we sat, as the people looked at us, fascinated. We talked and answered questions, and decided to go to church next door as the *Chèf Seksyon* had not yet arrived from Petite Rivière.

We were the first ones inside the church. There was one long bench and altar rails at either side of the altar. The altar was a wooden piece with four candlesticks, of which two had candles. The church walls were whitewashed and the floor was of random uneven stone paving. It was dark and smooth from the bare feet of hundreds of Sundays past.

The sacristan entered and told us the service would begin at nine. Marcellus, with great delight, brought out his watch and said it was nine-twenty. With a great flurry the bell was rung in the churchyard and the people began to pour in. Their clothes had been unfolded only a few hours earlier and lifted out of the Haitian tin trunk found in every Haitian household. As each man entered, he advanced to the altar rail, crossed himself, and placed his hat on a shelf behind the altar. People sat on chairs they had brought or they leaned against the *kampèch* posts that held up the church structure. The posts were long and heavy, hand hewn manchèt. Some were easily twenty feet long.

I was seated on the bench. Jeanette and I moved farther and farther apart as more of the arriving people sat between us. Happily my end of the bench was next to the wall and I had a soft seat that bridged the gap. I saw an old lady enter, smile, and draw up a stone to sit on. I squeezed harder to port and beckoned to her to sit beside me. During the service, whether it was the sermon, the prayer, or the hymn, she would hiss at someone who entered. The new person would immediately and dutifully come over and be introduced to me as *"tifi mwen"* (my daughter), and believe me, she had plenty of them.

The sermon was about the loaves and fishes, and was read in *kreyòl*. Afterwards, the minister asked if they wanted an explanation and the answer was yes, so the whole story was repeated in the minister's own words in *kreyòl*. There was plenty of time to look and to watch as I knew none of the *kreyòl* prayers or hymns, and there were no books. At the beginning of the service I saw a tarantula enter and be killed on the floor in front of me. Before the end, the vestige of the cadaver had been carried away by ants. One girl sitting on the rail of the altar had a five-cent piece braided in her hair. I thought she would take it out for the collection but no collection was made. All women who entered had come to the altar and handed the sacristan a pink card which was returned to them at the end of the service. It could have been that they gave money to the church three times a year at harvest time. We walked out of the church to find the marketplace a sea of activity. Every inch of the space was filled with people or things to sell. Nothing too unusual: the routine *kochon* (pork), *sik* (sugar), *pen* (bread), *konkonm* (cucumber), *militon* (squash), *pitimi* (millet), *mayi* (corn), *pwa kongo* (pigeon peas), *pwa blan* (white beans), *pwa rouj* (red beans), *tabak* (tabacco), and *zepis* (spices). There was the usual red, white, and blue tablecloth material, as well as the cotton dress goods. There were live chickens for sale, and dried fish of two varieties: guppy-sized, and fairly large goldfish-sized. These fish are caught in the marshes or canals, dried in the sun, and salted and sold by the *mamit* (tin can, canful).

We went back to meet the *Chèf Seksyon* who finally had arrived from Petite Rivière. We again took up chairs under the palm leaf shade and met all the local officials with their official *makak* sticks.

Madanm Philip had a shop and a large whitewashed house. We entered the house and sat down. Three chairs painted bright yellow were enchanting. They were like old, French wicker chairs and were comfortable.

We left for a few moments to visit a boy of eighteen who had been sick for the past week. He lay on the floor on a mat, in real pain with pleural pneumonia and probably TB. He coughed constantly and had been spitting blood. A rope hung from the ceiling over his mat so he could pull himself up.

Larry offered to drive him to the hospital if they could carry him on a litter to Drouin. The boy was in real pain and might have gone, but his family would not let him.

We returned to *Madanm* Philip's house to wash our hands. With due formality we were given water, soap, and a towel. We were first offered alcohol in a bottle full of herbs, which we refused. I was anxious for more than water to wash my hands. I took *Madanm* Philip aside and asked for the "water." When she registered no interest, I ran the whole gamut of words. For future reference the word is *"latrin."* I was taken out into the *lakou* behind, saw immediately the obvious building, and took off towards it. I was stopped and told abruptly to wait while a boy ran into the next yard and came back carrying the door. I entered the *latrin* and the same boy propped the door up for me. Soon he came running back, tilted the door open, turned away, and handed me a copy of *Le Reflet,* the popular Haitian weekly. I left the edifice carrying the door with me to be returned to the neighbor. I knew that the *konbit* was a highly-cooperative enterprise, but when neighbors can devise an amicable system of using the same door, it is concord at its highest and something to be emulated.

Madanm Philip's house had more than the usual niceties. There was a lovely old tin trunk covered with designs made by using nail heads. There was a French "whatnot" in the corner. There was the usual waist-high mahogany cabinet with shelves and glass doors above. This seemed to be the vital piece of furniture with which to begin one's married life and every household had one. That morning before we left, the grandson of Marcellus opened their cabinet and took out a piece of cellophane and a small rubber ball. He looked through the cellophane and returned both to the shelf. I could see bread and some figs in the case, too.

We decided to ride down to the river's edge to eat our lunch. There was a great delay in my horse being brought to me, and I discovered that they had been pouring water on the saddle because my horse had been standing in the sun. My hair was greyer than usual due to a dusty ride, but they heaped indignity on me by bringing out a chair to help me mount my horse. I refused it, and got up with such forced agility that I almost landed on the other side. We sat on a nice log and divided lunch for three five ways when Jeanette and a local politician arrived unexpectedly. Afterwards I produced a small box of twenty Chiclets. They handled them like peanuts and I watched them chew and swallow them four and five at a time right before my eyes. It was a lovely day and we arrived home at about four. We chose our own methods of relaxation. Mine was the bed and Larry's was the flute.

Our head pediatrician Dr. Skeets Marshall, Miss Pete, Larry and I went to visit Caroline Bradshaw in Port-du-Paix. Hot and tired after the long drive, we were all sitting in a guest bedroom, well into gin and tonics, when Caroline knocked and said dinner was ready. We had just enough time to shove our guilty pleasures under the bed. When Larry and I returned two years later, Caroline handed us the half empty bottle of gin and said, "I've kept this for you." This time we had ice in our drinks.

We went to Caroline Bradshaw's another time when Minister of Health Dr. Boulos asked us to take a trip to La Tortue. It was not until halfway there that Dr. Boulos told us President Duvalier wanted Larry to take on the management of the hospital on Tortue Island. He explained that Dr. Duvalier thought Larry could do it easily without interfering with his responsibilities in Deschapelles. The heavy seas and currents of sunrise necessitated a 2:00 a.m. departure to the island in an aging government *chaloup*.

We had slept briefly at Caroline Bradshaw's, and were given a sustaining breakfast that had to last us for twenty-four hours. But at the dock in Port-de-Paix, we were told the sea was too wild and we could not leave. The next morning we did depart after another of Caroline's wonderful breakfasts. We were no sooner offshore than the motor died. The crew, with lighted matches, tried to solve the problem. We and the gasoline motor survived the investigation, but we were careful to arrange for a local sailboat to return us to the mainland before the government *chaloup* reappeared.

On the mainland side of the island we saw a large iron ring imbedded in rock by the shore. Buccaneers would tie their masts down to the ring and hide, lying in wait for merchant boats en route from Europe to Jérémie or Port-au-Prince.

As the sun rose, we arrived at the top of the cliff where the hospital stood. The La Tortue hospital had been built and run by Swiss psychiatrists who were now preparing to leave Haiti. The hospital had several patients and a community agricultural program underway. It had good buildings, water, and a future for someone, but it was not a project for us.

Fort Liberté, in an isolated northeast corner of Haiti, had a privately-owned sisal factory with several stone houses similar to our fruit company houses, a swimming pool, and a small hospital. When we were there in the early years, there had been a manager, employment for many, a plane, and a landing field.

The sisal factory had machines that combed the green flesh off the sisal leaves, leaving white veins of strong fiber to be used for rope. The green waste was left to rot until someone thought of using it for sheep feed, since it was rich in chlorophyll. The sheep were indeed fat and healthy but their wool was a bright green. I never heard what the market was like for green wool.

The sisal factory became obsolete when Dupont synthetic rope was introduced. All was left behind. The hospital is in the process of being revitalized and a community health program is being established, but there are many holdups. The road today is a challenge.

At the western point of Haiti's long northern peninsula is Môle St. Nicolas. It is at the end of a long and dry road. When we went there, the town was almost nonexistent. There were a few shacks, but no goats, no pigs. We did see an abandoned three-story colonial building, probably a French seminary in past days. Through the open shutters of a top-story window, a man peered down at us. He never came any closer.

There were two French cannons, a powder house, and an enormous French cemetery. It had monuments with stone lambs lying on carved pillows. It had marble angels. Each grave was enclosed by an intricately-forged iron fence.

The white sand beach was long and wide, with not one footprint on it. The multi-strand French cable ran from the rocky north side and disappeared into the deep water.

Larry and I jumped into the sea with respectable but scanty suits. We had picked up a missionary couple along the way, and the wife appeared from behind some rocks in a long-sleeved, long-skirted costume plus a rubber bathing hat. Her husband sat on the beach, ready and watching should she need help.

In the past two years, this desolate spot has become an open port of small boat traffic. Charcoal, sugar, beans, and rice are brought to Môle St. Nicolas for distribution inland to St. Michel and other spots. With its extremely low population and the steady boat traffic, this community has today the highest incidence of HIV-positivity in Haiti. What a sad thing for this beautiful spot.

We once went to La Gonâve on what was called the Gospel Cruiser. The sea was rough and the wind blew hard, but with everyone's prayers we arrived safely. Indeed, there was a scarcity of water and a lack of human fellowship among the small mission group. We had the foresight not to have brought gin, but Skeets Marshall and I felt the need to smoke frequently. It was hard, however, to find a suitable hidden spot. In the middle of the night, Skeets felt an all-consuming desire for a cigarette and started to creep out of the house. Her other companions in the bedroom thought she had risen to pray. With the kneeling and the praying her desire for a cigarette was lost!

Since my first days in Haiti, Sister Joan in Port-au-Prince had been a good and strong friend. She had arrived in the country a couple of years before we did, and like us, she never lost hope for Haiti. She was loved and appreciated by all the blind, deaf, and handicapped children she cared for.

At St. Vincent's school, Sister Joan accepted all handicapped children and provided them with living quarters and education. These children were trained to learn productive skills in spite of their disabilities. The children could receive help from the brace and limb clinic, where many of the deaf children were trained to work. It was at St. Vincent's that my boys from Deschapelles cared for, dressed, and loved the handicapped children, bringing them back and forth from their *pansyon.*

In one year, we sent five blind children from our clinic to St. Vincent's. This was before we knew of the importance of vitamin A in a child's diet. All five of these boys led useful lives, became financially independent, and raised families. Today, one is the director and first violinist of the Port-au-Prince Symphony.

When Sister Joan came to Deschapelles with orthopaedic patients, I always made sure that she had drinking water for her return to Port-au-Prince. The containers of choice were Gordon's gin bottles, which I always kept because of their flat sides. Returning to her convent and placing the empty bottles on the dining room table needed some explanation!

Sister Joan and I used to visit two monkeys down in a courtyard by the sea at Carrefour. Although miserable and moth-eaten, they were a joy to watch. Finally, she took them up to Fermathe where it was cooler and they were somewhat happier.

The Frédérique family got its start in Deschapelles when Esh and Freddy met and married. Their three children were born in Deschapelles and continued to be close to me after Esh died. Later, I would go to Port-au-Prince knowing I could stay with her oldest daughter, Lise, and share in many nice days and evenings.

At lunch one Sunday at the restaurant, Kilometre 1,300, United States Ambassador Adams came over to speak to me. At his table were his wife and three snappy guys with black suspenders. I told Lise and her new husband Gary how happy it made me to see men wearing suspenders again. Not at all, Gary informed me. They were secret service men with sidearms.

Once, in town for a funeral, I was persuaded by my friend Larry Peabody to stay over and come for dinner that night. The guests were Ambassador and Mrs. Adams and Lise and Gary. I was tired and hoped the Ambassador would leave early. I kept waiting. All of a sudden it dawned on me that the dinner was being given for me and I should get up first.

A few months later I had dinner at the embassy and reminded Ambassador Adams of the time I kept everyone up late. He told me to be careful, it was up to me again that night, too.

The Ambassador was anxious to come to HAS. Twice it was arranged. The first time, he canceled. The second time, I did, because of anti-American sentiment.

Administrator Sandra Wadley and I went to a reception at the Embassy Residence. I went mainly because I had canceled the Ambassador's trip to Deschapelles. We drove up the long drive in a pouring rain and were stopped. There was too much traffic and too much rain. An aide told us to park, and said that a taxi would come soon. Indeed a car did come, the door opened, and in we jumped. It was the private car of the self-appointed wel-comer of all who came to Haiti, the colorful character of the Haitian press, Aubelin Jolicoeur! On the ride up the driveway, Jolicoeur said he had a pic-ture of me and Dr. Mellon in his wallet. I asked him if I could have it and he gave it to me. I sent it back to him the next day.

I entered the Embassy as Ambassador and Mrs. Adams stood at the doorway greeting everyone, with Jolicoeur swinging his cane beside me.

Mrs. Adams was a lovely hostess who cooked all the reception food herself. She passed me egg rolls. I chose two. She removed them from my plate and carefully chose two others.

Once, eating dinner in a restaurant in Port-au-Prince with our friend Issa, he said, "That waiter eats cat." He said he could tell by the waiter's eyes. When we doubted him, he said he could prove it. He called the waiter over to the table and asked, "When you roast *mimi* (cat), what do you put in your sauce?" Without hesitation, the waiter went into full culinary detail about what spices and herbs were needed. Issa was accurate. That same evening, we had discussions with three more waiters and each suggested something to add to the sauce. I began to wonder just what had been on my plate!

After the French rule ended, Haiti was not put on the back burner of the international world. Instead, Haiti played host to eminent visitors, including the Pope and Haile Selassie.

Big excitement! Haile Selassie, the "Lion of Judah," was coming to Haiti in his own plane with an entourage which included two lions. Port-au-Prince arranged a gala dinner and accomodations suitable for a guest accustomed to a palace. A new long red carpet was rolled out for the Emperor's airport arrival. He was received by the President in the palace, and, to everyone's surprise, returned immediately to the plane and took off. No one ever knew why.

The long red carpet was used for the short visit of the Pope when he spoke at the airport. It might well be the same one used at the wedding of Jean-Claude Duvalier and Michelle.

Our days in Haiti were always filled with unexpected and unplanned events which taught us a great deal about the country and people with whom we lived, endearing them to us.

Larry always picked up people on the road if they were traveling in his direction. A few cases backfired.

Once, on our way home from Port-au-Prince, we stopped for a man walking along the road. He got in, sat between us, and it became obvious that he was disturbed. The Saint Marc hospital would not accept him. Neither could HAS, so we had to drive all the way back to town. The only thing he got out of it was a long ride, a bath, and a couple of good meals before we let him off at Pont Bedet, the only place that accepted disturbed people. It had two large dormitories, one for men and one for women. They were released on alternate days and free to walk in the village. Food was prepared in the huge, cast iron, sugar-boiling caldrons, but few eating utensils were in evidence. A few years later there was a psychiatrist in residence and sedative drugs were introduced with some success.

Another time we stopped for a naked crazy woman on the road. Larry gave her his blue underpants, and I my blouse. She wanted to get out at Pont Sondé. When we opened the door, she was off, quickly throwing his blue underpants and my blouse to the ground.

We came across a man sleeping half off and half on the main road. We tried to awaken him, and discovered he was heavily drunk and unreasonable. Not daring to leave him to again choose his spot of rest, we put him between us and drove to Montrouis. There we presented him to Delegue André who made us wait while he put on his full uniform. He then told us to take him and the passenger to the police station in Saint Marc which was on the way to Deschapelles. The police put the man in a corner for the night, and we left with a clear conscience to continue on our way home. But it was not to be. We had to return Delegue André to his post in Montrouis some twenty miles behind us before finally heading back to the hospital.

Another disturbed friend was a frequent visitor to Deschapelles. She wore ankle irons connected by a very short chain. She shuffled with short quick steps all the way from Verrettes, asking for nothing, just making new friends. This might seem a cruel type of control, but the woman was free to come and go, and pregnancy was avoided.

Because Joseph Bernard had to leave for his temporary post in Africa, he asked Larry to take his place as *parenn* in the marriage of a couple who had worked in Community Development. It seemed a simple duty to perform, but complications quickly arose. The wedding was to be in Port-au-Prince, not in nearby Verrettes. The bride had to be driven in one car, and the groom in another, all the way to the city. The wedding ceremony was long and there was a longer reception afterwards. Larry asked if he could please provide the couple with a hotel room for that night, so all of us could avoid a long dark drive back to Deschapelles. There was no way. The couple insisted on returning that evening to the home they had prepared.

We started back at nightfall with the couple in the back of the jeep. Driving across the Artibonite plain, we came upon a badly injured horse lying in the road. Larry stopped, took off his dark suit to avoid staining it, and prepared to give the coup de grace with his Swiss knife. I moved the car ahead to spare the newlyweds a gruesome scene. Suddenly a truck came down the road. At that moment Larry was not a bit happy to be caught in the headlights in his blue underpants.

A husky driver leaned out of the truck and offered help. From the glove compartment, the driver pulled out a big revolver. Holding it in trembling hands, he aimed at the horse. Finally he admitted, *"Manke kouraj."* (I lack courage). He got back in the truck and drove off. Larry's Swiss knife did a neat and merciful job.

The couple returned to their house, which had been well prepared for them. The pajamas and the front porch awaited their arrival.

Toupuissant was a great and supportive friend. When sent for he would come running across the fields, pulling on his official uniform and his straw hat with its gold emblem. Every *Chèf Seksyon* in our district rode into Verrettes on the first Saturday of each month. They rode good horses and had good saddles, and many of them had telescopes. Their uniforms were blue and starched, and the government insignia glistened on their hats. They provided law and justice in their areas, expected and received respect, and, for the most part, deserved it.

When I broke my knee and was in a cast, Toupuissant came all dressed up to call. Saying he had decided at last which woman to marry, he asked if I would *"kondwi"* him to the wedding. I thought it meant to drive him in my car. I said that I could not with my leg in a cast, but that I would ask Doc to drive him and I would go along.

The day came and Larry went in to get him. Toupuissant asked where was his *marenn?* *"Kondwi"* had meant he wanted me to be his *marenn* and to be the witness to his wedding. Well, I hobbled into the house to get him and the four of us were off to church. I sat between the couple and held his gloves, his hat, and his wife's pocketbook.

It all had some unexpected complications. The Catholic priest thought Toupuissant must be a church member if I was a *marenn*, and did not find out until well after the ceremony that being a *chèf seksyon* did not preclude his also being a *bòkò*. The wedding was a happy one and I was proud to be part of it. Since then two of their many children have been employed in the hospital lab.

During the construction of the Tapion Dam, a friend of long standing, Acelom Congo, came each day to work with us, or he sent one of his many adult children. By hard work he had become an extensive land owner, and with three hearths and households that I know off, had fathered many children. Each year he would appear at our house leading a horse laden with a *rejim* of *bannann* and another of *fig,* and help hang them up in the garage.

He came to the hospital for surgery that was complicated and threatening, but was successful. When he returned later, our physicians refused to operate a second time. He was too old and it was too emotional a procedure. It involved a colostomy, which he found hard to understand. Then we heard he had gone to Bon Fin near Aux Cayes for the same surgery we had refused him, and had returned to Payen. Luquece, Anny, and I went to see him. I had sent word that we would come, and he had prepared for us by setting chairs in the shade. He was thin but well. However, he was alone. He had only a yellow cat and two scrawny chickens. There was none of the usual *diri* or *pitimi* drying on the large *glasi* (concrete slab).

Small children were at the gate, but none would enter. His dignity was intact but he seemed to have neither worldly goods nor family around. He said he slept badly, and when I produced a pillow from the boutique he was delighted. I was carrying Larry's Malacca cane, and I am sure he had never been as surprised as when I twisted and pulled out the concealed épée. He talked about his recent surgery and said the earlier surgery at HAS had been a veritable gift from Dr. and Mrs. Mellon. Bon Fin had asked for money up front. A lot of money. I was curious to know how they compared with our fees. His son had handled it, but he knew that his *bèf* (cattle), *chwal* (horse), *kabann* (bed), and *latè* (land) had to be sold before he was able to have enough money for the surgery. At Bon Fin there is no bed or board. It is necessary to rent a local room and to buy your own food. Care at HAS is indeed a gift.

He spoke of his many children, all with courtyards of their own, explaining that most went to the States and returned with things to sell. I told him I wore my new birthday hat in honor of our visit. Eyeing it carefully, he said it suited me. The visit ended by his saying that when Doc and I would no longer be there to help everyone, we would still be there as others had learned from us. He took us to the gate and admired my red car. He stood waving goodbye.

On the drive there and back we passed no vehicles, but we did stop at two ditches cut across the narrow road. Since the rains had come they were full of irrigation water on its way to lower fields. Strong men with *wou* and rocks were happy to help us over. Along the whole length of this road there was not a single concrete block house. All were of rock and mud. The roofs were thatched. On a road less than a half-mile below, were concrete houses with tin roofs. There, irrigation was available and one could be a successful rice farmer. If the pipeline from Coquille to Payen is re-established as is hoped, this community on higher ground, too, will profit from irrigation.

Recently I stopped to see Acelom at his son's house on the main road. He was well taken care of, lying on a mat with clean sheets. He was glad to see me and was cherishing the yellow pillow.

I went to Liancourt one day, to buy a case of beer. Handing the owner, Propheta, three fifty-*goud* notes, I took the beer and left the boutique. When I was halfway home, a motorcycle overtook my car. The rider said Propheta wanted to see me. I said I'd just come from there but he insisted I return. Propheta took me aside and showed me that what I had given her was not three fifty's, but two fifty's and a five-hundred. It was an error of ninety Haitian dollars, which she handed me. She had known Doc and me for years, and knew well that my eyesight had betrayed me. It's not often that friendship and money are good partners, even in Haiti.

Mr. Paul was a very important *bòkò* from Port-au-Prince. He used to call on us every New Year's morning at daybreak. Dressed in a black suit, he would thank us and tell us what we meant to Haiti. He was an important figure in the palace in the time of Duvalier, but he never mentioned politics. He did tell us how very busy he was kept by palace demands. He had good gardens in Deschapelles, and he sold me one of his sub-irrigated rice gardens which I gave to Ti Blanc. Mr. Paul was a dear friend and I am sad that New Year's Day now begins without his visit.

There has long been a Chinese Embassy in Haiti, but it has never been too active. At Mauger, an area under irrigation, they created a project growing high-yield rice and garden vegetables with success. We went down to introduce ourselves and to see what they were doing. They had a group of Taiwanese using hand tools and pulling hand plows. The four Haitian *agwonòm* that they had taken to China for training had returned to Mauger and were working side by side with the Chinese. They grew beautiful vegetables, but unfortunately their high-yield rice could not fit into local mills, so distribution of this crop was limited. We congratulated them all and they gave us vegetables as we left.

The following Sunday, the Chinese group unexpectedly arrived our house at noon. We invited them for lunch but they then stayed for the rest of the day. They spoke minimal English, no French, and no *kreyòl*, but smiled and giggled constantly. The came back the next Sunday with their tennis rackets. We sent them up to play and excused ourselves. The third Sunday we left early in the morning and came back after dark. They were terribly lonely I am sure, being all men in a truly isolated spot.

Larry did not like Carnival in Port-au-Prince or Saint Marc. He said he would take us to La Chapelle for the Carnival parade and *fèt*. Katie Strauss, very pregnant, happily came with us. At ten in the morning no one in La Chapelle had begun to think of a parade, so we went down to eat our picnic and swim in the creek below the town. Eating peanut butter sandwiches and sitting in fast running water, we were happy. We did notice two women upstream scrubbing something big and turning it over and over. When they got up to leave, we saw that each had the clean head of a *vach* (cow), complete with horns, perched on her head.

We often received unwanted and useless gifts from the States. Once, at the height of political unrest, we received big boxes of toy guns, complete with leather belts and bullets. They were very realistic and could have easily been mistaken for the real thing. Nowhere on the cartons were they referred to as toys. What to do with them? We put them in our jeep and drove to Amani beach. We hired a man with a *boumba,* went out over the "Big Hole," opened the boxes, and threw them in. The toys were in airtight plastic bags and they floated. Larry had to rip each bag open and throw the gun, belt, and bullets into the water. The owner of the *boumba* was rightfully nervous, but we finished and were left with the cartons and the empty plastic bags. We were worried when the owner of the beach came down the hill and insisted on helping us carry the boxes and bags back to the jeep. When we got back to HAS we stuffed the cardboard and plastic into the incinerator.

Later, Sister Joan told us she received the same gift for St. Vincent's in Port-au-Prince. She was smarter than we and turned them over directly to the police.

Soccer has always been a big game in Haiti. It was especially fun in the early days when no big betting was involved. We were asked to make shirts and provide shoes for the local teams, since up to then they had been playing barefoot. At the end of the season we were asked to give a cup to the winning team. Larry said he would think about it. We had been given twelve busts of Albert Schweitzer for our hospital. All were terrible and not one of them looked like him. The first year, we carried one of these big, heavy burdens to the middle of the soccer field and presented it to the winning team. They were surprised since they had been expecting a silver cup. This became an annual event, and at the end of twelve years, twelve winning teams had trophies and we were rid of all our busts of our good friend Albert Schweitzer. We had many better things to remember him by!

The telephone service arrived miraculously in the small town of Verrettes. It consisted of a tiny house with an operator in the back room and a wall telephone in the front room. Everyone was fascinated but usage was slight as it was a facility they had never before encountered. However, they soon learned its value and convenience.

One day, our Italian physician wanted to talk to Europe and needed my help. A half-a-day later she was talking to her mother in Milan, but the call was only halfway successful. She could not hear her mother talking to her.

The telephone service did not last for long. All too soon the line was cut, repaired, cut again, and left that way. Later, it was discovered that Liancourt, wanting to be the town with the phone, had cut the line that connected Verrettes to the service.

One Sunday, during especially hard economic times, my longtime friend Freyel came all dressed up to call on me. Over the years, he was the one who came daily with his wheelbarrow and one or two dogs to pick up our trash and garbage. This day he had one of his sons with him. As we sat down together on our bench in the garage, they said they'd come to thank me for the steady work Freyel had had over the years. It had enabled him to send all of his children to school. This boy, the last and youngest, had just completed his secondary education.

Dr. Duvalier had great respect for Larry and for HAS. He never abused his referral rights as a physician and sent us only two very legitimate cases. He never questioned our government contracts with their highly-desirable tax exemptions for hospital supplies.

When Jean-Claude Duvalier took over as President For Life, we had reason to be worried. Once, the Minister of Agriculture, Gus Menager, told us that Michelle Duvalier wanted to come out to visit HAS. Larry said that he would prefer to leave things as they were.

Jean-Claude was an avid bird hunter. Our farm at Drouin had plenty of wild guineas and wild doves which gave him good reason to go there. Even though, when en route to Drouin, Jean-Claude passed the Carrefour Alexandre entrance to Deschapelles, he never entered. One wonders if his father had told him to leave us alone.

When Dr. Duvalier was still President he sent word that he wished to see Larry. This required a white suit and tie and a fast trip to town. We had Larry driven in by a chauffeur. Should Larry not come out of the Palace, the chauffeur was to return immediately to inform us. At the steps, Larry was stopped and told that even though the President sent for him on a Saturday, he should come back on Monday. Three bad, nervous days were spent speculating as to why he was called in. Larry returned to Deschapelles Monday afternoon with the decoration *L'Ordre National Honneur et Mérite au Grade de Chevalier* pinned on the lapel of his white linen suit.

CHAPTER 13

Cherish What We Have, Value It For The Future

L arry was lucky. Since his broken shoulder forty-five years ago, he
had been well and strong until his last illness which lasted more
than two years. During this time we would take trips to Miami for his X-ray
therapy and to visit Dr. Harrington.

No matter how unexpected our arrival, Dr. Harrington was always ready
to see us. His huge conference room, with a bathroom, kitchenette, Larry's
bed, table, chairs and a sofa, was there waiting for us. We also had rooms in
a motel across the street for our family and a nurse. Larry's older sister
Rachel, Mike, Jenny, and Ian came, individually, several times. The big room
became a corner of the world that belonged to us all.

The trips to Miami were always for a sad reason we tried to push into
the background. The trip would begin in the middle of the night with Larry
saying we must leave early the next morning. Our passports and my suitcase
were always ready with dollars in hand. In Port-au-Prince, no matter how
crowded the plane, American Airlines always found us space.

In spite of Larry's treatments, we did manage to find some joy on these
trips. It was a treat to have one of the children drive us in a rented car to La

Boussala restaurant in Miami, or to Bay Shore for Nicaraguan music and chili beans. These were gay evenings.

One evening in Bay Shore, on our way to the Nicaraguan restaurant, Larry wanted to buy sneakers. Anny was wise in the way of sneakers and advised him, and they both were so pleased. The next day he sent Anny back to get a pair for herself exactly like his.

Fresh from winter quarters in Sarasota, the Barnum and Bailey circus arrived in Miami. We wanted to go, and we decided the matinee would be less crowded. It must have been a holiday or a Saturday. The moment we stepped out of the car we were swept up faster and faster in the middle of a whirlpool of children and balloons. Nothing could stop the stampede. We were in the middle of it and were carried up to the top of the quivering bleachers. Standing we were okay, but seated we were at the mercy of the spun sugar at head level behind us. The circus was wonderful, and for a few hours we were fifty years younger.

Mr. Fairchild, our friend from Maui, had duplicated his Hawaiian garden in Miami. We often spent a happy hour or two on the small rail car that circled the garden. It was a peaceful and beautiful time, removed from the tests and treatments of the hospital.

We planned to visit Larry's brother Matthew who lived near Fairchild Garden. He was over ninety and ill but was waiting for us, beautifully dressed and welcoming. Jenny and I sat on one side of the room and listened to Matthew and Larry talk and laugh and tell old stories. All of a sudden Matthew said, "Do you ever see Larimer?" Larry said, "Matthew, I am Larimer!" We all laughed, but no one laughed harder than the two brothers.

On one of Rachel's visits to Miami she said she and Frédérique would do the laundry. The ride to the motel's top floor was Frédérique's first trip in an elevator. For both, it was their first encounter with a laundromat. Realizing they needed quarters, they went down again to the drug store. With the quarters in place and the machines going, they watched, their heads rotating in rhythm with the clothes and soap suds. The sequence was repeated with more quarters until all the clothes had gone through the dryer. They sat in chairs, looking at each other and smiling, unable to speak or understand one word of each other's language. It was a newly-learned accomplishment, but one that neither would be apt to use again.

When I decided to do something about my hip, the doctor in New Haven asked me exactly why I wished to undertake this major surgery. I said it was because I couldn't see. He asked me how that could be. I replied that I had tears in my eyes with every step I took.

I did have the operation, was upright in hours, and was almost immediately transferred to a hospital bed in Jenny's home at 183 Bishop Street. Larry's treatment was transferred to New Haven so we could be together. Settled in their library, I was in the geometric center of Jenny and Ron's daily life. I had television at my fingertips, and crutches and canes with which to try out my newly found freedom. Larry was upstairs in one bedroom, and his nurse, Rani Toltin, in another. She drove him to his daily X-ray therapy, which meant one less car for the household. Mike, Ian, and LeGrand all came to see us during the time we spent there. We were wined and dined, me mostly in my bed. But I did lots of exercises and eventually was up and mobile. In a remarkably short time, I was able to return to Haiti with Larry, who was frantic for us to be on our way.

Ian came to New Haven in a rented car with driver to take us to Kennedy Airport. LeGrand was on hand to meet the car with two wheelchairs. Larry had canes, I had crutches and canes, and we both had our usual large allotment of baggage consisting of all necessities, but few clothes. The drive to Kennedy was difficult as it involved much sitting. LeGrand left us at the plane door and Larry's nurse and Ian flew with us. By the time we arrived in Port-au-Prince I was close to tears as it was the longest period I had spent in a sitting position since my surgery. As Ian later remarked, we were met at the Port-au-Prince airport by seven people in various vehicles, and we needed every one.

The drive out was rough and muddy and I am sure it was the hardest trip I ever made. Larry and I were so glad to be home that it was well worth the torturous traveling. On our front door, Frédérique had fashioned *"Bienvenue"* in wire.

The first letter we received was from Jenny, who despite the weeks of demands we made on her and her household, was able to write, "We miss the fun couple."

One day, after the hip surgery, I noticed a stainless steel paperweight on our administrator's desk. Surgically wiser than before, I asked him to store his paperweight in the OR. It was a long and heavy hip pin, just like the one that has me walking well once again.

On our last trip to Miami, Dr. Harrington had synchronized Larry's therapy treatment with the University of Miami's graduation. Larry, always reluctant to receive any recognition, could not bring himself to refuse Dr. Harrington's wish for him to accept an honorary degree from the University of Miami. The many honors given over the years to Larry have been accepted with almost a feeling of guilt. He reasons that there are many who, if they were financially able, would do the same thing. He was only doing with modesty and deep abnegation what he wanted most to do in life: Give service of self to others. There is no doubt that the honor Larry valued most highly was Dr. Schweitzer's referring to him as "*mon fils adoptif*", or "my adopted son".

At the outdoor graduation, Larry was brought in his wheelchair to the back of an elevated stage where the President of the University and guests of honor were to be seated. The campus was beautiful with its big trees and flowers, and vast lawns. The graduation was for the entire University; the Schools of Medicine, Law, Dentistry, Nursing, Agriculture, Horticulture, and Arts and Sciences. It was a veritable sea of caps and gowns. The anthem was played and the ceremony began. When Larry's citation was read, he stepped forward and the whole audience, students and parents, spontaneously stood up and applauded. Larry left soon afterwards to return to the hospital. When I asked him what he thought when everyone stood and clapped, he said he had not noticed it! But what he did notice was the young Haitian who came up and thanked him just as he was getting into the car.

Larry, during his illness, had good and loving care. In Haiti, Frédérique and Luquece were always available but unseen. Later he had nurses. Sometimes they were the hospital staff, but more often they were people Ian had found for us. They were young and fun and played music, and they became our close friends.

At the head of each dining table is a sliding piece of wood that can be pulled out to serve as a tray. This was just right for Larry's plate as he sat low in his wheelchair.

When Larry was so sick, each of the children came to Haiti and took an eight-hour shift to sit with Larry and read to him. Larry really loved that. Mike read works from Larry's favorite poets: Robert Service and Rudyard Kipling.

Larry enjoyed his CD player, but most of all he loved his well-used and well-cared-for records. Right up to his last days, he enjoyed his turntable and tapes. When he could no longer play an instrument, he made oboe reeds. If they crowed like roosters they were successful. He sat on the sofa with the French horn he loved by his side.

When Larry was ill at home, he once placed his false tooth inaccurately. It was Thursday, and luckily Dr. LaRose, our dentist, was in his office. He came to the house and was able to remove it. He said, "I will take it to the garage and adjust it." Larry was so weak and I was too shocked to object. Soon he came back. Not knowing what he and Bòs André had done, we found the tooth had been aligned and adjusted to perfection.

Larry never complained of pain, and accepted his limitations philosophically. He kept his mind busy and positive. He had tremendous will, and up to the last day he lived, he insisted on walking to the bathroom.

On my seventy-eighth birthday, Larry cut the cake. Forty pieces for forty guests. He was dressed for the last time and in his wheelchair. He had no present for me and it worried him. Reading the magazine section of the *New York Times*, I saw a full-page picture of a red Alfa Romeo convertible. I tore it out, folded it up and said, "Give this to me for my birthday." He asked if I had ordered it and I explained it was only the picture I wished. Some time later, he said, "Don't worry, I'll be there to meet you in that little red car," and added, "No problem about clothes as we'll both be wearing feathers."

Larry wanted me to leave him to go to the August 2nd HAS Alumni Reunion in Burlington and read his speech. I said I did not wish to go. Later he asked me, "Is your suitcase packed?" I said it was not, and that I was not leaving. "*Bondye bon*" ("God is good"), he said.

The reunion was crowded with people expecting to see Larry. It was a stunning blow to hear of Larry's death as the meeting opened. Ian read Larry's speech. Then Ian described Larry sitting behind him teaching him how to tie his shoelaces, a lesson he had never needed until he graduated from boots to shoes on leaving Arizona.

Jenny and Susannah and Dr. Harrington were all in Deschapelles when Larry left. Dr. Harrington stayed the whole last week of Larry's life and saw to his peace and comfort through his last days. He stayed until Larry was covered with the land he loved so well. After Larry died, Dr. Harrington continued to come and see me, and to look for prospective Haitian doctors to serve a year's residency with him in Miami.

To lose my friend and companion, and to lose the daily love and support that we had for each other, would have been a death's knell had Larry not foreseen it. He had called Bill Dunn in to dictate a letter to be read to me. It asked if I would accept Larry's place as President of the Grant Foundation. Without hesitation, I agreed.

Among Larry's last words were, "Gwennie, I leave with no regret." These are words not many can honestly say. When he left my side, it was with serenity and peace.

The coffin had already been arranged for. Earlier, Dr. Mellon and I had gone to Petite Rivière and ordered cardboard coffins made by our good friend Maître Delinois. Larry died in the early evening. Early the following morning the pickup truck came to the front door. Larry, in his coffin, was placed in the back. Jenny and I buried him with his simple comforts: his glasses, his small round magnifying glass, the Parker pen his mother gave him in his shirt pocket, his bedroom slippers with holes and string to tie them, his blue underpants, his blue socks, and his handkerchief. I think we put his old Swiss knife into his pants pocket at the last minute.

The truck was driven around the whole compound, and as it passed the front of the hospital, the entire staff, with the men dressed in white shirts, black ties, andblack pants, stood quietly on the hospital steps. The pickup rounded the hospital and the coffin was carried by chosen employees to the grave site in the small hospital cemetery. Larry was buried almost before the community had realized he had died. It was just as he had wished.

The ceremony was simple but full of silent grief. We all said goodbye to our good and great friend, and walked back to the house. There was a young tree at the head of the gravesite. A gardener stood beside it to protect it during the service. At that time, the tree was just his height; now it must be sixteen feet tall. For two months, the cemetery had a guard twenty-four hours a day. It was feared that people would steal his "power." Luquece made the iron grill cemetery fence, though Larry probably would have liked the goats and cows to be near him.

After August 2nd I went right to work, shedding no tears except personal and quiet ones, and started the job Larry had given me to do. It was on this day that I decided to give up my nightly gin and tonic, and it continues to be a part of my past life.

Jenny and Susannah stayed and helped me in the sad aftermath without Larry. Our grandson Andrew was here and he was proud to be given many of Larry's clothes. Larry's good friends all got something. Larry had given me a list indicating where all his instruments were to go. The octagonal squeezebox to Bill Dunn, the oboe and French horn to the Pittsburgh Symphony. His cello went to Jeff, Jenny's son.

Jenny and Susannah helped me arrange my physical life so I could face living alone. My bedroom is lonely, but it is still the most beautiful room I have ever seen.

It was hard for me to pass by Larry's library, so Jenny, Susannah, and I made it into a warm and liveable guest room. Some good friends would still rather not sleep there. Anny Frédérique is one of the brave ones who can face the nostalgia. She was with me when Larry died. She was close to me in the house, but we each respected and valued independence and privacy. Sometimes I sit on the wall in the cemetery. It is a beautiful spot with shady trees, quiet and peaceful. One day, a woman riding her horse along the canal, stopped and said, *"Madanm, pa chita la. Mouche ou, pa pale ak ou. Pa rete la. Leve kò ou, tanpri. Nou pa vle ou genyen chagren."* ("Madame, don't sit there. Your dear one will not talk to you. Don't stay there. Get up please. We don't want you to be sad.")

Most words of comfort from my Haitian friends are unspoken but they are always evident. The local people have real concern for me, for which I am grateful. They have seen me over many years working with Larry, and they understand the loss in my life.

There is little one can do for a loved one after a death. I was so lucky to be asked by Larry to take on his responsibilities. It was a miracle that gave me the strength to face life without him. May I be given the time, the patience, and the wisdom to do it well.

I had to learn to stand alone. In some ways it is a lonely job; one's judgment must not be swayed by close friendships. Ian's advice and support were important in helping me to fill the new position Larry asked me to take. He gave me a gift of an "I am the Boss" badge that I always carry in my basket, but have never needed to bring it out.

Despite the fact that I stated I would not leave Haiti for a year after Larry's death, a toothache altered my decision. When leaving Port-au-Prince, during the two-hour required wait at the airport, I met the shoeshine man Larry had always welcomed. The man had tears in his eyes when he saw me alone.

Once, after a board meeting, Bill Simpson, Mr. Vestal, Bill Dunn, Larry, and I were on the plane to New York. The stewardess asked us why we were all together having such a fine time. We explained briefly about the hospital. She returned later and handed the Secretary, Mr. Vestal, a check for one hundred dollars.

Now, as I entered the plane alone, the stewardess cried, the steward cried, and I cried. They were all good friends and on so many trips had seen that Larry and I were both carefully and well taken care of. This trip, the same lovely stewardess handed me a check for five hundred dollars for the hospital.

By the middle of August I was back at work at the hospital. I was asked if I wanted to choose a spot as my own; nothing seemed comfortable. It soon solved itself. With no electricity from six a.m. until one p.m., there were few places where there was adequate light. The best place in the hospital is today mine. I have a table and extra chairs in the center courtyard under a beautiful almond tree. To be sure, the noises of the surgery ward bathroom are over my shoulder, but I am busy and can ignore it. For security reasons, all staff enter and leave by the front door of the hospital. Therefore, most of the staff passes before my table. This passing group is a barometer of the staff's morale. It would not be easy to walk by with a guilty conscience.

Opposite me in the courtyard are the four pediatricians at clinic tables with their patients. Mothers and children wait their turn nearby. The addition of an open-air, tiled bathroom with low faucets enables the mothers to take care of, and bathe their children. Another big, beautiful, spreading almond tree baffles the noises from the other side. A pool with running water lends a peaceful tone to the intensely busy clinic day.

At Larry's memorial service a year later, many friends came from around Port-au-Prince: the Episcopal bishop, Catholic priest, ambassadors, many alumni, and, of course, all our local friends who missed the funeral that had taken place so quickly. Acelom Congo, our valued and good friend of the Tapion Dam project, gave his great speech in *kreyòl* and ended with a heart-touching dance. The horseyard was crowded, and people sat on all the available benches and chairs. There were speeches and prayers, and in the middle of Gérald Augustin's eulogy the skies opened up and it poured. In spite of the rain, not one person stood up and ran for shelter. All sat as if the sun was shining, such was their respect for Dr. Mellon. I said goodbye to each person as they left at the gate, each one wringing wet, and happy that I was staying in Haiti.

Feeling fairly secure about the morale of the hospital, I decided to take my granddaughter Wendy, newly graduated from medical school, on a trip to Hong Kong and Bangkok. I wanted to see what changes had taken place in the last sixty-five years. The changes were enormous, but the beauty of the two cities survived the changes.

I saw Gene and Florence Szutu in San Francisco, and Tai and Sylvia Kong showed us all of Hong Kong.

In Bangkok we had a letter to the Queen Mother and were treated royally. The Queen Mother's equerry and his wife took us out for the day. High in the mountains, they kept talking about the monkeys we would soon see. The car was stopped and the equerry gave me a few bananas. In the distance was a troop of angry little spider monkeys making obscene gestures and advancing toward us. Not wishing to appear nervous, I offered a banana to the equerry and his wife, which they took reluctantly. It seems the bananas were for me and Wendy to distribute to the band of monkeys.

We had a dinner party with the Queen's family. It was a lovely evening, but on leaving we realized we were the only two who spent the evening with shoes on. All the others had left theirs in a neat line at the entry.

After a week spent enjoying the luxuries of the Mandarin Hotel, when checking out I was told my credit card was refused. I was shocked and called Bill Simpson in Pittsburgh. His office at Mellon Bank did not answer so I called him at home. Bill said, "I am afraid, Gwennie, I can't help you." After what seemed a long pause, he said, "It is Sunday and 4:00 a.m." We were able to use Wendy's credit card and were on our way to Thailand.

My return to Hong Kong with Wendy convinced me how quickly and how completely things can change. It gave me a good perspective on changes that were taking place in Deschapelles, and made somewhat easier the adjustments I had to face on my return.

When it first opened, the hospital presented a unique service previously unknown to the local people. Medical care was given, marveled at, and deeply appreciated. It was also valued as a personal gift. The inclusion of Public Health and Community Development broadened the importance of the hospital. Now, with the community into its third generation, the interpretation of the gift seems to be in a process of change. A feeling of ownership of the hospital has grown among the local community and staff. This reflects pride and personal responsibility. It also opens up an area of criticism of the administration in Deschapelles and Pittsburgh.

We began taking social residents from the University in Port-au-Prince in medicine, pediatrics, and surgery for their year of service after graduation. The first three came at a time when the medical school had been fraught with dissension. These students were vocal and articulate. Clandestinely, they organized the entire local staff. An important meeting held in the open courtyard was broken up by three Demosthenes-like doctors abruptly stopping the administrator's address and openly criticizing the Grant Foundation and the Board. All the nurses seated together in crisp, white uniforms clapped at the appropriate moments. The situation was electric.

They were asked what they wanted. They replied that they would let us know. It took some time for them to produce the report but HAS continued its daily work, often without the help of the three who were busy drafting a response. Some of their demands were reasonable, others were left to be arbitrated. A lot of time and energy was put into the solution, and when they left at the end of the year of residency they were good friends, both of mine and the hospital. Whenever encountered afterwards, it was obvious that they wished to forget the part they had played in this stormy era.

Hard on the heels of this came the confrontation with the business office. With special consideration for the difficult economic stresses within the country, we budgeted and planned raises for all employees. Each department head helped in deciding the ration and distribution of each raise. The results when presented were found satisfactory, but never with any expressed gratitude.

The business office called Bill Dunn and me to a meeting with its seven accountants and one department head. Two of the accountants were spokesmen but the department head did not speak. We were told that the raise was most inadequate, and instead of the percentage we had granted they demanded a fifty per cent raise. When we said it was not possible and that we had already taken their needs into special consideration, we left. The office members continued to sit at their desks but did no work. We tried to bargain but to no avail. We tried to speak with individuals but they refused, saying they were *aji nan blòk* (acting as one).

This impasse took place just days before the annual *boni* (end of the year bonus) was due, and a week before the Christmas and New Year's salary, payments which are extremely important to every employee. We knew we could not hold up the payments and decided to fill each employee's envelope ourselves. These envelopes were essential as they contained not only the amount of their monthly salary, but also noted the deduction if they had a debt. When we asked for the envelopes, the paymaster refused to open the safe. The only alternative was to agree to the fifty per cent raise. The *boni* was paid and the December payroll was met on time.

On January first, the day the new raises were to go into effect, the two business department spokesmen were called into the office of Ward III. Bill and I sat with them. These two had been highly vocal, extremely arbitrary, and verging on rudeness at every meeting we had with them.

It was up to me to speak out. I told them the fifty per cent raise had been granted, but because of this increase the budget was unable to meet their office salaries. Consequently, the business office must be reduced by two staff members. I looked right at them and said they were the two we could best do without.

It was the only alternative, but created two strong anti-hospital individuals. One left for the US. The other was made *Judge du Paix* in Verrettes and we often have to rely on him for legal papers and decisions.

The business office struggled to operate with two fewer employees, but the staff was inadequate for the demands put on them. The financial report was sometimes three months behind. We discussed the idea of bringing an accountant from Pittsburgh to help them establish a new system of bookkeeping. The business office staff came to us again and asked not to have someone brought in, saying they liked and trusted each other and worked together well. We listened, and the office manager said he wished to place each employee on a higher echelon with a compensatory raise and hire and train one person who would begin at the bottom. As of today this works well. The financial reports are late, but the delay is caused by two other departments who have yet to submit their reports. Last month, for the first time, the report was submitted on time.

The impasses with the doctors and the business office have ended with positive results. Strong words were spoken, but there was give and take. It took time, patience, and always diplomacy. Through it all, the real leader and catalyst was our administrator, Bill Dunn. Day and night he worked on a solution, and it was due to his tact and foresight that HAS stands stronger and more united than ever before.

The result was the autonomy of department heads and their responsibility to allocate the budget, decide the raises, and define their needs and programs.

Bill and I worked together closely and supported one another during these events. When we had similar problems with the Community Council, we relied heavily on our hospital counselors' wisdom and experience. It all took time and patience.

These incidents were heartbreaking but this documentation should give an idea of what we faced, and we may well be glad that Larry was not present for these confrontations.

One of the hardest decisions that had to be made was for me to agree to the importance of Bill and Irene Dunn leaving Deschapelles and heading up

At my desk in the courtyard.

an office in Sarasota, where Bill would be Executive Vice-President of the Grant Foundation. Their presence in Deschapelles is greatly missed, especially by me, but their value serving the hospital from Sarasota has doubled their importance. Both Bill and Irene have a twenty-four-hour a day responsibility. They are the veritable lifeline between the States and Deschapelles.

I can be found at my desk each morning. The Medical Director Dr. Michel Jean-Baptiste comes daily and tells me of what has passed in the evening and early morning hours. My administrator stops on his many trips through the courtyard. Yvon, head of security, Bòs André, head of maintenance, and all four pediatricians on their way to and from their ward rounds pass before my table. Each month there is always a new face, or two, as short-term doctors come and go.

My presence on the wards and clinics each day gives a boost to morale, for the staff as well as for patients. In recent years my influence has been indirect. A strong administrative team meets every Friday morning and all are free to advise when attention is needed or change is warranted in any aspect of the hospital. Members of the administration are available to me at any time.

Jan Flanagan and I used to sit under the almond tree discussing residences for our new staff. Until her work called her elsewhere, she was my ever-ready companion helping to choose suitable and acceptable housing for the residents. This is truly a challenge and I miss Jan's participation very much.

I have a great interest in the housing we offer. One of my greatest pleasures is to turn a small, square, concrete-block house into an interior of warmth and charm. There are plenty of things to help me. To enlarge a room, I can have a wall broken out and the scars mended and painted within a few hours. The wood shop can supply pieces copied from my own furniture. The weaving shop makes rugs and material for woven pillows and swing covers. White water paint is always available and makes a dingy house immediately look fresh and clean. The empty paint buckets are made into scrapbaskets by removing the handles, painting them flat black, and having De Louis decorate them. TB treatment-related drugs INH and PAS arrived in round tin containers which were saved for me and made into lamps. The electric parts had to be bought in the States, and even though the cans were free, the fixtures and shades for the lamps represented a sizeable investment. Because there were no alternatives to be found locally, this was a welcome substitute. When in New York, I always buy material from Far Eastern Fabrics and Phoenix Pan-American with our houses in mind. Gifts of printed sheets often make good curtains. A shipment of army sheets proved extremely useful. By sewing off the two vertical blue woven stripes, each sheet can be made into white curtains for two windows.

Luquece has learned to copy iron furniture of good design. Sponge rubber can be bought in Port-au-Prince and cut to size. I cover them with my chosen fabrics, removable and washable. Paintings, carved wood, and iron works are available for the white walls.

Thank-you letters take up a lot of my time. I wrote to four hundred donors during a recent two month period. I enjoy it as I know so many of them, and I am truly grateful for their support. The stories of a troubled Haiti have not seemed to lessen people's interest in HAS. In fact, it seems stronger.

When Larry was still active but not driving, he rarely went to the hospital. He would periodically go to the business office to sign checks and purchase orders, and he went only to important meetings.

Once, there was a schism in the hospital. Larry told his physicians he wished to meet with them in the library. The entire medical staff was waiting. We entered through the morgue door and sat in silence for what seemed a long time. Finally Larry said, "This is no way to run a good hospital." Then we got up and left. There were no longer any differences.

Some time after Larry's death, it fell on me to face a similar situation in the hospital. Long hours and frequent patient deaths take their toll in stress on the doctors. There had been too many complaints of a physician being impolite to patients and children's parents. I called a meeting of all medical staff and addressed them thus: "Today, I call you to meet me in the library as we face a serious problem that can be solved if you recognize it and work together. I remind you of a prior meeting five years ago that Dr. Mellon had called relating to a similar issue. I ask that you be sure that the help you give to each other is not only with wisdom and knowledge but also with love and concern.

"The reason the hospital was built is the ethic *Reverence for Life*. It is this foundation that makes it strong. As you pass in and out of the hospital, help each other not to forget the words carved in stone at the entrance."

Dr. Roger Jean-Charles leads a group of doctors, nurses and other local professionals who are volunteers staffing a clinic serving the Haitian community in Boston. This help by Haitians for Haitians is of great importance to new arrivals in the States. *kreyòl*-speaking patients face an enormous hurdle when meeting with English-speaking physicians. Good histories and good medical care can be obtained only when bonded with a like language and its unique expressions and explanations of their ills. *Konbit* Clinic aptly fills this role. The doctors and nurses rotate and cover duty seven days a week plus evenings. Quietly at home, enjoying my serene life in Deschapelles, I received via Bill Dunn an invitation from the *Konbit* Clinic. They wanted me to come there and receive an award they wished to give to

Dr. Mellon and me for what we had done in their country. I did not hesitate to accept this offer even though it meant two days of traveling for a two day stay in Boston, a hard schedule in view of the Deschapelles to Pont Sondé road in late May.

The *Konbit* Clinic event was beautiful, with twenty-four red roses on the long table and some twenty-five round tables with ten guests apiece. There was a Haitian flag at the entry, and we were welcomed by beautiful children of the doctors and nurses. They wore sashes with Haiti's strong national colors, and all the doctors wore beautiful, wide-striped ties. The room was filled with about two hundred and fifty Haitian friends, most of them volunteers at *Konbit* Clinic. Boston is known to have a hardworking group of Haitians. All seemed professionally successful and glad to be American citizens, but all, as always, spoke of returning to Haiti. No person wishes to lose his identity as a Haitian.

I was introduced by our first Haitian surgical resident at Deschapelles with a lovely speech which I include later. I had spent a great deal of thought on my speech, and luckily had it firmly in mind because as I stood up with notes and eyeglasses in hand, there was no light! I gave it without forgetting a thing: *Konbit* Clinic - what a wonderful name. It means working together. As I left the Artibonite Valley, the rains had come and I passed friends and neighbors on the way to their gardens, each with a *wou* over their shoulder. They more than any know the meaning of *konbit.*

"When I told my staff yesterday where and why I was going, they were proud that it was for an award for Dr. Mellon and myself. I told them that it was equally a tribute to all of them who had stood beside us over the years while others came and went. The future of HAS is in their hands.

"I was asked to tell you how it happened that Dr. Mellon and I built a hospital in Haiti. It is a simple story. We read an article about Dr. Albert Schweitzer, who started a medical mission in Africa, and his reason for doing so, choosing the area of greatest need and his ethic *Reverence for Life* that motivated it. His answer to our asking for advice on following a similar path was realistic, pointing out the disappointments and pitfalls we would face, but he did not discourage us. From that moment on, life changed for us. Correspondence with Dr. Schweitzer continued until his death eighteen years later. We now had a mentor and we had a goal. We knew what we wanted to do, but we did not as yet know where. We had traveled in South America, Central America, Mexico, and Africa but none seemed right. It was after a summer spent camping throughout Haiti that we decided that Haiti would be our choice.

"We were fortunate that property was available halfway between the two main cities and midway between the ocean and the border. Your government granted us the use of this property for as long as we ran the hospital. The next step was plans for the construction and the laying of the cornerstone. Dr. Mellon, in his cornerstone speech, spoke of his hopes.

"First, that it would meet the medical needs of our local friends and help them to lead a better life.

"Second, that it should be a center of learning, not just teaching. From the moment we came to Haiti, we learned the value of hard work, the importance of loyalty, and the need of politeness and sensitivity.

"At this point I implore you not to let your children forget this heritage that is so easily forgotten in this busy life. It is the strength and the charm of Haiti. The third point Dr. Mellon made was that the hospital would ultimately be in the hands of those of Haitian nationality.

"The last and most important hope was never to forget that no matter how well-equipped and how well-staffed the hospital might be, that if the help that is given does not have love and concern, the hospital is but an empty shell.

"Carved in stone at the entrance of the hospital are three simple words, *Reverence for Life,* which means respect for all living things. They were planned to be there when the hospital was but a blueprint.

"My hope and prayer is that all help given at HAS in Haiti is help given with love and concern.

"To see you before me, new and good friends, gives me strength and enthusiasm. While you are here and I back there, *ou fè'm kenbe dwat. Ou fè'm kenbe fò. M'genyen bezwen ou. M'ap rèmesi ou.* (You keep me righteous. You make me stand strong. I need you. I am thanking you.)"

At six the next morning, Bill, Irene, Jenny Miller, and I were off to the airport after a full and happy four days. My only regret was that Larry had not known this group of friends and felt their gratitude.

Less than a month later I was back in the States for hip surgery. Once again, Jenny and Ron made a post-op nest in the heart of their home for me, complete with hospital bed and elevated toilet seat, not to mention Ron's architect's lamp at my bedside. Jenny's garden was lovely, but it did not take the place of my nostalgia for my own.

Jenny and Ron left on a sailing trip. Gene McGovern, and then my sister Cornelia, came to help me. Neither Cornelia nor I knew what buttons to push for the washer and dryer, the butane stove, the microwave, the coffee maker, or the garbage disposal. Ian arrived, took two hungry octogenarians out for a meal and taught us the button sequence of all the mechanical household aids.

Both Mike and Ian came for the day. I made them laugh. I said I had altitude sickness. I had conquered the stairs to the second floor. It was great to have both my boys together marveling at my dramatic progress.

HAS alumni Roger Williams and Julian Strauss found two army vehicles from WWII that were older than HAS. We bought them reconditioned with extra parts. They were painted white over the camouflage paint and were ready to be shipped to Haiti. It is rumored that the sands of the Sinai can still be found in the trucks.

These two heavy trucks help meet our transportation needs. Our hauling equipment suffers from exhaustion due to overuse and bad roads.

Strict regulations controlling export of US military equipment delayed the trucks' arrival in Haiti. We had to get involved with the Pentagon, and it began to seem almost impossible. Shipping papers were finally secured via the Mennonite Central Committee. It was ironic that the pacifist Mennonites broke this deadlock and even stored the army vehicles for over two years in the open, in front of their main headquarters.

The two trucks finally arrived in Port-au-Prince and were released from customs. Our head mechanic, pessimistic about their future, had planned to make them mobile, immediately sell them in Port-au-Prince, and replace them with one new vehicle for the hospital. What a surprise when he turned on an ignition and a truck came to life. Our whole attitude changed. When the first truck arrived in Deschapelles, our administrator picked me up and we drove around the hospital grounds. I was filled with nostalgia for our Dodge Power Wagon and our first summer in Haiti. Recently, when repairing one of the truck's tires, an Arab coin dropped out.

The bicycle man is due again. His trip was postponed by the embargo when he was unable to bring his supplies. His first trip was a wild success. He repaired bicycles and made special seats on the backs for children. He made trailers for the bikes. They were two-wheeled strong carts, easily pulled, with frames to carry oxygen and butane tanks. He made a one-wheel litter that needed only two people to roll it down a mountain. This could take the place of a relay of eight people carrying a patient on a door. He started a shop in Borel and turned it over to one of our local friends. During the gasoline shortage, the roads were filled with bicycles comparable to the early morning traffic around the Zuider Zee.

The poor state of our X-ray department was the result of a long period of neglect by the department head and hospital supervision. The darkroom, by its nature, could hide a lot of neglect, and the department's staff members were not anxious to look under the duckboards surrounding the developing tanks. The files were bulging out of their racks, and not having been transferred to the X-ray file depot, they held much more than the allotted three years of records.

That depot of two rooms was an even bigger disaster. A leaking water pipe had created piles of damp and sticky envelopes and X-rays. It took seven workers over four days to restore order. Now the depot consists of one room with files limited to two years of X-ray procedures.

The Boutique was given the extra room and it is basking in a renaissance with space to display paintings and furniture to advantage. The front door is painted black with bright yellow trim. On either side of the door on the outside wall there are murals of banana plants.

Since the closing of the dining room, we have Christmas dinner on my lawn at noon on the twenty-fourth of December. Lunch is served in two relays because medical services in the hospital must always be covered. The first year, the hospital kitchen staff cooked the dinner, but they were so tired they were unable to sit down with us. Since then, Luquece and his wife Micheline have cooked the dinner and served it with help from foreign staff.

It becomes the gala affair that it is because of my daughter-in-law Lucy's effort to see that the thirty tables are covered with festive cloths, plates, and cups as we give lunch to the staff of four hundred under the ficus tree. It gives me the opportunity to thank each member personally.

Gifts are handled strangely in Haiti. They are always given or received carefully wrapped up. They are opened only in privacy and one seldom hears if they give pleasure or not.

Each year, every staff member receives the same gift, and no one ever knows what it is beforehand. It is never an easy decision. My Christmas gifts are never wrapped. Instead, they are laid out so people can have a choice of color. One year the gifts were fanny-packs in different colors with "Hôpital Albert Schweitzer" printed on them. Another year, we ordered baseball caps in assorted colors, also with "HAS" on them. It became evident in December that although the order was paid for, the process of filling the order had never begun. Luckily a good friend worked forty-eight hours and filled the order, and a doctor arrived on December 23rd carrying two duffel bags filled with the caps. What a disappointment it might have been for the staff who eventually found themselves on my lawn having Christmas lunch under their 385 hats! Yet another year, everyone received a bath towel in their choice of one of twelve colors. One recent gift was a double-sided mirror on a metal stand.

Dr. Menager told me that as he was driving some of his staff home after the Christmas party, he heard one of them say, "If I could, I would give Mme. Mellon a year of my life."

I was appointed to take Larry's place at the laying of the cornerstone for the new addition to Carnegie Mellon University. We had a family dinner where Big Pa's achievements were spoken of. During the courses, I asked to speak. I began, "'Big Pa' had a dream and it became a reality. His youngest son had a dream and it too became a reality. Almost all of you here tonight have the same genes. You too may have a dream and you too can make it a reality.

"I was lucky enough to be a part in the realization of 'Big Pa's' youngest son's dream. I wish Larry's father had been able to live to see that Larry's vision had an impact greater than Gulf Oil, Mellon Bank, or a ranch. He and Larry's mother would be so proud of their cowboy son who became a strong leader and influenced in a profound way the lives of so many."

These stories have run easily from my black felt pen, but now I find this last era is hard to recount. There have been so many problems, so many responsibilities, and so very much sadness. Suffice it to say I will not give details. Most solutions have been obtained and disappointments filed away to be forgotten. I have never lost hope in Haiti, but for friends and neighbors I suffer deeply.

The military coup in 1991 which overthrew President Aristide brought many challenges to Haiti. Haitians had fewer opportunities. This caused an exodus of primarily the young and able from Haiti, and this exodus had a deep effect on life in the provinces. Many chose to make the perilous trip by boat, a difficult choice between starvation and disaster at sea. When a family member was chosen to leave, it usually meant that a piece of the family heritage had to be sold. A broken family was left behind awaiting news of a safe arrival, eventual success, and then hope that a place had been established for another family member. Those with no visas were returned, and there were many with visas and proper working papers who could not find employment abroad.

The lack of fuel had unseen implications. A ferry between Jérémie and Port-au-Prince was dangerously overloaded in an attempt to obviate a second trip. With no rafts or life preservers, the ferry foundered and sank in a heavy sea with a tremendous loss of life. Despite the wealth of protein in the sea, no one today will eat fish in this area.

Loads on vehicles doubled. The result was the breakdown of the vehicles and an increased danger of accidents. The bridges on each side of Deschapelles developed ominous cracks.

The people-drain affected all strata of Haitian life, from the elite who left on American Airlines, to the poorest of the poor who helped construct the boats that they hoped would take them to the Florida shore. In Deschapelles, we saw the drain not only on our employees but also on our friends in the community. Hospital personnel can be replaced, but broken homes are not easily repaired. It is a miracle that Haiti adjusted to the embargo's effect on the destruction of the stability and strength of the local home life.

The embargo challenged life in Deschapelles. The US State Department advised all American dependents to leave Haiti. The staff returned to Haiti as quickly as possible and picked up their work where they had left it.

Even though we had been left with a minimal expatriate staff, a strong nucleus remained. Especially touching was the outstanding support the Haitian staff gave the foreigners who remained. It was as if they held an umbrella over us. Without the leadership and the caring philosophy behind the work at Deschapelles, the hospital would be, as Larry had said, an empty shell. It was with the support and strength of our *konfrès* that stability was secured. Gasoline and many other items became impossible to get. The Sarasota office and the Agape mail service became our lifeline to securing essential supplies unavailable in Haiti. Shortly after the coup, I went to see Dr. Liautaud, a dermatologist in town. At the end of the consultation, he stood up, shook my hand and said, "Thank you, Mrs. Mellon, for staying."

Closing the hospital would have been a calamity, not only for those who needed medical care, but also for the 385 employees whose jobs would have been lost. Each had an extended family that was directly dependent on the salary paid on the first and fifteenth of each month. The huge market next to the hospital would have have dissolved, and so too would have the *taptap* traffic that transported its daily overload of passengers. My continued presence gave an assurance that we would not leave and thus gave strength to the community around us.

During those hard days, one felt a strong and unspoken support, not only from staff but also from the local community. At one point our oil tank came close to sludge level. Finally, humanitarian oil arrived. When the driver turned off the main road at Pont Sondé to go to Deschapelles, a crowd stopped him and asked where the oil was going. This was a scary question since everyone wanted oil. When they heard it was for the hospital all the crowd clapped. All along the road to Deschapelles the same question was asked with the same reaction. The driver was bewildered but we were reassured.

Peace and hope were for the most part by our side. There were periodic roadblocks but HAS vehicles were usually given special permission to pass. The blocks were piles of rocks, burning tires, or fallen trees across the road. They were formidable but, for the most part, just inconvenient and more a local statement of unfulfilled government promises than an expression of anger.

Though Port-au-Prince shuddered, Deschapelles remained calm. Our staff was intact and the hospital's daily work was effective. We were able to adjust to the embargo with its disciplines and limtations, and continued to give care to all those who came.

Those who return to Haiti, outwardly successful, are quickly devoured by relatives and they are soon anxious to return to their new homes. This new group created by the economic and political upheaval is referred to as the "diaspora." They return only to visit. There are many great success stories of arrivals making excellent professional contributions to their adopted country and many Haitians quickly earn respect for their honesty, courtesy, and willingness to work hard. Parents make a gallant effort to ensure that their children remember their beautiful Haitian heritage.

A lot will have to change in this country in order to produce a chance of basic human survival. The resiliency of the people is a strong element on which to begin.

The time will come when HAS will have no co-founder as leader, but preparations have been made to face the inevitable. The Long Range Planning Committee has worked out a design for the transition to new leadership and management of inpatient load, as well as an extension of health-related services into the community.

The Committee is a group of thoughtful and wise good friends headed by Dr. Jack Bryant. Over the course of several months, they worked in small groups with subcommittees, and a leader from each group was chosen to meet in Haiti to smoothly fit the pieces of this puzzle together.

I am happy indeed that this group understands well the roots and the philosophy that have been here since the beginning of HAS. This process can well be compared to Larry's decision to name me as President of the Grant Foundation just prior to his death. Both are efforts to assure that the continuity of the original precepts of the hospital will not be lost. This is done in the hope that we will avoid the calamity that occurred in Lambaréné at Dr. Schweitzer's death in 1965, when the leadership was suddenly no longer there. Only after several years of strife has the hospital at Lambaréné recovered, but only with the combined efforts of American, European, and Gabonese support.

Our focus is the solid integration of the hospital, the Community Health program, and its satellite dispensaries and workers. It should result in a chain which reaches from the hospital itself to the farthest corners of our district, and brings to the surface those who, up until now, have not yet taken advantage of what the hospital has to offer.

Recently my eyesight betrays me, a natural consequence of age. My peripheral vision is good and I do not miss much. I can write with good light and a heavy black pen, however I can no longer read a book. I have found a good substitute to fill the evening and the often lonely bedtime hours: books on tape. I am educating myself, and choose wisely what I read. The books are unabridged and fill a definite need in my life. Having become dependent on these tapes, my life was torn apart when, during the embargo, mail went undelivered for long periods of time.

With my visual world getting smaller, I am lucky to have had the time to train myself to live a life of order. Everything in the house has its rightful place. My biggest challenges are my ubiquitous basket, my six pairs of glasses, and Larry's cane, all of which are continually needed and none of which has a specific place. My good household support have trained themselves to watch where I leave things and are always quick to retrieve them for me.

Many friends have played an integral part in the warmth and success of our life in Deschapelles. The bond among the daily staff, loyal alumni, and the Grant Foundation board gives the hospital the strength that it has today. Our young friends of forty years ago have now become adults and responsible citizens.

How to explain the importance of Anny in my life! She was born in Deschapelles, the child of my dearest friend, Esh, and our ophthalmologist, Gérard Frédérique. I was present at her baptism. I saw how effective she made her refusal to go to school by throwing her shoes out of the car window in heavy traffic. Her love of animals and her early decision to be a vegetarian directs much of her life. She is a breath of fresh air, cooking and mixing strange combinations in the blender.

One of her first jobs in Haiti was to work in marine biology. She filled in as secretary at the hospital, and she now works at HAS in the areas of reforestation and agriculture. Her heart and her life will always be in Haiti.

313

As I have had the chance to get to know her husband, John Chew, I have grown to love him for his obvious care and concern for Anny. One evening, as I left them to go to bed, they were undecided as to whether they would go camping. When I went to eat breakfast at sunrise, the pup tent was pitched on the front lawn and John was sitting on the wall playing his clarinet. He has a free spirit equal to Anny's.

Anny grew up knowing Larry and me. Her presence when Larry died was of enormous importance to me.

My life has spanned the better part of the twentieth century. Attaining an age of better than fourscore is a privilege not granted to all. It has been a kaleidoscope not only of opportunities but also of love and warmth from those who have walked beside me.

I have many happy memories. So many involve the kindness and consideration of my children and their pride and interest in what Larry and I have been able to achieve. The children, all of them, come when they can, and would always be here if I needed help. One is always here to speak for me at the HAS and WLM birthday. Another big occasion is Christmas dinner. They rarely forget my birthday, or August 3rd, the date of Larry's death.

Once my three children were in college, they made their own decisions. They were seldom handicapped by financial limitations.

Haitian tradition values highly the involvement of family in any enterprise. The children and children's children give their impetus to the original works of the parents, by observing, learning, and following. Our family exhibited this tradition in our first summer, when Ian and Jenny joined the volunteer work team in building the HAS chicken house. During the opening days of the hospital they worked along with me at the front desk.

Ian came with three college friends, each carrying his own instrument. It meant the fulfillment of Larry's dream to play in a brass quartet under our ficus tree.

Billy returned from college in time to supervise the placing of his gift on the stone wall of the center courtyard. It was a bronze plaque engraved with Albert Schweitzer's quotations. Soon, Billy and LeGrand began to publish an annual hospital brochure. Later, they made two movies. The first was of Dr. Binder's medical mission in the Upper Amazon. The second movie, which is of untold value to us, is *A Beginning in Haiti.* Today we are able to see and to hear Larry tell us about his work. This also enables people who have never known him to get a sense of him as a person.

We joined Michael in Italy, and he showed us Rome. When he came to Haiti he worked side by side with Larry in the field. He was always ready to lift the heaviest rocks when making levels for the pipeline and he was the first to jack up the car and change the tire. It was fascinating to watch him play ball with his blind dog.

Lucy and Ian took on the whole family in Lebanon. It was a beautiful and memorable ten days, seeing the incredible ruins of Sidon, Tyre, and Petra. Lucy gave all the historical background in a lively and entertaining way.

Later, Ian took Larry and me to a ranch in Montana where I was able to ride once again, and this time in the snow. Larry waited for us in the log cabin and lit a wood fire to melt our frozen bones. Ian's day in Great Falls, Montana, was made when the bank president said he had never heard of the Mellon bank in Pittsburgh and refused to cash my check. Mr. Vestal, in Pittsburgh with a four-way phone hookup, gave the bank president a few words he will never forget. Typically, Larry sat reading in a waiting area. Ian could not stand it and left the scene of action.

Billy was Larry's only child. He was born of extremely young parents who were soon to be divorced. Larry was a devoted and dutiful parent, making frequent trips to visit his son in California. Some summers, Billy went to Beaumaris in Canada with the extended Mellon family and Larry joined them when possible. The entire Mellon family thought of education in terms of the East coast. After much discussion it was agreed that Billy should go to St. Paul's school in New Hampshire. He was now closer to us, with the extra bond of his cousins and Mike at the same school. From there, the next step to Princeton was inevitable. In 1955 he graduated, majoring in English Literature. He fullfilled his military obligation in the Air Force, and earned his wings and the agreement of a wonderful girl to marry him when he decided on a direction for his life.

After the Air Force, Billy travelled through Africa recording programs for NBC Radio. With Dr. Emory Ross, he had the chance to meet Dr. Schweitzer at the hospital in Lambaréné.

Billy had been writing a novel, and he came to live with us in Deschapelles to finish the book and then claim his bride. When the book was completed, Billy and LeGrand did get married and moved into a lovely home on Cape Cod. He continued his discipline of writing, but his early success as editor of the Princeton Review did not assure his entry into the wider world of literature. It seemed hard for Billy to find and fill a niche for his life. The marriage was soon troubled and a separation was decided on. Billy was offered a teaching position in Virginia. The night before his early morning departure, LeGrand and Billy had a sad farewell dinner with much drinking.

It was not alarming when morning came and the packed car and Billy were gone. Not until the school called asking why he had not arrived had there been need to worry. Billy was found in the car parked in a spot where he often went to watch the sun rise when he couldn't sleep. An autopsy showed a heavy ingestion of sleeping pills, but this was a time before the lethal combination of pills and alcohol had been recognized. Larry and I both strongly termed it an accident. Others did not agree. We all adored Billy and we grieved with Larry over his tragic death. It might well have been that Billy, like his father, would have found his dream late in life. It was a sad end to an unfinished life.

Larry asked to go alone to Cape Cod to Billy's funeral. That was hard for me because Billy was one of my devoted children. At the funeral, Billy's mother asked Larry to thank me for having been such a good mother to her son.

It was a difficult era for LeGrand as she considered her future. She was always assured of our strong support, and she valued this highly.

After Billy's death LeGrand continued to come to Haiti to put together the annual brochure. And she continued to play music with Larry, as she and Billy had done before.

Through the first thirty-five years, all the children were able to learn by working with Larry. It was a privilege granted to all too few, but to those who were exposed, it became pivotal in their lives.

Since Larry's death, all of the children have become more deeply involved. They feel a sense of responsibility for Larry's dream to continue strong and vibrant, even if it is surrounded by a world that is shuddering and reaching out for expression.

Mike comes, often with Martine and the four children, the youngest two of whom are named Glen and Grant in honor of my brother. Mike always expressed his devotion to Larry in a sensitive way, especially during Larry's last illness. Now Mike brings gifts that always give joy to the household, such as the ice cream maker, the bread machine, and the fountain that sings in the center courtyard of the house. Not the least of his contributions is the sharpening of my tools and replacing them in their designated spaces on the tool board above my work table.

LeGrand no longer comes alone with her guitar, but with her husband, Herb Sargent. Two or three times a year, they bring me frozen raspberries, honey-cured ham, comfort, and fun. LeGrand is a very dear friend and has entered personally and deeply into the workings of the hospital. Her job as archivist is demanding and time-consuming. She does it well. She provides her love and admiration, which I need and bask in. Herb not only contributes his honoraria to the hospital, but having finally been persuaded to come to Deschapelles, today leaves his clothes with us to guarantee his return.

All serve on the development committee, and Ian is now a member of the Board of Directors. Both Ian and Jenny have run successful fund-raising auctions of Haitian paintings.

Jenny is a story in herself. My beautiful and loving daughter is so generous of her love, her time, and her children. They make life, especially after Larry's death, full of plans and hope. Jenny was one of many who worked on compiling the written correspondence between Larry and Dr. Schweitzer. The search and translation demanded hours of time, but the result, *Brothers in Spirit,* has been published. Jenny also collected and printed an enchanting book, *The Spirit of HAS.* It contains vignettes of Larry's life by those who knew and worked with him. It is the basis of an orange-bound library of all available writing and information on Dr. Schweitzer, our hospital, and Larry's and my part in it. Jenny seems to have all the needed instincts to do things right. I am grateful to her also for encouraging me to write these stories, and it was she who sent me Jenny Miller equipped with a gift of a laptop computer. My daughter has also always been present for the awards and degrees that Larry and I received.

Jenny's friend Ron has given architectural advice on changes to HAS's clinic area in order to accommodate and plan for a faster flow of the many patients. Jenny and Ron took me on a beautiful barge trip on the Nivernais canal in France.

In addition to the children, Larry's two sisters, Rachel and Peggy, have come frequently, each time bringing with them one of their own children, and in later years their grandchildren. These trips allowed a second and third generation of Larry's family to appreciate and learn of Larry's vision and its importance.

The family's awareness spreads wider and stronger. Our grandchildren take part in HAS; Wendy as an M.D., Nicole as a nurse in Community Health, and her husband Ethan in Community Development. Jeff comes to work in Community Health when he has time off from medical school. Charlie, Rachel's husband, has also worked in Community Health. Susannah, a screenwriter, and Andrew, a photographer, recently picked up the responsibility of the brochure, which takes on added importance these days.

When most of my twelve grandchildren were beginning lives of their own, many had debts for medical education or special training of some kind. It was a time when they were not financially solvent and life held many choices and the need for freedom. Three times I was in a position to give each of them, at the beginning of the year, a gift that opened doors to undertake new challenges. It is Larry's planning and generosity that gave twelve young people and myself this pleasure.

One by one, these grandchildren are getting married. At each wedding when asked, my spoken advice to them as a couple is, "Cherish every moment you have together." They are choosing their own ways of life and have always shown real interest and support in what Larry and I have created. This group brings joy to my daily life.

Personally, Larry and I have never lost hope for Haiti. We commenced our dream and we began its expression standing alone but together. Our faith lies in the strength of the people that are the closest to us. Through all the vicissitudes of the past forty years, these people have maintained their honesty and their integrity, and have never lost their humor or their ability to enjoy life. Added to that is the security that our family stands steady and is willing and able to see that HAS continues to hold the ethic of Dr. Schweitzer's *Reverence for Life,* not only in future plans, but in daily work.

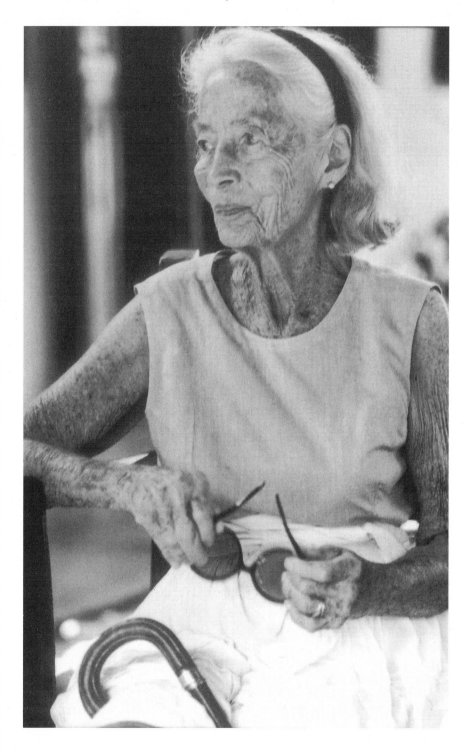

The involvement of our families, the loyalty of my staff, and the support of the alumni groups strengthen me in the work here in Deschapelles.

We also gain strength from a whole new group who wish to hear about Deschapelles and learn what it has meant to Haitians in this corner of Haiti, as well as to hear from those who have worked in Deschapelles. They hear from local and foreign staff, past and present, of the impact of days spent here, what it meant, and how it influenced their lives.

I truly believe that Larry's and my success with the hospital's firm foundation is due to our awareness of the rightful pride, dignity, and sensitivity of our hosts as we work with them in their own country. The future of the hospital rests on never losing sight of these three basic truths.

We have a roster of wonderful staff. All of them, in their own ways of making niches for themselves in their lives and work in Deschapelles, have left us gifts that we treasure. Many write to say how grateful they are for the time spent here and how it changed their focus on their future lives. It is a gift one gets in giving and a gift one gets in receiving.

Our challenge is to keep this spark of the founding ethic burning bright. We must keep close to alumni and friends who have taken part in the work here. We must find new friends to help us for the future of Haiti.

Many people asked Larry to put up a better "Hôpital Albert Schweitzer" sign at Carrefour Alexandre. His answer was, "No." He felt that even though the two-foot square sign was old and hardly visible, it was adequate. Today, even this vestige has disappeared but those who need help have no trouble finding the road to Deschapelles.

In the hearts and minds of local people, "Doc" is very much alive. Some hear him drive by in his Land Rover and half await his return to pick them up. For those ill-prepared for the departure of loved ones and for those about to embark on a new and unknown future above, there is no fear. There is a strong belief that "Doc" is preparing for their arrival and even that he is building another hospital.

These are lovely stories and would fit in well with Larry's telling me he would be waiting for me in the little red car.

Potpourri

CORNELIA WARD HALL

(A letter written on February 2nd, 1937, by my mother, Katherine Hall Grant, describing her mother, Cornelia Ward Hall.)

Although it is nearly fifteen years since she died, I still consider her, as I did then, one of the most attractive older women I have ever seen.

Her coloring, almost to the day of her death, was lovely, as were her expressive brown eyes. She knew above all how to dress suitably for her age and to grow old gracefully. She cared little for jewelry although she had many beautiful pieces, and she had the fine art of wearing them suitably and correctly.

Her laces, both black and white, were noted in a day when gentlewomen wore only those that were handmade. Also she took pleasure in fine furs, black velvet and rich brocades. She always dressed for dinner.

During her later years, she suffered much from rheumatism, chronic bronchitis, and heart trouble, but never did she utter a word of complaint.

Everything about her was the epitome of neatness. Nothing in her room was ever out of place. Her sewing was of the kind that now is almost a lost art. During my Father's lifetime I know she allowed no one but herself to do his mending. The maid, of course, attended to the others, but not for him.

Needlepoint was her delight, and she was never without a piece of work in her hands when she was not reading, and she kept up with world affairs and current doings to a remarkable extent.

One will never know of the kindnesses to her less fortunate relatives, or the extent of her charities and her personal interest in them. She would cut out garments by the hour to be given to the poor to make up, and for long years she was indefatigable as President of the Bethlehem Day Nursery.

Her disposition was the most unselfish I have ever known. She never raised her voice but somehow things were done.

She had a nice sense of humor. One of her sayings comes to mind. "What is obstinacy in others, my dear, is firmness in myself."

During her later years she would rise about five o'clock and attend to her business affairs (which were quite a burden after her husband's death) before breakfast. She was meticulous about paying all her bills the first of the month, and later on, when her income had decreased, it troubled her greatly if it could not always be done. She never cared for an automobile and her smart brougham and pair were among the last seen in New York.

A fine appreciation for all things beautiful in music and art was hers, and in travelling, her interest never flagged in visiting churches, galleries, and museums.

A proud woman, a true aristocrat, always thoughtful and considerate of those less fortunate, but her friends were only those whom she considered worthy.

She was really a shy woman. Society did not appeal to her, but she was most hospitable in her own home, and before I left home the house was full of young people coming and going.

Fortunate were her children that they can look back on a home with a mother like that at its head, a gracious home beautifully appointed and apparently managed without effort.

My most cherished memory is that she always called me "her sunshine."

(Signed) Katherine Hall Grant, oldest daughter and third child of John Hudson Hall and Cornelia Ward Hall.

I must add that she never married until she was thirty three years old. My Father had long wished to marry her, but until the death of her own father, Augustus Henry Ward, she who was his inseparable companion, would not leave him. She used to play backgammon with him nightly, and she told me more than once of her pleasure once when she opened the board and found a beautiful watch inside. That watch was lost in the San Francisco fire many years later, and the blue enameled watch with pink flowers on it was made to order by my Father to replace it.

K.H.G.

GLEN GRANT

(Excerpt from a letter from my brother, Glen Grant to Larry and me.)

Everyone tells Jane and myself that we look very well and healthy which we are most happy to hear. Our main problem is lack of energy which for a Grant is catastrophic. We both miss Deschapelles and you both more than I can ever convey to you. You gave us two of the happiest years of our lives. Keep up the good work. You are two very rare people.

Affec.

Glen

WLM BROUGHT FROM HIS OTHER LIFE:

The stone mask and the wooden box from Dr. Schweitzer.
His accordion and his guitar.
His tools, normal and mini size.
His transit and stadia rod and steel tape.
His drawing tools.
His small hatchet with a leather guard.
His Swiss Army knife.
His pocket size whet stone.
A small round pocket magnifying glass.
A Brazier telescope.
A jaw brace to float horses' teeth.
His false tooth.
His eyeglasses.
His silver folding traveling spoon.
His Arizona driver's license - good for life.
His five-year diaries, that he discontinued soon after our arrival in Haiti.
A leather box that had been tooled by him. It was 12"x 4"x 4",
    and he used it to carry checks, etc.
A blue knitted scarf Jenny made for him.
His leather suitcase with false bottom - from OSS days,
His garters from Colmar, Alsace.
His Malacca cane, concealing an épée.
A carved box from Spain. It was copied hundreds of times in our
    carpentry shop, and sold in our boutique. It finally
    succumbed to termites.
A big round-top chest from Argentina.
A black teak desk from Korea.
Four Georgian silver candlesticks.
A beautiful red Kashmir shawl from his father's house.
His two-sided desk from his mother. He gave this to Chip Burnette.
His Parker pen, a gift from his mother.
A photograph of his mother's portrait.

GGM BROUGHT FROM HER OTHER LIFE:

Tools from Father.
Mother's desk and sewing table.
Two sewing machines, Singer portable.
My beautiful set of three sewing scissors from Granny Rawson.
Beds, with new mattresses and springs.
Bureau I bought at age fourteen.
Chosen furniture from Geneva, Slingerlands, Arizona and New Orleans.
   Most have been copied many times for the boutique and houses.
Flat silver and other silver dishes from Mother.
Baccarat glasses and dinner plates from Grandmother, via Mother.
Three trunks of Grandmother's.
Jewelry from Grandmother, Mother and Larry.

BILLY MELLON

(Excerpts from a letter from Billy to his father on the occasion
of Larry's graduation from medical school.)

Sunday, May 31, 1953

Dear Dad,

Well, I've waited a long time to write this letter and can't tell you how
glad I am that the big day has finally come. It's going to be strange, for a
while, to be writing Dr. Mellon instead of the Mr. Mellon I've known for so
many years.

Dad, I sure am proud of you, as proud as any son could be of his old
man, for what you've done. It took an awful lot of guts and determination to
go through with it.

It seems to me the greatest thing in the world, that a person should find
his life's work and be going in a straight line toward a goal. Without such a
cause a person is just wandering and really can never prove anything monumental or hardly even worthwhile. In my opinion you've picked the best. I
want you to know that I'm behind you all the way, and though I guess I
haven't shown it outwardly, I would like to be part of whatever you're doing.
That means everything in the world to me.

However, you are not the only figure in the spotlight. Without
Gwennie's love and help, I doubt if I would be writing this letter now. I sure
envy you, Dad, for having found such a wife.

Dad, I've racked my brain trying to think of a present for you. I'd like to
give you something special but can't think of a thing you need or would like.
For some strange reason, parents seem to have everything. If you think of
anything, please let me know.

Love always,

Bill

A SONG FOR GGM BY WLM

When Gwen and I were seventeen
   Am   *C*
And life and love were new
  C   *G*
The world was just our paradise
  G7   *G7*
And we knew what to do.
  D7   *G7*
Though we've had our fling - and everything
          Am   *C*
She's still my beautiful Queen.
  C7   *Dm*
But I'm appalled at getting bald
  Fm   *B7*   *C*   *A7*
While Gwen looks seventeen!
   Dm   *G7* *C*

FROM LARRY'S LITTLE BLACK POCKET NOTEBOOK

"Civilization and Ethics", *The Philosophy of Civilization,*
by Albert Schweitzer, p. 310-311, 509.

It is good to maintain and to encourage life;
it is bad to destroy life and obstruct it.

Ethics are responsibility without limit towards all that lives. A man is truly ethical only when he obeys the compulsion to help all life which he is able to assist, and shrinks from injuring anything that lives. He does not ask how far this or that life deserves one's sympathy as being valuable, nor beyond that, whether and to what degree it is capable of feeling. Life as such is sacred to him. He tears no leaf from a tree, plucks no flower, and takes care to crush no insect. If in summer he is working by lamplight, he prefers to keep the window shut and breathe a stuffy atmosphere rather than see one insect after another fall with singed wings upon his table. If he walks on the road after a shower and sees an earthworm which has strayed on to it, he bethinks himself that it must get dried up in the sun, if it does not return soon enough to ground into which it can burrow, so he lifts it from the deadly stone surface, and puts it on the grass. If he comes across an insect which has fallen into a puddle, he stops a moment in order to hold out a leaf or a stick on which it can save itself. He is not afraid of being laughed at as sentimental. It is the fate of every truth to be a subject for laughter until it is generally recognized.

I sought my soul, but my soul I could not see.
I sought my God, but my God eluded me.
I sought my brother and I found all three.

A QUOTE FROM LARRY'S SWISS GOVERNESS

"Do you remember I told you: *Plus le mal est grand, plus sera grand le bien qui fleurira sur les ruines."* (The greater the evil, the greater the good that will blossom in the ruins.)

ADDRESS BY LARRY MELLON
PARK AVENUE CHRISTIAN CHURCH
NEW YORK, NEW YORK
DATE UNKNOWN

This morning we come together to worship God - to praise Him and thank Him for his continuous blessings. Among his many blessings were the gift of his only son and the pattern of love He bequeathed us. Jesus' disciples tried to live in the way their teacher did. According to the understanding and physical construction of each individual, men and women have tried to copy the example of the teacher, and love has been the motivating force. Life holds many mysteries but one thing seems clear - and that is that love acting on the individual heart is the great fact of life which supports our universe.

All successful teachers have themselves been faithful and devoted disciples. Last Thursday the world took pride and joy in celebrating the anniversary of one of Jesus' faithful disciples, Albert Schweitzer. The influence he exerts on human hearts - and on a good many other living hearts, not human - will go on and on. His example will be as eternal as the source from which he received his intellect and his strength.

I would like to read from a familiar book of Dr. Schweitzer's called *Out of My Life and Thought:* "Whatever you have received ... etc."

Gwen and I are here with you today in honor of our friend, Dr. Schweitzer, and of his lifelong friends, Dr. and Mrs. Emory Ross, whom we met through Dr. Schweitzer. To Emory and Myrta we owe our affiliation to this church and to this larger group of devoted friends. We thank the Rosses for this, and we wish to thank you from the bottom of our hearts, all the men and women who have given so generously of their time and substance to the patients of the Albert Schweitzer Hospital in Haiti.

LAPRIYÈ - NWÈL 1966
PA
LARRY MELLON

Ann priye Bondye,

Bondye ki konn bay lapè,
Fè ke kè-nou gen trankilite
Pou nou kapab tande chante zanj yo.

Pi wo pase enpòtans bezwen, fè nou santi nan kè nou,
Pi wo pase tèt chaje ke nou kapab genyen, asire nou mesaj
    espwa-a.

Fè nou resevwa Pitit Bondye nan kè nou nan sezon Nwèl sa-a, tankou
    gadyen mouton yo ki bay byenveni nan ansyen peyi, malad ke yo
    te genyen lontan pase.

Fè vini pou nou sila ki konn pote espwa, sila ki bay limyè, paske nou
    genyen tèlman bezwen. Toulède pou klere chemen ki lonje devan
    nou. Nou mande sa O non Jezi, sovè nou.

AMÈN.

TRANSLATION
PRAYER - CHRISTMAS 1966
BY
LARRY MELLON

Lord, let us pray.

Lord, who gives peace,
Grant our hearts serenity
So that we may hear the angels sing.

Instead of our needs, make us feel in our hearts,
Instead of our problems, assure us of your message of hope.

Let us receive the Christ Child in our hearts during this Christmas
    season, like the shepherds of the old countries welcomed their
    sick so long ago.

Grant to us, that which gives hope, and that which gives light,
    because we need them so much. We need both to light the way
    that goes before us. We ask this in the name of Jesus, our Savior.

AMEN

LAPRIYÈ - DIMANCH RAMO 1967
PA
LARRY MELLON

Papa nou, nou rekonèt ou pa temwayaj Moyiz avèk profèt yo, e pa pawòl yo avèk jès Jezi, pitit ou. Ede nou pou nou konprann yon ti mòso mirak nou rele "Pak." Mete tèt nou ansanm sou prinsip lamou. Konbat linyorans, neglijans, avèk sipèstisyon, e ba nou plis kouraj pou nou swiv ekzanp Jezi-Kri.

Nou lapriyè jodi-a pou ba nou plis pasyans avèk vwazen nou yo e mwens pasyan avèk nou menm. Fè ke nou respekte lide vwazen nou yo e ke nou sonje ke lide nou yo pa toujou bon.

Aksepte lapriyè nan men tout moun ki vini devan Ou aswè-a. Rekonfòte sila ki malere e rejwi sila kap soufri an silans. Beni sa yo kap sèvi nan kongregasyon sa-a, avèk sa yo ki fè kado pou soutni-li.

Nou mande benediksyon sou peyi Dayiti. Proteje-li, kont tout malè, tout aksidan, tout kalamite, tout enjistis. Klere avèk sajès Ou, Prezidan Divalye avèk tout moun ki okipe pozisyon otorite.

Fè ke volonte nou anvayi kè tout moun ki rete an Ayiti e fè ke vrè relijyon an pral gaye lagras pami nou e soulve nasyon sa-a an dwati e an jistis.

Lapriyè pou tout moun va konnen ke nan pwen Bondye apa ou menm. Se ou menm sèlman ki vrè Bondye. Se ou menm ki te fè nou, ki siveye nou, ki renmen nou. Lamou ke ou te mete nan kè nou, fè nou montre li devan frè ak sè nou yo, nou mande sa nan non Jezi.

AMÈN

TRANSLATION
PRAYER - PALM SUNDAY 1967
BY
LARRY MELLON

Our Father, we know you through the testimony of Moses and the Prophets, and through the actions of Jesus, your Son. Help us to understand but a small part of that miracle you call "Easter." Join our minds in the principle of love. Combat ignorance, negligence, and superstition, and give us more courage to follow the example of Jesus Christ.

We pray today for You to give us more patience with our neighbors, and less patience with ourselves. Let us respect the ideas of our neighbors, and let us remember that our ideas are not always good ones.

Accept the prayer brought by each person who comes before You today. Comfort those who are unfortunate, and reward those who are suffering in silence. Bless those who are serving in this congregation, and those who are bringing gifts to support it.

We ask Your blessing for the country of Haiti. Protect her against every evil, every misfortune, every disaster, and every injustice. Enlighten with Your wisdom, President Duvalier and every person who holds a position of authority.

Let our will invade the heart of everyone who lives in Haiti, and let the true religion spread grace among us and raise this nation with right and justice.

We pray that all people come to know that there is no other God but You. It is You alone who are the true God. It is You alone who made us, who protects us, who loves us. The love that You put in our hearts, let us show it before our brothers and sisters. We ask this in the name of Jesus.

AMEN

LAPRIYÈ - NWÈL 1968
PA
LARRY MELLON

An Nou Lapriyè Bondye.

Bondye nou, sa ki konn fè nou kado lapè, fè ke tout bri, tout troub ki nan nanm nou vin trankil pou nou kapab tande chanson ke zanj ap chante. Pi fò pase ti ijans pesonèl ke nou kapab santi, fè nou konprann mesaj lespwa ke Ou genyen pou nou.

Fè kè nou louvri pou resevwa pitit ou, menm jan tankou gadyen mouton yo te akeyi'l lontan pase. Fè ke li va pou nou sa ki va vini pote lespwa, sa ki pral fè kado limyè-a. Ou konnen, Bondye, kòman nou bezwen toulède (lespwa ak limyè) pou montre nou bon chemen pou swiv.

Padone tout plent kap sot nan bouch nou kont sikonstans nou yo. Fè nou konprann ke malè ke nou kapab genyen yo pat soti nan men zanmi nou yo, men pito nan lide nou menm.

Ke tout tan nou pap chase movèz panse an deyò kè nou sikonstans yo pa pral chanje non plis.

Nou lapriyè ke lide nou yo va devni pi pwòp, pi pi, pi charitab, pi plen lamou anvè pwochen nou yo.

Nou mande sa nan non Jezi, ki te fè Nwèl vini nan lemonn.

AMÈN

TRANSLATION
PRAYER - CHRISTMAS 1968
BY
LARRY MELLON

Let Us Pray To God.

Our Lord, who knows to bring us the gift of peace, let all noise, all troubles in our souls become quiet so we may hear the song that the angels sing. Stronger than the little personal problems that we feel, let us understand the message of hope that you have for us.

Let our hearts open to receive your son in the same way that so many shepherds accepted Him long ago. Let Him come to us, He who brings us hope, who brings us the gift of light. You know, Lord, how we need both (hope and light) to show us the good road to follow.

Forgive all complaints that we speak against our circumstances. Let us understand that the problems that we have do not come from the hands of our friends, but instead from our own ideas.

If we don't reject our evil thoughts, our condition will remain the same.

We pray that our thoughts will become more acceptable, more pious, more charitable, more full of love for those near us.

We ask this in the name of Jesus, who brought Christmas to the world.

AMEN.

SOM 23
RESITE PA
LARRY MELLON
30 MAS 1969

Letènèl se gadyen mwen:
M-pap manke anyen!
Li fè-m kouche kote gen frechè.
Li mennen m' bò dlo ki kalm pou repare nanm mwenn.
Li kondwi-m bò jaden ki vèt.
Menm si m' tap pase nan galèt lamò,
M' pa krenn okenn mal ka ou menm akonpaye m'.
Baton-ou ak zam-ou ba m' konfyans.
Ou pare manje mwen devan lenmi m' yo.
Ou mete tèt mwen alèz.
Gode m' plen ap debòde!
Se sèten, tout sa ki bon, tout sa ki dous
Va swiv mwen toulejou nan lavi m'
E ma rete Lakay Letènèl jouk dènye jou m'.

AMÈN

TRANSLATION
THE TWENTY-THIRD PSALM
RECITED BY
LARRY MELLON
MARCH 30, 1969

The Lord is my guardian:
I will lack nothing!
He makes me lie where there is shade.
He takes me where there is calm water to repair my soul.
He leads me where there are green gardens.
Even though I cross the river on sharp stones of death,
I don't fear any evil, because you accompany me.
Your stick and your weapon give me confidence.
You prepare my food in front of my enemies.
You make my head at ease.
My cup is overflowing.
It is certain, all that is good, all that is sweet,
Will follow me every day of my life,
And I will live in the Lord's house until my last day.

AMEN

LAPRIYÈ - NWÈL 1976
PA
LARRY MELLON

Papa Nou.

Plen kè nou avèk remèsiman pou tout sa Ou fè pou nou. Pa janm kite nou bliye vwazen nou yo ki pap santi menm konfò yo ke nou jwi nou menm. Sonje nou ke nou pa isit poukont nou. Frè nou avèk sè nou yo isit tou. Nou lapriyè pou jou tout pèp ka vini you sèl gwo fanmi.

O non Jezi, nou mande l'.

AMÈN

TRANSLATION
PRAYER - CHRISTMAS 1976
BY
LARRY MELLON

Our Father.

Fill our hearts with gratitude for all that you do for us. Never let us forget our neighbors who are not feeling the same comforts that we, ourselves, enjoy. Remind us that we are not here alone. Our brothers and sisters are here, too. We pray for the day when all men become one big family.

In the name of Jesus, we ask this.

AMEN

MESSAGE DE PAQUES
PRONONCE PAR
LARRY MELLON
DATE INCONNU

Lorsque le jour de Pâques s'approche et que nous voyons devant nous la Résurrection de Notre Seigneur, Jésus-Christ, nos coeurs débordent de joie et de gratitude. Des chants de louange et de triomphe s'élèvent de nos lèvres.

Qu'est-ce qui nous a amené à Deschapelles? Bien certainement c'est l'exemple de Notre Seigneur, Jésus. Sans la doctrine chrétienne l'Hôpital Albert Schweitzer n'aurait jamais existé.

L'amour que Jésus nous a apporté est la force motrice de cette entreprise. En y répondant nous avons appris la première leçon de l'amour du prochain et de l'un pour l'autre.

Ce que nous disons ici n'a guère d'importance. Ce que nous faisons ici peut avoir des conséquences, bien au delà de nos faibles compréhensions. En vivant notre crédo chrétien, nous sommes en quelque sorte, arrivés à mieux nous comprendre et à mieux nous respecter les uns les autres.

Ici à Deschapelles les préjugés de nationalité, de croyance, et de race ont tendance à perdre leurs pointes aiguës. Les différences qui nous caractérisent deviennent de moins en moins séparatistes et les forces motivées de l'amour nous font paraître comme des membres universels de la famille humaine.

Espérons que quand l'histoire du 20ème siècle sera écrite, l'unité du dessein sera parmi ses accomplissements et qu' en quelque mesure, les résidents de Deschapelles auront gagné une partie du crédit, pour avoir aidé l'homme à avancer un peu plus près du Royaume de Dieu, sur la terre.

Voici, la manière par laquelle Saint Paul exhorte l'Eglise de Corinthe à s'unir à nouveau: "Mais je vous conjure, frères, par le nom de Notre Seigneur Jésus-Christ, de tenir tous le même langage et qu'il n'y ait pas de divisions parmi vous, mais restez bien unis dans un même esprit et un même sentiment."

Continuons maintenant notre pèlerinage vers le jardin de Gethsémané.

TRANSLATION
EASTER MESSAGE
BY
LARRY MELLON
DATE UNKNOWN

As the day of Easter approaches and we see before us the Resurrection of our Lord, Jesus Christ, our hearts overflow with joy and gratitude. Songs of praise and triumph are brought to our lips.

What has brought us together in Deschapelles? It is most certain the example of our Lord, Jesus. Without the Christian doctrine, Hôpital Albert Schweitzer would not exist.

Jesus' love for us is the motivating force of this enterprise. In response, we have learned the first lesson of love for our neighbors and for each other.

What we say here is of very little importance. What we do here may well have importance far beyond our feeble comprehension. In living our Christianity, we have in some measure come to understand ourselves better and to respect each other more.

Here in Deschapelles, the prejudices of nationality, creed, and race tend to lose their sharp edges. The distinctions which characterize us become blurred and the driving forces of love emphasize our universal membership in the family of man.

Let us hope that when the history of the 20th Century is written, that the unification of purpose may be one of its achievements and that somewhere in the scheme of things the residents of Deschapelles may have earned part of the credit for helping mankind advance one step closer to the Kingdom of God on this earth.

Here is the way in which Saint Paul urged the Church of Corinth to reunite: "Now I beseech you, brethren, by the name of our Lord Jesus Christ, that ye all speak the same thing, and that there be no divisions among you; but that ye be perfectly joined together in the same mind and in the same judgement."

And now, let us continue our pilgrimage toward the Garden of Gethsemane.

ACCEPTANCE SPEECH BY LARRY MELLON

(Award and date unknown).

For half a lifetime his example has inspired Gwen and me to greater usefulness - and as a consequence, to greater happiness. I'll treasure your medal to brighten rainy days. The cash prize I intend to use for the health and comfort of our Haitian neighbors.

Honesty compels me to confess that without the devoted and efficient efforts of my wife, no committee on earth would have accorded me such an honor as this. Please therefore consider Gwen Mellon the joint recipient of your generous recognition.

Thank you.

August 2, 1989
Saturday

Dear Jenny,

How wise you are - to know not to delay, but to act immediately and get to Haiti.

I am enclosing Larry's opening comments as I presented them, with some added comments. We put it first on the agenda and somehow I got through it. Please pass this on to Mother at the appropriate time.

The reunion is proceeding, somewhat in shock, because each person heard the news about Larry as they arrived, and the fact has not yet begun to be processed.

Please take a quiet moment to pass on to Frédérique my personal condolences to him - he has lost a good friend - and my thanks for the love and support which he provided Larry.

Let me know, through Bill Dunn, your personal plans - we will schedule full-time family coverage through early September. Just tell me your target date to leave.

Bill Dunn gave a wonderful talk easing through a review of the recent past to a forecast of the future. The naming of Mother as President of the Grant Foundation was very well received - the most logical move.

We got the obituary out to all the target newspapers on Friday - Jeff doing some today for Arizona and New Orleans papers.

We're looking forward to Wendy's talk tomorrow.

With lots of love to you there from all of us here,

Ian

1989 ALUMNI REUNION SPEECH
GIVEN BY IAN RAWSON

I have been asked to share these thoughts with you as a representative of the family - my sister Jenifer, as you know, is in Haiti with my mother; Michael is bringing one of his research vessels into safe harbor, and I am pleased and honored to be here with all of you today as are Lucy, Edward, and Rachel Rawson, and Wendy, Jeff, and Jerry Grant. On behalf of these and others of the family who are not here, let me express my heartfelt thanks to all of you who have shared Larry Mellon's mission and who have given of yourselves to those in need, as Dr. Schweitzer has counselled us to do.

At a time of loss and sorrow, we can ask for nothing more than to be with people we know and love, so I am grateful for this opportunity for us to be together at this time.

I feel that the spirit of Larry Mellon lives on in all of us, in so far as we dedicate our lives to the principles of *Reverence for Life,* as embodied by Larry and by Dr. Schweitzer.

I think that we all knew Larry well enough to know that he would want for us, at this event, to express our sorrow, but also to take this opportunity to celebrate his life, and the inspiration which it provides to all of us, and would want us to continue in that spirit.

Had mother been here, she would have said the following: Larry is weak - he is extremely thin. He has kept his indomitable will and spirit and retained his sense of humor. Music is still one of his greatest joys - sometimes Mahler, sometimes Willie Nelson.

This is the message Dr. Mellon sends to all of us: THE PRINCIPLE JOB OF THE ALUMNI ASSOCIATION IS TO KEEP ALIVE THE SPIR- IT OF ALBERT SCHWEITZER UPON WHICH THE HOSPITAL IS

CREATED. Gwen and I think often on the meaning *Reverence for Life.* Albert Schweitzer's own words furnish the answer. The following text contains the profound truth:

"We must never let ourselves become blunted. We are living in truth when we experience these conflicts (taking or suppressing of life) more profoundly. The good conscience is an invention of the devil.

"*Reverence for Life* is an inexorable creditor! If it finds anyone with nothing to pledge but a little time and a little leisure, it lays an attachment on these. But its hardheartedness is good, and sees clearly. The many modern men who as industrial machines are engaged in callings in which they can in no way be active as men among men, are exposed to the danger of merely vegetating in an egoistic life. Many of them feel this danger and suffer under the fact that their daily work has so little to do with spiritual and ideal aims and does not allow them to put into it anything of their human nature. To others the thought of having no duties outside their daily work suits them very well.

"But that men should be so condemned or so favored as to be released from responsibility for self-devotion as men to men, the ethics of reverence for life will not allow to be legitimate. They demand that everyone of us in some way with some object shall be a human being for human beings. To those who have no opportunity in their daily work of giving themselves in this way, and have nothing else that they can give, it suggests their sacrificing something of their time and leisure even if of these they have but a scanty allowance. It says to them, 'Find for yourselves some secondary activity, inconspicuous, perhaps secret. Open your eyes and look for a human being, or some work devoted to human welfare, which needs from someone a little time or friendliness, a little sympathy or sociability, or labor.' There may be a solitary or an embittered fellow-man, an invalid, or an inefficient person to whom you can be something. Perhaps it is an old person or a child. Or some good work needs volunteers who can offer a free evening, or run errands. Who can enumerate the many ways in which that costly piece of working capital, a human being, can be employed? More of him is wanted everywhere! Search, then for some investment for your humanity, and do not be frightened away if you have to wait, or to be taken on trial. And be prepared for disappointments. But in any case, do not be without some secondary work in which you give yourself as a man to men. It is marked out for you, if you only truly *will* to have it...'"

THE WORDS *REVERENCE FOR LIFE* ARE CARVED ON THE OUTSIDE ENTRANCE WALL OF THE HOSPITAL IN DESCHAPELLES. THEY WERE THERE WELL BEFORE THE FIRST PATIENT ARRIVED. LET US NEVER FORGET THEM.

THE SPIRIT OF LARRY MELLON
BY
GWEN MELLON

(Read at the first Board Meeting when she was made President of the Grant Foundation by Dr. Mellon.)

We here today are lucky enough to be a witness of it. It is like a piece of crystal with many facets.

It is found on the handle of a door, on the end of a stethoscope, on the edge of a scalpel and under the saddle of every horse.

It is a letter of love written by illiterates on the rocks, the hills and within the homes of thousands in Haiti. It is something learned by having seen and having learned. It is a legacy for you to teach by example.

It cannot be stifled,

It cannot be abused,

It is a real and living thing.

PITTSBURGH ALUMNI MEETING SPEECH
AUGUST 7, 1992
GIVEN BY GWEN MELLON

Rereading Larry's cornerstone speech - the aims he spoke of on that day still are constant in the hospital. It provides medical and physical care and aims to improve the conditions of lives. It is a center for learning as well as teaching. We are close to fulfilling his wish to make the staff all of Haitian nationality. *Reverence for Life* is still the keystone of H.A.S. It is a powerful ethic that includes all life, all sects and religions, and the surrounding ecology.

We have come far in fulfilling these aims and we must not let the spark of this philosophy fade. It is a flambeau to be held high and passed on to others.

Our alumni, doctors, nurses, and other staff members are a powerful group. Now there is a second generation that follows.

The long term strength of H.A.S. lies in the ethic *Reverence for Life*. It lies in our Haitian employees who are the backbone of our staff. They are here and they will stay while doctors, nurses, lab technicians, and pharmacists come and go.

As we make plans and decisions we must be particularly mindful of the rightful pride, the dignity and the sensitivity of our hosts as we work with them in their country. It is in this awareness that lies the future of the hospital.

LETTER TO DONORS, JANUARY 1993 WRITTEN BY GWEN MELLON

These are heartbreaking times for Haiti. Our staff and local communities are vocal and wish to be heard. We listen carefully and hold a balance of hopes and the hospital's needs.

Your interest and your concern give us the strength and enthusiasm needed for the job at hand.

Despite the frustrations and disciplines imposed by the embargo, we are able to be a beacon of hope to many.

Should the embargo be tightened and our electricity further limited, we will still be able to do what we came to do - care for the sick and the needy. These days there seem to be more of both.

We are grateful for your partnership with us in our work for the future of Haiti.

Please extend to each member of the community who participated in this gift my personal thanks.

LETTER TO THE
LONG RANGE PLANNING COMMITTEE

(Written after the ten-day meeting was postponed due to local unrest and acute complications of transportation.)

To give up ten days of your busy life to work on plans and hopes for H.A.S. is an enormous contribution. To have the event postponed at the last moment was a bitter disappointment to all concerned. So much thought and planning has already gone into the early structure of the components and so much was dependent on the synchronizing by you all with your collective wisdom in these planned ten days.

It might well be providential. A new government could have proved counter-productive and made our plans not viable.

I am grateful for the collective work done by all and I wish to thank you for the personal part you play. I can assure you that this effort will not be lost. It can be picked up and ridden in on the undercurrent of hope that exists here today in Haiti. It will surface as an important part of progress and change that is needed at H.A.S. and throughout the country.

BOSTON ALUMNI REUNION, MAY 1993
SPEECH GIVEN BY GWEN MELLON

When I left Deschapelles, the roads were muddy but life was full of hope. People were preparing their gardens and the mangoes were ripe. The roads were just passable.

The gestion of the hospital is now almost completely Haitian which was one of our original hopes. Many of our departments have no foreigners. Nursing has only three and of the sixteen permanent physicians, we have only four foreigners.

Plassac, our first and successful demonstration of almost complete community participation had its formal opening, with great interest from many communities, including Port-au-Prince, St. Marc and Gonaïves. It is a pilot project and others are planned in our district.

The health care plan for employees and staff is underway.

There is a new volunteer project, the Institute for Transportation and Development Policy, simply BIKES. It is help for the transportation problem and many bikes have been donated to Community Health workers. Five new employees are teaching relays of applicants to assemble and repair bicycles, ultimately to open their own repair shops with parts available for them to purchase.

Larry's pipelines and wells are being repaired. Grants are in hand to fix the stanchions and dalles of the Tapion Dam. The dam itself stands as strong as ever.

There are international contracts from Carrefour Rotary, from Biel for pediatric and nurse exchanges.

Haitian alumni plan a medical conference to be held in Port-au-Prince with the cooperation of H.A.S. for two days in November. We hope to have foreign medical participation.

A Long Range Planning Committee meeting is scheduled - a good successful program with vision. No one is ready to unseat me yet, and I am not ready to go. We all welcome everyone's constructive suggestions.

SPEECH GIVEN BY DR. GÉRALD REID
KONBIT CLINIC, MAY 23, 1993

Ladies and Gentlemen, Mrs. Mellon and friends, friends of Haiti, it is a real pleasure for me to be here to talk about what I remember of Hôpital Albert Schweitzer.

Twenty years ago, in May, 1973, to be exact, I went to the Albert Schweitzer Hospital in Deschapelles to be interviewed by the late Dr. Muller Garnier, who was then H.A.S. Medical Director, for a position in the surgical department. I was not aware that the official language of H.A.S. was English. I could read English then. I could write some. I could not speak or hear the spoken words if my life depended on it. Needless to say, I was scared. The late Dr. Larry Mellon put his hands on my shoulders, noticing my obvious nervousness and whispered in my ears, "Doctor, everything is going to be O.K." Somehow, I regained my confidence and managed to finish the interview. I was accepted as the first surgeon trained in Haiti to work at H.A.S.

Too often you hear that you should not attempt to do anything unless you can do it with perfection. Dr. Mellon used to tell me that perfection is only a goal, that nothing is perfect in this world. The issue is not perfection, the issue is growth. The issue should be progress, improvement. The issue is to continue no matter how high or how hard are the obstacles. That is one of the many things I have learned from the Mellons, and believe me, there were many obstacles. The Mellons did not have an easy passage or an easy stay in Haiti.

This past week the TV sitcom "Cheers" came to an end after being on the air for close to 11 years. One of the "Cheers" characters gave a pretty good definition of love. For Norman, loving someone or something had to be complete, full, without judgment. In other words, love has to be unconditional. Let me tell you the love of Dr. and Mrs. Mellon for Haiti and the Haitian people has been without judgment and has been unconditional.

355

Let me tell you why.

Dr. and Mrs. Mellon did not go to Haiti to feel sad or sorry for the people. They did not go to Haiti to criticize or have pity. They went to give compassion, to care and become one of the people of the Artibonite Valley. "Go to the people. Live among them. Learn from them. Love them. Serve them. Plan with them. Start with what they know. Build on what they have" -words by Dr. Y.C. Yen in Dr. Mellon's handwriting hung in Dr. Mellon's office.

Dr. and Mrs. Mellon are immigrants to Haiti. There are different groups of immigrants: People looking for better lives, maybe freedom of religion, freedom of speech, economic opportunities, etc. When Dr. and Mrs. Mellon went to Haiti they were not looking for any of those. They had freedom of speech, freedom of religion and they were doing pretty well in the States. There are other people who go to Haiti, like the missionaries and other religious groups or even political appointees or recently, the Peace Corps. No one asked Dr. and Mrs. Mellon to go to Haiti. They were not appointed by anyone. They were not forced to go. They were not being persecuted by anyone. They are among a small group of philanthropists whose only mission is to promote human good will to fellow men. That is a definition of philanthropists given by *Webster's 9th New College Dictionary*. Dr. and Mrs. Mellon are true philanthropists. In that regard, Dr. and Mrs. Mellon should be counted along with Dr. Schweitzer, whose philosophy of *Reverence for Life* they adopted, Mother Teresa of Calcutta and a handful of other good humanitarians.

What have they accomplished? They founded a private institution in the Artibonite Valley, serving an area of 982 square kilometers which represents 5.7% of the total surface of the Republic of Haiti. They are serving a population of 178,000 people which is 3% of the Haitian population. I am going to tell Mrs. Mellon something that she might not know but probably she already does. I think you are serving more than 3% of the Haitian people. As you know, Haitians have friends and families all over the country. Everybody from Les Cayes, Cap-Haïtien or Gonaïves has a relative living in Verrettes, and they can come there and get full care at Albert Schweitzer Hospital, the best there is. So I think you are serving 15, 20, 25% of the population or maybe more than that. I have worked there and I can tell you that you are doing more than you think.

By World Health Organization standards, H.A.S. has the highest level of hospital complexity in the whole Republic of Haiti. In other words, this is the highest, the best served, the best run hospital in Haiti. The big teaching hospitals with hundreds of millions of dollar budgets are not doing as much as that 116 bed hospital in the Artibonite Valley. Adopting that policy of decentralization, they have been able to serve the people better, to take care of the people who have come to be admitted, and to keep those who can be treated as outpatients outside and closer to home.

One other thing that really amazed me - that is a word that I've learned at Deschapelles; everyone used that word. I asked one of the surgeons with whom I worked, "What is amazed?" He said, talking about Dr. Marshall, "She is amazing, and then you talk about a difficult case and that is amazing." What is amazing? Well, I was amazed to see, although the word *"Konbit"* was not in use at H.A.S., Dr. and Mrs. Mellon were practicing *Konbitism* without using the word. Think about it. At H.A.S. you have a community of people coming from all over the world. They came from the Netherlands, from Africa, Canada, from every state in America. They were Mennonites. They were Hindus. They were Muslims, Catholics, Protestants and Jews. There was never any religious war. There were never territorial battles or gang fights. They were all in there together putting their heads together to serve the people of the Artibonite Valley and they did that under the leadership of Dr. and Mrs. Mellon. By seeing the Mellons really give so much of themselves, everybody who stepped in Deschapelles had to follow in their footsteps.

The Mellons also taught discipline to the Haitian people, for example, the necessity of being there on time. One morning I was going to work and the Land Rover pulled in. Dr. Mellon got out. It was five minutes of seven and he literally dashed into the place. He ran in. I said, "What is going on?" and went running in after him. Every day at 7 o'clock we started x-ray rounds. He made a commitment to be there every single morning at 7:00 o'clock before going out into the community. When I worked at H.A.S. he was no longer practicing medicine, but he kept a hand inside the hospital to know who was in, who was out, what you needed, what could he do for you, etc. This is work that Mrs. Mellon has been doing since her husband's passing and I again, thank you, Mrs. Mellon, for continuing such good work. So he ran in and everyone ran after him. So I went to Dr. Garnier and I said, "Tell me one thing. Why does he have to run to be there on time?" and Muller said, "You know, I think discipline is something that is physiologic to these people. We have to learn it. But, if we keep watching him we are all going to be there on time and we will never be late." I think that is another good lesson we learned from the Mellons. It was important to be there on time because people were coming all the way from the mountains and they walked for days to get there.

I was talking with Exanus, who was an interpreter at H.A.S., and I told him about a man who came from the mountains. The man had a perforated ulcer. He was very sick and Dr. Bart Saxbe, who was visiting from Brigham Hospital at the time, and myself took care of him. He got better and in six or seven days was ready to go home. I said to him, "Sir, you are doing fine. You are going home." He said, "I have nothing to eat. I cannot got home because I have an ulcer. I have no food at home." He got a job at H.A.S. and I think he is still working there. That is the type of commitment that the Mellons had and they continue to do it for everybody. They could not hire the whole country but they tried every time there was a need.

Dr. Mellon, with his leadership, brought people together. He started literally a *konbit* in Haiti. I would also like to quote someone who called this kind of situation a "unified diversity:" To have people from all over the world and to bring them together to serve people to whom they have no relation. They have nothing basically to do with them, and yet to watch them work, you cannot think for one minute that they are not one of them. You cannot separate the people from the Artibonite Valley from Dr. and Mrs. Mellon when you see them hold a full-bellied child with kwashiorkor and take that child, feed that child, teach the mother what to do with that child. To see them have the support of many friends who come from everywhere, who leave important responsibilities, great homes and everything, to go to Deschapelles and work for the poor, needy people, just like Mother Teresa and Albert Schweitzer.

There is a Chinese saying: "To know and not to give or to know and not to share is to really not to know." Dr. and Mrs. Mellon have learned. They have shared. They have given, and we are grateful forever. I do hope some day I will be able to go back in Deschapelles, and I mean that as a pledge, to work, to volunteer, to give my time and to follow in the footsteps of this great leader and his distinguished wife.

MESAJ - NWÈL 1995
PA
GWEN MELLON

Byenvini tout moun.

Ane sa nou gen anpil chanjman depi 40 ane pase. Konye-a Sèvis Sante avèk Developman Kominotè lonje bra lwen nan chak pwen nan distri nou, e la li gen moun ki konn non lopital, men yo poko konnen nou. Nou pote nan men dwat sa-a, nou pote remèd, nou pote piki, men se pa menm si nou pa gen respè nan figi nou lè nou pote sa.

Fò tout moun konnen lopital isit bay respè ak tout moun nou rankontre nan distri nou. Se trè inpòtan. Konsa yo konnen nou la pou fè lavi pi bèl.

Map mande chak moun gade nan miwa ou te resevwa jodi-a. Gade andedan pou wè si je ou gen respè. Si doktè gen respè pou doktè, si mis gen respè pou doktè, si intèprèt gen respè pou malad, si tout moun gen respè pou mekaniksyen ki travay tout joune pou fè lopital mache byen.

Fò ou gen respè. Se pa sèlma andedan lopital, fò ou gen respè nan tap-tap. Pou moun ki chita avèk ou. Fò ou gen respè pou moun ki mache nan kominote. Fò ou gen respè lè ou antre nan lakou ou. Answit, mwen mande ou, fò ou gen respè pou moun andedan kay ou.

Mwen pa bezwen gade anndan miwa, paske je mwen gen anpil respè pou chak moun isit ki bay mwen konkou, ki fè lopital mache byen. Mwen invite ou isit pa sèlma pou manje lakay mwen, men mwen te invite ou sitou pou di ou yon gro mèsi.

Mèsi tout moun!

TRANSLATION
GREETING - CHRISTMAS 1995
BY
GWEN MELLON

Welcome, Everyone.

This year we see many changes in the hospital since its beginning 40 years ago. Today Community Health and Community Development reach their arms into each area of the hospital district. We carry medicine and vaccinations in our right hands. But that is not enough if we do not have respect in our faces.

Each person must know that this hospital has respect for each person in our district. It is very important. Thus they know we come to improve their lives.

I ask each person to look in the mirror you received today. Look to see if you have respect in your eyes. If doctors respect doctors, if nurses respect doctors, if interpreters respect those who are sick, if you respect the mechanics who work all day to keep the hospital running well.

You must have respect. Not only inside the hospital, but for people you sit with in the *taptaps*. Have respect for others in the community. You must have respect when you enter your homes. Additionally, I ask you to respect the people you live with.

Myself, I don't need to look in my mirror because I know my eyes respect each person here who assists to help make the hospital a success. I don't invite you here today only to eat, but to give you my appreciation.

Thank you everybody.

WILLIAM LARIMER MELLON, JR., M.D. AND GWEN GRANT MELLON
HÒPITAL ALBERT SCHWEITZER
DESCHAPELLES, HAITI

Honors, Awards, and Degrees

WLM   Diploma
        Choate 1929

GGM   Diploma
        The Shipley School 1930

GGM   Bachelor's Degree
        Smith College 1934

WLM   Doctorate Degree
        Tulane University School of Medicine 1953

WLM   Louisiana Medical License 1953

WLM   Intern Certificate
        Charity Hospital, New Orleans 1954

GGM   Elizabeth Blackwell Award
            for Outstanding Service to Mankind
        Hobart and William Smith Colleges 1958

WLM   *L'Ordre National Honneur et Mérite*
            au Grade de Chevalier
        République d'Haiti 1958

WILLIAM LARIMER MELLON, JR., M.D. AND GWEN GRANT MELLON
HÔPITAL ALBERT SCHWEITZER
DESCHAPELLES, HAITI

Honors, Awards, and Degrees

GGM   Honorary Doctorate in Humane Letters
        Smith College 1959

WLM   Honorary Doctorate in Humanities
        Trinity College 1961

WLM   *L'Ordre National Honneur et Mérite*
        au Grade d'Officier de Chevalier
        République d'Haiti 1961

WLM   Cunningham Award
        The International House, New Orleans 1961

GGM   Citation for Creative Service
        The Shipley School 1963

WLM   *Diplôme de Mérite Agricole*
        au Grade de Chevalier
        République d'Haiti 1972

WLM   *Diplôme de Mérite Agricole*
        au Grade d'Officier de Chevalier
        République d'Haiti 1976

WILLIAM LARIMER MELLON, JR., M.D. AND GWEN GRANT MELLON
HÒPITAL ALBERT SCHWEITZER
DESCHAPELLES, HAITI

Honors, Awards, and Degrees

WLM   Honorary Dotorate in Humanities
Bethany College 1976

GGM   Honorary Doctorate in Humanities
Bethany College 1976

WLM   Albert Schweitzer International Award in Medicine
Educational, Historical and Scientific Foundation
University of North Carolina, Wilmington 1981

GGM   Margaret Bailey Speer Award as Distinguished Alumna
The Shipley School 1981

WLM   Award in Recognition of Creative Leadership
& GGM   and Dedicated Service
The Family of Man
World Convention of Churches of Christ 1985

WLM   Humanitarian Award
Jackson Memorial Medical Center
University of Miami 1988

WILLIAM LARIMER MELLON, JR., M.D. AND GWEN GRANT MELLON
HÔPITAL ALBERT SCHWEITZER
DESCHAPELLES, HAITI

Honors, Awards, and Degrees

WLM　　Honorary Doctorate in Humanities
　　　　University of Miami 1989

GGM　　*Reverence for Life* Award
　　　　Boston *Konbit* Clinic 1992

GGM　　*Reverence for Life* Commendation
　　　　Albert Schweitzer Institute for the Humanities
　　　　Quinnipiac College 1994

WLM　　Schweitzer Institute Award for Excellence
& GGM　　(to WLM posthumously)
　　　　Chapman University 1996

GGM　　*L'Ordre National Honneur et Mérrite*
　　　　　au Grade de Chevalier
　　　　République d'Haiti 1996

GGM　　Smith College Medal,
　　　　　Which Conveys the True Purpose of a Liberal Arts
　　　　　Education and Service to The Community or
　　　　　to the College
　　　　Smith College 1997

February 25, 1996

Mrs. Gwen Mellon
c/o Hospital Albert Schweitzer
Deschapelles
Haiti

Dear Mrs. Mellon:

In late 1943 or early 1944 I treated a beautiful Gwen Grant for pneumonia in Jerome, Arizona. This was the first case of pneumonia I had treated since completing my internship and the last also, since I went into the Navy shortly after where we had Penicillin.

I sat up all night with Gwen, but I also had Larry Mellon sitting with me and questioning me with questions like, "Did you get a 'sputum test' on her before you started the Sulfa?" Even then he was very knowledgeable about medicine.

Very shortly after this I was in the Navy and in the South Pacific, on my way to the invasion of Leyte when I heard that you and Larry were married and then went on to medical school.

It was in a Reader's Digest article that I read that you were in Haiti, doing what I had planned to do instead of going into the Navy.

In the April 24, 1995 People magazine, I read about Gwen Mellon. I saved the article and planned to write, but since retirement I move much slower. It wasn't until I had pneumonia and was cured in 6 hours with Zitheromax that I recalled that case of pneumonia that I treated with Sulfa. It also was the only case I treated with Sulfa since I went into the Navy where we had Penicillin.

It was wonderful to read how much you and Larry have done with your lives - the "Albert Schweitzer's of Haiti."

I believe the article mentioned that you had family in Southern California. If you do come here on a vacation, I would like to hear from you and see you. I still can drive around Southern California but not much farther.

Sincerely,

Blenn Whitaker

Blenn Whitaker, M.D.   (formerly M.D. at Jerome Arizona)

From my Arizona doctor.

367

Glossary Of *Kreyòl* Words And Phrases

Word or Phrase	Meaning
Abitan	Farmer
Agwonòm	Agronomist
Ajan	Agent
Aji	Act
Ak	With
Animatris	Health Worker
Anmwe!	Help Me!
Ap	Denotes "Ing"
Atelye	Studio
Avoka	Attorney
Azil	Asylum or Home for the Aged
Bagas	Sugar Cane Pulp
Bak	Barge
Bannann	Plaintain
Bèf	Cattle
Bezwen	Need
Biwo	Office
Blan	White Person

Ble	Blue
Blòk	Alliance
Bòkò	Voodoo Priest
Bon	Good
Bondye	God
Bondye Bon	God Is Good
Boni	End of the Year Bonus
Bonjou	Good Morning
Bonswa	Good Afternoon, Evening
Borlet	Numbers Game
Bougenvil	Bougainvillea
Boul	Ball
Boumba	Dugout Canoe
Branch	Branch
Chagren	Sadness, Heartbreak
Chaloup	Motorboat
Chèf	Chief
Chèn	Oak
Chita	Sit
Chwa	Choice
Chwal	Horse
Dechouke	Uproot, Pillage
Degi	Bonus
Diri	Rice
Dwat	Straight, Righteous
Elèv	Student
Fè	Make, Do
Fèt	Festival
Fig	Banana
Flach	Flash, Flashlight
Flanbwayan	Flamboyant, Royal Poinciana
Fò	Strong
Fòjon	Blacksmith
Gagè	Cockfight
Genyen	Have
Glasi	Concrete Slab
Gonm	Eraser

Goud	Haitian Monetary Unit
Grate	Scraping
Grenadin	Granadia, Passion Fruit
Griyo	Spicy Fried Pork, a Delicacy
Gwa	FatF
Gwo	Large
Gwo ble	Denim
Ha-Ha	Retaining
Jako	Parrot
Jij	Judge
Jij Lapè	Justice of the Peace
Jou	Day
Joumou	Pumpkin
Kabann	Bed
Kafe	Coffee
Kajou	Mahogany
Kampèch	Logwood
Kavo	Burial Chamber
Kay	House
Kenbe	Stand, Hold
Kleren	Sugar Cane Juice for Rum
Kò	Body
Kochon	Pig
Konbit	Peasant Work Team
Kondwi	Escort
Konfrè	Colleague
Konkonm	Cucumber
Kontwolè	Controller
Koton	Cotton
Kouraj	Courage
Krab	Tarantula
Kreyòl	Creole
Kreyon	Pencil
La	There
Lagon	Pond, Marsh
Lakou	Courtyard
Lakrè	Chalk

Lapè	Peace
Latè	Land
Latrin	Privy
Lavi	Life
Lè	Hour
Lespwa	Hope
Leve	Lift
Li	He, She, It, Him, Her, His, Hers, Its
Li Chwa	Her Choice
Lonè	Honoro
Machann	Vendor
Madanm	Madame
Madi	Tuesday
Madi Gwa	Fat Tuesday
Makok	Official Club, Stick
Makout	Straw Bag
Mal	Bad
Maladi	Sickness
Mamit	Tin Can, Canful
Manchèt	Long Flat Iron Knife
Manke	Lack
Mapou	Kapok
Marenn	God Mother
Matènite	Maternity Hospital
Mayi	Corn
Melanj	Mix
Mereng	Popular Dance Rhythm
Militon	Squash
Mimi	Cat
Mouche	Husband, Loved One
Mwen	My
Myèl	Bee
Nan	In
Nan pwovens	In the Country-Outside Port-au-Prince
Nou	We, Us, Our
Nwi	Night
Oksilye	Auxiliaire, Nurse's Aide

Ou	You, Your
Pa	Not
Pale	Speak
Pansyon	Dormitory
Parenn	God Father
Paspatou	Passkey, Passport
Pen	Bread
Pitimi	Millet
Planch	Plank
Plasaj	Common-law Marriage
Pou	For
Poul	Chicken Yard
Pwa	Pea
Pwa Blan	White Bean
Pwa Grate	Pea Scraping
Pwa Kongo	Pigeon Pea, Green Bean
Pwa Wouj	Red Bean
Pwovens	Country
Ra-Ra	Noisemakers
Rejim	Regime, Stalk
Rele	Limpet
Remèsi	Thank
Respè	Respect
Respè Pou Lavi	Respect For Life
Rete	Stay
Sante	Health
Seksyon	Section
Selibatè	Bachelor
Sèptè	Sickle
Siam	Muslin
Sik	Sugar
Siwo	Syrup
Siwo Myèl	Honey
Soup	Soup
Swa	Afternoon, Evening
Ta	Denotes "Conditional Tense"
Tabak	Tobacco

Tanpri	Please
Taptap	Small Passenger Truck
Tavèno	Sabicu
Te	Denotes "Past Tense"
Ti	Little
Tifi	Daughter
Tinis	Tennis Shoes
Toro	Bull
Toro Lagon	Bull of the Marsh, Bull Frog
Va	Denotes "Future Tense"
Vach	Cow
Vennkatrè	Poisonous Insect
Vin	Come
Vin' ou	Come Here
Vle	Want
Wou	Hoe
Zepis	Spices
Zonbi	Living Dead

Photographs

The photographs in this book were taken over the years by family, friends, colleagues, and visitors who have generously allowed us to use their pictures in our brochures and publications. Whenever possible we have given proper credit.

Anderson, Erica - Albert Schweitzer Collection, Department of Special
    Collections, Syracuse University Library - front jacket cover, pages 50,
    75, 76, 157, 198, 201, 203
Baldeck, Andrea, M.D. - page 319
Killam, Frank - pages 149, 162, 228, 254 bottom, 260, back jacket cover
Mellon, Gwen Grant, page 31 bottom
Mellon, LeGrand - pages 142, 144, 147, 148, 156, 164, 167, 172, 173, 177
    top and bottom, 183, 194, 212 bottom, 227, 229 top and bottom, 230,
    232, 238 top and bottom, 240, 243, 244, 246 top and bottom, 250, 253,
    254 top
Mellon, William Larimer, Jr. - page 31 top
Phillips, Robert - page 174
Sargent, Herb - pages 208, 210, 212 top, 213, 216 top and bottom, 302
Tarnay, Tim - page 47

Haiti

N

District served by the
Albert Schweitzer Hospital

Ille de la Gonave

Caribbean Sea

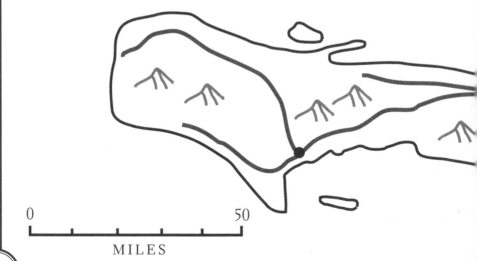

0   50
MILES